To Emily
thank you so much
for having us
Janice 郑玫 & 沙叶

SCALING THE DRAGON

ADVENTURES IN CHINA

SCALING THE DRAGON

JANICE MOULTON **GEORGE ROBINSON**

Cross Cultural Publications, Inc.
CrossRoads Books

Published by **CROSS CULTURAL PUBLICATIONS, INC.**
CROSS ROADS BOOKS
Post Office Box 506
Notre Dame, Indiana, 46556, U.S.A.
Phone: (219) 272-0889
FAX: (219) 273-5973

©1994 CROSS CULTURAL PUBLICATIONS, INC.
All Rights Reserved
ISBN: 0-940121-29-8
Library of Congress Catalog Card Number: 94-71584

PREFACE

The title of this book is a five-fold word play. The *Dragon,* of course, is China, and the several meanings of *Scaling* are the ways we present our experience of that country. By reading on you will find out what is in the book, but here we want to tell what is missing.

We came home with our portable computer filled with the equivalent of nearly a thousand pages. Some of it, we discovered, was interesting only to us and a few specialists—details of Chinese syntax, *Ding Ding* comic books. Some was available in other sources—descriptions of scenic and historical places. Some, if published, would harm or embarrass people we cared about—political and illegal behavior, personal relationships. To this last category belonged such interesting material we couldn't bear to leave it all out. We compromised by disguising identities, combining some characters and splitting others. Changed are names of people, institutions and locations to conceal the identity of our friends and to offer others the courtesy of denying their inclusion.

Chinese editors, deciding whether to publish works critical of Chairman Mao, were said to be guided by the rule that criticism is permitted if balanced by praise, the balance set at thirty percent criticism/seventy percent praise. Curiously, this ratio is exactly what Western psychological research determined to be optimally believable. *Scaling the Dragon* both criticizes and praises China; naturally, the ratio is thirty/seventy.

We are grateful to the State Education Committee of the Peoples Republic of China for generous financial support. To the many Chinese friends, colleagues and students who shared their lives and knowledge with us we have said, and say again, *Feichang Ganxie!* Thanks also to the Wuhan Office of the Bureau of Public Security for many hours of informative detainment.

1
JOURNEY TO THE MIDDLE KINGDOM

Warnings and Worries

The airline check-in area was stacked with cardboard boxes, squat and cubic, bound with double strands of rope. Where were the modern plastic and leather suitcases, the ones equipped with straps and buckles and wheels? This luggage was too makeshift, too informal, out of place at a US airport, and the first sign we were entering an alien culture. We were about to check in at CAAC, the national airline of the People's Republic of China.

Standing next to or astride their boxes were Chinese returning home, equally informal—men in loose white summer shirts, straight hemmed, not tucked into their trousers, the few women mostly in slacks. We felt reassured by the look of these people. They seemed pleasant, gentle, very subdued for passengers about to board an airplane.

Our appraisal was not shared by Mother Demetra who was seeing off her middle-aged child on its first adventure. She stage-whispered that we must be careful, that we shouldn't trust foreigners because they didn't think like we did. She knew, she said, because her parents were foreigners. And all Chinese must need glasses, she added, "with those eyes." We knew it was her fear speaking, worry about us living in a strange land with strange people, her last chance to warn us. Our worry was that the people with "those eyes" might hear her.

The personnel at the counter were not Chinese, but Americans in the uniform of a US airline. The CAAC officials stayed in their office on the fourth floor of the building, inaccessible without a special security pass. The Chinese passengers quickly assumed the role of host, smiling at us, nudging their cardboard boxes aside and insisting that we, with our wheeled American Tourister and Samsonite cases, precede them in line. We tried to decline but they smiled and bowed and extended their arms in a gentle, firm insistence until we yielded with a mumbled *"Xie Xie"* (thank you), suddenly aware that ours was the less gracious culture.

Our overweight luggage was accepted at the counter with no surcharge. For a moment we imagined we were getting special treatment until we saw that baggage twice as heavy as ours went through unnoted, as if the scale were merely a resting place. Were such rules ignored in China? There was so much we didn't know.

And why were we about to board a Chinese airliner? We were timid academics who only read about exotic journeys. We never took airplanes if we could avoid them, and those few times we'd had to fly, we tried to check the wings and fuselage for missing rivets and leaking hydraulic fluid. Unlike our colleagues and students we had not spent our junior years abroad, or taken sabbatical leaves in France. We had never visited Oxford or Cambridge, never even gone to Club Med. The most exotic place we had ever seen was Tucson, Arizona. While we wrote recommendation letters for our students to study abroad, received postcards from colleagues traveling in Europe, and saved foreign stamps for our nephews, our holidays had been spent renovating our house and making our life at home more comfortable. We admired, but didn't envy, our friends who returned from abroad with anecdotes of pickpockets in Bogota, medical emergencies in Romania, strip-searches at international borders, hepatitis, bandit taxi drivers, oppressive poverty, terrorist attacks. Brrrr.

While waiting to board this flight, we compared ourselves with Bilbo Baggins, the Hobbit who gave up his comfortable life and traveled to the land of the dragon. Bilbo never figured out why he set off on his great adventure. So why were we going to China, we asked ourselves, not for the last time.

We had once written a book on linguistics that attracted a good publisher and a small readership. We had hoped our book would revolutionize the field. It didn't, or rather hadn't yet. Instead of waiting for posthumous fame, we had moved on to other things, occasionally reviewing grant proposals and answering letters about our work, delighted that a few people were still interested.

Our relatives and friends asked, in the same way they would ask about the accomplishments of progeny, "How is the language book doing?" We answered, "Oh, it's doing fine. We still get royalties." We neglected to say how much, that is, how little.

So when we received a letter about our book from a professor at a Chinese university, his inquiry inspired us to reply with more than a reprint of a research paper. We wrote an accompanying letter, trying to combine the self-deprecation we believed appropriate for a Chinese audience with a little self-promotion about our book. Our correspondent answered: "Let me be a student of yours through the air. You would be welcome to China and my house as my guests and good friends."

We sent another letter, a reprint of another article. He answered: "Dear professors, are you interested in coming to teach for some time in my university?" We responded in what we hoped was the same courteous style: "We would like to visit your wonderful country someday. We earnestly wish for continued friendship and cooperation between our peoples." We hoped our prose would gain in translation.

The exchange of letters continued, two weeks there, two weeks back. Then we received a surprise, a formal invitation to teach at our correspondent's university. We could teach graduate courses in our specialties. The Chinese government would pay our way, give us housing and salaries lavish by Chinese standards. His colleagues "all expressed their warm welcome." But we had to stay for a whole year to receive these benefits.

This was an offer we had been waiting for all our lives, although we didn't know it: a chance to live on the other side of the world, in a place we knew nothing about, to get to know the people, the customs, maybe some of the language, to teach and do research as well as travel, to have a real adventure.

But wait. Adventures could be dangerous. Bilbo knew that. We weren't going to jump into anything too quickly. We sought encouragement, reassurance, social support. When we told our colleagues, some said, "What a wonderful opportunity." A few said, "How do you get invited to these things?" meaning how come we had been invited and not them. But they all said, "You must go."

Easy for them to say, the people who passed along a certain London flat from one member of the faculty to another; who vied to lead tour groups of alumnae through Japanese or Greek Islands; who themselves were born in Europe or Africa, or at least Canada. Still, we were encouraged by the enthusiasm of all, by the envy of some, and by their offers to send us toilet paper in case there wasn't any in China.

That there might be no toilet paper in China quickly became a symbol of all our fears about an unknown culture, a way to joke about going to a place where so much of what we had taken for granted all our lives would be different. Every discussion about China led us to the topic of toilet paper until a more knowing acquaintance assured us, in the patronizing tone our worry deserved, that the Chinese did indeed have toilet paper.

Still, there were other problems. We who read and wrote and talked for a living were not eager to relinquish the communication power of our native language. The Chinese scholar wrote that we didn't have to know Chinese because our students would be fluent in English. Had he thought of what would happen if we left the university campus? We had visions of ourselves—starving, stricken with some terrible disease, unable to make ourselves understood as we begged for food, medical care, or toilet paper.

At this point we turned to the tools of our own profession. We would learn more before making any decisions. And so we found ourselves in the introductory Chinese language class, watching Teacher Fong's long braid pendulate as she chalked incomprehensible symbols on the blackboard. Our competence in our own disciplines was no help here. When Teacher Fong called on us to respond in Chinese, the room was suddenly hot, our faces burned and our minds went blank.

With the fearless self-confidence of youth, the students in the class all planned to go to China. We were not sure that we ourselves were going, but the students swept us up in their obsession with learning Chinese characters, seeing Chinese movies and finding out about China.

Teacher Fong gave us all Chinese names, and we practiced writing ours over and over, cherishing them as precious gifts. Janice became *Zhen Mei*; Robin became *Luo Bin*. *Zhen* is the surname of a character in the classic Chinese novel, *Dream of the Red Chamber*, a name that is rare now, so it marks the bearer as unusual and romantic. *Mei* means rose, a proper girlname. *Luo* is a common surname in China, one of the mere hundred surnames used by most of the billion Han Chinese. *Bin* means refined and courteous, a proper name for a male, but like "Robin," appropriate for a female too.

Some of our classmates' names were easy: *Ma Duona* was an angelic blonde who we remembered as "Madonna" from then on. *Ou Die* (pronounced Oh Dee-ah) was another blonde who flustered and flubbed when asked to speak and we thought of her as "Oh dear." There were *Shen Lisha* and *Shi Mishan* whose melodic cadences were so attractive that we overheard *An Kezhi* say jealously to *Zhang Zhen*, "Wouldn't you know I'd get a stupid name and they'd get the good ones." *An Kezhi* had an "attitude," our classmates said, and later dropped the course.

We read books about China: Fox Butterfield's *Alive in the Bitter Sea* explained the effects of the Cultural Revolution on contemporary China. We learned the Cultural Revolution was not, as we had previously thought, an extension of the Chinese revolution of

1949, nor a version of our student protests in the sixties, but a violent, chaotic upheaval driven by paranoid jingoism. Universities were closed, education stopped, families uprooted, thousands humiliated and tortured, killed and maimed and starved. Butterfield's bitter disillusion was apparent. "He was too negative," some Chinese told us. As we read other books, *Son of the Revolution* and *Life and Death in Shanghai*, and as we talked with Westerners who had taught in China, we learned more than we wanted to know about the problems of modern China.

To escape these depressing accounts of reality we dove into *Journey to the West*, a delightful Chinese fable about Sun Wu Kong, the Monkey King, whose blend of resourcefulness, humor and hubris got him into and out of a long series of adventures. He sometimes did evil, sometimes caused harm, but that didn't lessen his impish charm. We never imagined any lesson in the fable.

We interviewed everyone we could find who had visited or lived in China. We heard good things—kindness toward strangers, enthusiastic students, beautiful children. The good things we learned were general; the bad things were more specific—dirty toilets, greasy food, shoddy construction. We listened to the complaints and drew our own conclusions.

"People spit bones onto the tables and floors of restaurants." We joked that we would have to practice spitting, that after returning from China, friends would have to lay drop cloths when they invited us for dinner. We didn't take this problem seriously because the only bones we'd ever seen in a Chinese restaurant were in spareribs.

"Hospitals are filthy." This criticism came from a friend whose home might have been a cat-hair-and-used-kitty-litter warehouse. Ah well, dirt was the eye of the beholder, we thought knowingly, and besides, we didn't plan to visit any hospitals.

"University officials lie and agreements are ignored." So what else is new? We reminded ourselves not to assume that Chinese administrators were less capable of deception than their American counterparts.

"Foreigners are overcharged. You spend the whole trip finding out about the two kinds of Chinese money." We knew the Chinese government subsidized its citizens. Non-citizens were not entitled to these subsidies so of course they should pay more. Besides, if we worked in China, we would be charged Chinese prices, not tourist prices. At least that's what we'd been told.

"The food is boring and greasy; everyone who goes to China loses weight, ten or twenty pounds." Sounded good to us. No more watching our weight; it would happen automatically when we got to China.

"The toilets are just holes in the ground." This got our attention. We had just built a new bathroom with bookshelves and an electrically-heated toilet seat. Sophisticated friends said, "Oh, squat toilets are all over Europe too." We tried squatting and lost our balance so this news failed to provide the intended comfort. Still, we had been told that our apartment in China would have a Western style toilet with a real toilet seat.

We talked with a young man who had just returned from teaching in China. He hated it. He was bitter and angry, with a long list of complaints: Students spat on the classroom floors. There was no heat. People lied to him all the time. Then we found out he had gone to China with his fiancee but came home alone. That explained it, we thought, and attributed his negativity to his broken engagement.

A musician invited to give a series of concerts in Tianjin told us about the woman whose job it was to dust the piano. The afternoon before the concert, she appeared while he was practicing. She dusted the legs of the piano. She dusted the sides. She dusted the top. And then, *while he was playing*, she dusted the piano keys and his fingers.

Another friend, studying acupuncture at Nanjing University, reported her experience at a bakery when she asked to buy a cake.

"No cakes."

"Why no cakes?" she said.

"We are not making cakes today."

She returned with a Chinese friend who knew the workers in the bakery. They had been saving their cakes in case important people or friends came by. To get a cake you needed to have *guanxi*, that is, connections. Since the friend knew the bakers, they sold her a cake.

Before these stories discouraged us, Teacher Fong arranged a Chinese New Year's Party. We offered our house and helped her prepare the huge bowls of chopped meat, vegetables and exotic spices to fill seven hundred *jiaozi* dumplings. The party was a huge success but the dumplings disappeared as people were still arriving. The Chinese guests rose to the occasion, taking over our kitchen, mixing flour and water and sending us to cut pieces of dowel in our basement workshop for them to roll out hundreds more dumpling wrappers. In no time the dumplings were filled, boiled and served, the pots were washed and the kitchen cleaned. Never had we had so large a party. Never had we had so much fun at our own party.

Our enthusiasm for China renewed, we practiced writing Chinese characters, listened to language tapes and attended class conscientiously, still blushing and sweating when called on to recite, still terribly nervous before each quiz. We joined the Chinese Language Luncheon each week, learning the words for chicken and eggs, but not for cheese, chili, tuna fish, lettuce, pizza and all the other foods we would miss in China.

We exchanged more letters with the linguist, with the Vice Chairman of the English Department and with the Foreign Affairs Office of the Chinese university. Their letters were full of polite enthusiasm and descriptions of our living conditions but no clear information about our teaching duties or salaries. The linguist wrote that we shouldn't worry, that everything would work out. "The cart will arrive at the other side of the mountain when it gets there," he told us, "an old Chinese proverb."

Unlike the proverbial cart, we needed work visas from the Chinese Embassy. To get work visas we needed letters of invitation from the Chinese State Education Committee in Beijing. For six months we waited for these letters, writing periodically to convey our anxiety that they might not arrive in time. Finally, barely two weeks before we were due to depart, the official letters arrived. Now we had to find out how to apply for work visas. We called the Chinese Embassy in New York. For two days no one answered the phone. We called every half hour and on the third day, made contact and explained our needs.

When we finished, the Embassy official said, "You! Need! Letter! From! Chinese! Government!" Each word was a sharply punctuated sentence. Was it a challenge, a refusal, or did the official think English words must all be pronounced in the Chinese fourth tone, the intonation used in English for commands?

"We do have letters of invitation from the State Education Committee," we replied meekly, humbly; our gratitude at finally making the phone connection dissolving in more worry.

"You? Do?" It sounded like challenging disbelief. Or was it Chinese second tone, the rising intonation?

We sent him the requested letters and passports, hoping the cart would get to the other side of the mountain in time.

Awaiting the return of our passports and visas, we concentrated on other business. The offer-we-could-not-refuse included round trip airfare, confirmed by a telex that arrived at what seemed to be the end of the last minute:

WILL RESERVE CAAC PLANE TICKETS AUGUST 20 NEW YORK TO BEIJING CABLE RESPONSE IMEDIATLY.

We made arrangements for leaving our house by August 20th, then called the New York office of CAAC, the Civil Aviation Authority of China.

"Yes we have prepaid ticket for your trip to China. We have reserve ticket for you August 23."

"Ohhh . . . but Central China University booked tickets for us on August 20th. They are going to meet us in Beijing. We need tickets for August 20th."

"Sorry. CAAC does not fly on August 20."

"Oh. When *do* you have flights?"

"Thursday and Saturday."

"August 21 is a Thursday. How about August 21 instead of August 23?"

"We have tickets for you on August 23."

"Can you reserve tickets for us to fly on August 21?"

"You *have* tickets on August 23."

"Can we *cancel* the tickets on August 23 and get tickets on August 21 instead?"

"Wait-a-minute . . . Yes . . . Okay. We reserve tickets for you August 21."

"How can we get the tickets?"

"Come to CAAC office."

"In New York? Can we pick them up at the airport? Can you send them to the airport?"

"Better you come to office. Mail not safe."

We agreed meekly and hung up. Then the thought of driving eight hours to pick up our tickets gave us the courage to call back.

"Hello. Do you have tickets to Beijing reserved for George Robinson and Janice Moulton on August 21?"

"Don't have."

"Do you have tickets for George Robinson and Janice Moulton on another day, August 23 or 20?

"No. Don't have."

"But your office just said there were tickets for us."

"What is your name?"

We tried reversing the order, "Janice Moulton and George Robinson."

"Wait-a-minute . . . Yes. We have."

"We live far away from New York and we would have to travel a whole day to get the tickets. Could you please mail them to us? We will send you our address and the stamps on an envelope."

"Yes. We can."

The tickets came in the mail a few days later. We had learned that our assumptions about business arrangements were not shared by everyone else in the world. We had assumed that our host university would make a reservation for us to fly on a day the airline would have a flight. They didn't. We assumed the people we spoke with on the telephone would volunteer helpful information. They didn't. We assumed they could arrange for us to pick up the tickets at the airport. They didn't.

We had also assumed that because the airline clerk said the mail was not safe, they would refuse to mail us the tickets. But they didn't. They didn't *offer* to mail the tickets to us; we had to ask. Sometimes it helps to push the cart a little to make sure it gets around the mountain.

And so we came to board the airplane, our home for twenty-three hours. It was a Boeing 747, a design with a decent safety record, no obvious flaws or malfunctions to add to our worries, and unlimited beverages with limited ice. From New York to San Francisco the plane was nearly empty so we tried to use the space to sleep. We were shy about lying together across the middle seats but after an uneasy nap we saw a young Chinese couple asleep together, his arm resting on her breast. No one seemed to notice.

At San Francisco the plane filled with Chinese passengers returning home. Our new seatmate was a doctor who had been studying in the US. His spoken English was about as good as our Chinese so the conversation required both languages and a lot of gestures. The dialogue was right out of our textbook—name, age, home city, family, how long he spent in the US and how long we would be in China. He showed us a valise filled with cartons of cigarettes, explaining that he himself did not smoke but was bringing the cigarettes for friends, as "little bribes." Little bribes, huh? No one told us about this before.

The flight attendants served a meal of stir-fried snow peas, pepper steak and rice, and we thought eagerly, "Ah, Chinese food," but our companion lifted the foil cover and said disappointedly, "American food." From then on familiar comforts diminished—the coffee got weaker, the English announcements more awkward and the restrooms dirtier. The flight attendants insisted we close our window blinds for the movie—five hours of "Marco Polo," in which John Gielgud and Burt Lancaster spoke dubbed Chinese. Hardly anybody watched the screen, but the flight attendants used the opportunity to sleep.

And then the plane began its landing descent. We watched through the window as the earth loomed and the airport became visible. Ours was the only airplane in sight, and bicycles were riding across the runway.

Asian Cool and Money Talks
It was the middle of the night and we worried that no one would come to meet us. Had our ticket changes confused our hosts? Had we accounted for crossing the international date line when we telexed the date of our arrival? Again we asked ourselves, what were we doing here?

Scores of signs were held aloft in the area past customs, and to our relief one of them had our names on it. Its bearer introduced himself as Zhou (pronounced "Joe," the same family name as the beloved premier, Zhou En-Lai).

Zhou was the Vice-Director of Central China University's Foreign Affairs Office. His handshake was firm, his smile was warm, his determination to carry our luggage was unstoppable. In a few minutes we were in the back seat of a new air-conditioned Toyota, Zhou and the driver in front, luggage in the trunk. The taxi driver tore down the middle of the broad street, swerving around crowds of pedestrians, cyclists, and pushcarts selling orange soda and ice cream. Using his horn and flashing the headlamps to punctuate his maneuvers, the driver slalomed through traffic in a way that helped us put any fear of air travel in perspective.

At the Beijing Friendship Hotel, Zhou escorted us to the rooftop restaurant and ordered quart bottles of warm Chinese beer, roasted peanuts that glistened with oil, and sweet dry cakes. It was clear that he was comfortable, confident and in charge. The open-air restaurant was level with the treetops; stars and strings of colored lights competed overhead. Nearby a group of Africans were speaking fluent Chinese; a summer breeze and their gestures kept their bright dashikis fluttering. In this *Casablanca* atmosphere we fell in love with China, an infatuation that would last for weeks. Our emotions focused on Zhou, our host and protector, the dark-eyed, bronze-skinned master of this new world. What kind of person was he and how did he fit what we knew about China from the books we had read? During the misery of the Cultural Revolution had he been a victim or a perp? Not a victim, we decided, sensing the power behind his smile, a mystery about his past.

Relaxed, confiding, he leaned close and told us about new Chinese social customs—that people now chose their own marriage partners, that girls sometimes changed boyfriends, and some even decided not to get married, ever. He watched our reactions, encouraged us to speak Chinese, laughed at our jokes, and taught us new words. As he translated his given name for us: "*Jin*" meant gold and "*Liu*" meant smooth, flowing, we dubbed him "The Golden Smoothie."

The next morning the streets of Beijing were filled with traffic more varied and chaotic than we'd ever seen. Bicycles darted in front of buses causing them to brake suddenly, while trucks and taxis squirted past each other, missing by centimeters. We decided that Chinese traffic abhorred a vacuum, obeying Newton's laws and little else. We grabbed Zhou's arms in fright as a truck swerved toward us and, like a parent, he took our hands and led us across the street.

At every ticket window, restaurant, taxi stand and soda cart, Zhou negotiated the prices. "Wuhan is much cheaper, much better than Beijing," he assured us, and we shared his pride in the city that was to be our new home.

Zhou took us to all the famous historical sites but watching him wheel and deal was more intriguing than the dusty relics of the Forbidden City. At the Great Wall, the restaurant was booked full of Western tourists for the entire day, but Zhou struck up a conversation with the manager, dispensing comradely nudges and hearty laughter, learning that the man had a brother studying in Wuhan. This established a connection that was cemented by an exchange of business cards and an invitation to visit if the manager should ever find himself in Wuhan.

Still the man hesitated, clearly a hard case. Zhou offered a cigarette, then tucked the whole pack into the manager's shirt pocket. One of those "little bribes" our airplane seatmate told us about. The manager then fetched chairs from the dining room, invited us to sit down and promised Zhou that one of the tour groups, which had just arrived, would leave in twenty minutes and then we would have a table. The group did leave in twenty minutes, herded out by guides shouting into bullhorns.

The waitress informed Zhou that the price of lunch was fifteen *yuan* per person. He smiled and stepped very close to her. We didn't hear what he said as they walked away from the table, heads nearly together, sleeves touching. The waitress began to giggle. When Zhou returned to the table he said in a quiet voice that she would not charge us full price, after all. The waitress looked back at Zhou and smiled coyly. He explained that she would charge the tourist family at the next table twenty-five yuan per person to make up for the discount we'd received.

Except for the major tourist sites, Zhou did not know Beijing very well, so he arranged for us to tour the city with his friend and classmate, Shu, who had moved to Beijing to become an editor of China's English language newspaper, *China Daily*.

Shu was taller and paler than his friend, dressed in a loose white shirt and baggy trousers, the style favored by older professional men. In contrast, Zhou wore a polo shirt and slim trousers with a "Styled in USA" label on the pocket. With a European haircut, a pair of very stylish sunglasses and fashionable high-heeled sandals, Zhou looked very cool and he knew it. But as we got to know Shu, his indifference to Western fashion began to seem even cooler, as if he knew all about our part of the world and wasn't overly impressed.

Shu and Zhou got into a debate, a good natured disagreement. They explained to us that China had two parallel currencies: *renminbi*, or People's money, could be used only in China; the other currency, Foreign Exchange Certificates (FEC), were what tourists received in exchange for their foreign money and what tourists were required to use in China. However, the government announced it would soon change to a single currency.

Officially, one yuan FEC was equivalent to one yuan *renminbi*, but only FEC could be exchanged for foreign currency and used to buy imported goods such as Japanese washing machines and American cigarettes. This made FEC more valuable than *renminbi*. Clerks and merchants refused to accept *renminbi* from foreigners, and some tried to give *renminbi* in change for FEC. The flourishing black market offered at that time three yuan *renminbi* for two yuan FEC. By making it more difficult for Chinese to buy foreign goods, the dual currency system encouraged foreign money to flow into the country faster than Chinese money flowed out. Unfortunately, the black market reduced the effective value of Chinese money by one-third.

In order to get rid of the black market, the government had once again announced that it would soon eliminate the dual currency system. Shu and Zhou debated whether this time the promise would be carried out. We listened, grateful to them for using English, impressed with their speculation about government motives and policies.

Shu, whose newspaper had reported the government announcement, believed the dual currency system was on its way out. Zhou, more cynical about government announcements, thought the announcement was made just to frighten people so they would stop hoarding FEC. He argued that the two systems would remain, at least for a while. Zhou turned out to be right—the government did not give up the dual currency system until 1994.

If we recognized a little competition between them, it was a competition between old friends who had been study partners and sports rivals. They called each other *Xiao* ("Little") Zhou and *Xiao* Shu, inviting us to do the same. They told us how they had played basketball together when they were in school until Zhou broke his arm and both his legs during a game. Zhou explained that Shu's father, a surgeon, repaired the splintered bones that were poking through the skin and sewed him up.

"Dr. Shu did a very wonderful job," he said, "Do you want to see?"

Before we could decline, Zhou rolled up his sleeve and trouser legs to reveal long jagged scars on each limb. Shu's father hadn't wasted any of his skill on the outside of Zhou's limbs, but Zhou was proud of the scars.

Under Shu's guidance, we explored Tiananmen Square, the Forbidden City, and so many historical sites that only photographs and notes kept the experiences from blending together. Except for the magnificence of the Great Wall, little things made the strongest impression—a mahjongg game played by old men in an alley; the colorful pushcart of a street merchant; the similarity of the Ming Tombs to New York's IRT subway.

We did not want to quit, but Shu had to return to work the next day and jet lag began to catch up with us. Zhou announced proudly that he had reserved tickets on the next day's train to Wuhan and—he paused for effect, "It is an air-conditioned soft-sleeper berth." We didn't yet appreciate the need for special connections or special pleading to get travel tickets in China, so our mild reaction to his announcement must have been disappointing.

On the train Zhou arranged for us to have the lower bunks in the four-bed compartment, taught us the symbols for "Vacant" and "Occupied" (literally, "has person") on the washroom and toilet doors, and asked the conductor to give us washcloths (all the other passengers had brought their own). The train was our first introduction to the notorious squat toilets. We held our breath and appealed to the hepatitis antibodies in our blood stream to do their job.

In the morning Zhou charmed the waitress in the dining car to get a special breakfast of scrambled eggs and noodles. He wiped the table with toilet paper, gave us each a length to use as napkins, added enough red pepper sauce to his noodles to set them afire and urged us to have some of the large side order of sautéed garlic cloves. He ate our share when we declined.

And then we arrived in Wuhan, the fifth largest city in China, a major industrial, military, and educational center, not only of Hubei Province, but of the entire Central China Region. Except as a place to board Yangtze River Cruise ships, Wuhan is off the usual tourist circuit.

Zhou added a valuable bit of lore to our guidebook information. The people of Hubei Province describe themselves as spirited and indomitable; according to the locals, every Chinese revolution began in Hubei. People from other provinces are less complimentary; one folksaying translates roughly: "As in Heaven there is the Nine-Headed Bird (a mythical creature known for its bellicosity), so on Earth there are the Hubeinese."

After he delivered us safely to the university we did not see Zhou again for two weeks. At first we felt abandoned. Without our Golden Smoothie we had to confront alone all the things we worried about before we left home and all the anomalies we were unprepared for. We had to learn to order food from a dining hall staff that spoke no English, to gesture about stomach cramps and diarrhea to the doctors in the university clinic, and to cross streets without his help. But we had learned from Zhou to carry our own toilet paper for napkins and table wipers; learned the difference between *renminbi* and FEC; learned that love and romance were not taboo topics. And most important, we had learned to imitate his smile and good nature and to negotiate persistently whenever we were told "Don't have" or "No Way" or "It's Impossible."

2
FOODSTUFF

Banquets and Ptomainia

We had been warned about the food in China. Bonnie said it was too oily. Marcia said she lost ten pounds. Susan said the food was the hardest thing to get used to. They all reported the bones spat on restaurant tables and left for the next customer, the dishes and utensils merely rinsed off in cold water, the rarity of napkins. They complained that the ubiquitous orange soda was cloyingly sweet and smelled like perfumed soap and they cautioned us never to drink tap water. Forewarned and prepared for the worst, the reality turned out to be better than we expected.

During our first week in Wuhan we ate at the Foreign Experts' Guest House Dining Hall with two other foreigners, Daniel and Bud. The dining staff served us very small portions of what must have been their idea of Western food. The plates were the size of demitasse saucers and there were no napkins, but we brought enough toilet paper to share. They served no water or tea, only weak coffee in the morning and beer for lunch and dinner until we got brave enough to ask for soda. The August heat was tropical and we drank so much soda they soon rationed the four of us to one liter of Pepsi per meal.

Bud, who refused to try chopsticks, ate with a ceramic spoon. He also couldn't stand fried food. We explained to the kitchen staff that Bud didn't like food cooked with oil, but in Wuhan that was equivalent to saying that Bud didn't like food. Our appeal on Bud's behalf may have lacked enthusiasm because his refusal to use chopsticks in China seemed unreasonable, and besides, we got to eat his portion.

On the morning of the fourth day we received an invitation to a banquet to "Welcome Professor George Robinson and Janice." Janice's title and surname were missing from the printed notice but at least she was mentioned. Bud and Daniel were not listed and they didn't know they were invited until a few minutes before the banquet was to begin when they were told: "Hurry up. We are waiting for you." Bud did not attend; he was in bed with cramps, moaning that he never wanted to eat again.

Our hosts included four men from the Foreign Language Division, all named "Wang." They referred to each other by titles: Chairman Wang Xianming, Vice-Chairman Wang Yizhong and Chairman Wang Zhitao. The fourth Wang was Professor Wang Wei, the linguistics scholar who had invited us to China. Afterwards we dubbed them Wang W, Wang X, Wang Y and Wang Z. "My Wang is bigger than your Wang," Bud would chant suggestively, for he and Daniel were in the General English Department and their Chairman, Wang X, was very tall. "We've got more Wangs than you have," we would counter, for W, Y and Z were all in our English Department.

In addition to the four Wangs, the banquet guests included a bevy of lesser deans and minor administrators who were not introduced to us, and the Director of the Foreign Affairs Office, Fang Xijian. The Golden Smoothie did not attend.

Director Fang looked every bit an administrator. He had a round smiling face, chin pulled in until it doubled, and a long hank of hair carefully combed across the top of his bald head. Each time the oscillating fan blew over his head, the hank abandoned his shiny pate and curled into the middle of his forehead. Each time this happened he finger-combed it flat again.

The Director patted the top of his head before he spoke to us. He had a unique voice, pitched deliberately low, simultaneously resonant and nasal, seeming to originate deep inside his belly.

"Do you know how to use chopsticks?" he intoned.

We answered proudly, "Yes, we have used them for many years."

Director Fang nodded. "You will get used to them in time. They are very difficult for foreigners to learn."

We did not have time to ponder the significance of this remark because we were called on to make a speech. We each spoke for a few minutes in simple Chinese and this effort was met with much applause and praise. The linguistics scholar, Wang W, told us later that the vice-president asked him to recommend more foreign professors like us, that our speech had increased his status. This was no accident. It was Wang W who suggested we make the speech in Chinese and corrected our draft before the banquet.

The banquet table filled so much of the room that our chairs were backed against the wall. A huge lazy susan covered most of the table, allowing only a narrow space around the edge for our bowls, glasses and utensils. As soon as the speeches were over, the kitchen staff brought out five giant dishes, beautifully sculpted platters of dragons and phoenixes and blossoms made from vegetables, eggs, bean curd, and sliced cold meats, each dish a meal for a whole family. Daniel and we took generous helpings as the dishes rode by on the lazy susan.

Our hosts acted like Mediterranean mothers, coaxing us to eat more and placing choice morsels in our bowls. They poured beer and wine and orange soda into our glasses. The beer was served at room temperature, which was near body heat, the wine was sweet and medicinal (touted explicitly on the label), the orange soda was syrupy and deserved its bad reputation, but we were growing used to it. As we finished the food on our plates, satisfied with the quantity for the first time in days, the kitchen staff brought out another five dishes. Then another set and another and another and another and another—more than thirty dishes in all. Shrimp, Wuchang fish, Mandarin fish, yellow fish, crab, eel, several pork dishes, chicken dishes, beef dishes, vegetable dishes, *jiaozi* dumplings, duck, bean curd, quail eggs, fruits, and three giant soup tureens, each different.

The serving platters were stacked on top of each other as they were brought in. Some stuck out over the edge of the lazy susan and occasionally toppled a bottle or glass as it turned. Our confidence in our skill with chopsticks diminished as slippery quail eggs evaded the shiny lacquered sticks and delicate morsels disintegrated from too much pressure, splashing into our soy sauce. Robin's crab slipped away and dumped a bowl into his lap. Daniel dribbled orange sweet-sour sauce down the front of his white shirt. We gave up trying to eat the crabs with chopsticks and tore them apart with our fingers like Western barbarians.

Director Fang explained that a special cooking staff had been brought in for the banquet. He then asked us how we liked the food at the Foreign Experts' Guest House Dining Hall. We avoided a direct answer and instead we praised the banquet food, comparing it enthusiastically to our previous meals.

This one time, Director Fang was alert to the nuance in our response. Was there anything wrong with our daily meals, anything that might be improved? His question seemed so genuine that our complaints spilled out—the inadequate portions of food and beverage, the leftovers that the dining staff frequently served us. Director Fang asked what we meant by "leftovers." We explained: "Old food. Sometimes the food they give us was cooked the previous day for another group."

Everyone was looking at us. Director Fang vigorously finger-combed his hair and said he would "study the matter." He was clearly upset, as if we had complained about his own cooking. We tried to change the subject by praising the banquet food, but this only served to emphasize our earlier criticism. Wang W and Wang Z tried to cover the awkwardness by promising to show us a wonderful restaurant on the other side of campus.

Much later, we pieced together the following history. The Dining Hall used to have a very good cook who retired and had been replaced by the person next in line for the job. When the quality of the food deteriorated, the foreign teachers complained and the Foreign Affairs Office went to great trouble to find a replacement.

In China people were rarely fired for doing their job badly. Full employment regardless of ability or productivity, called the "Iron (unbreakable) Rice Bowl," was the alternative to a welfare system. As China's economy changed this policy was beginning to change. If people didn't work, they should be fired, several Chinese told us, naively believing that all US workers had to demonstrate competence to keep their jobs.

The Foreign Affairs Office had no authority to fire the cooking staff, but somehow they managed to get the cooks transferred to the carpentry shop. Since the present cooking staff represented the Foreign Affairs Office's best efforts to improve the food, our negative report was unwelcome news, a loss of face for their efforts.

Despite Director Fang's promise to investigate, the meals at the Dining Hall worsened. Bud recovered from his intestinal distress but vowed to eat nothing but peanut butter and jelly in his own room. Twice the Dining Hall staff forgot to prepare meals for us and we had to share Bud's peanut butter and jelly. They cut our ration of Pepsi to a half-liter per meal. That week Janice got abdominal cramps and a day later Daniel was stricken.

Janice recovered quickly but Daniel's pains did not go away so we escorted him to the university clinic. The medical staff spoke no English and our knowledge of Chinese, so easily supplemented by gestures in other realms of discourse, was suddenly inadequate. Doctor Ming, a dignified older woman, was unhappy that we understood so little of what she asked. In a frustrated pantomime, she bent over and made quick motions with her arm as if pulling something from her rectum. She was trying to ask if Daniel had diarrhea, *la duzi*, literally, "pull stomach." We laughed. "Bring a translator next time," she said in Chinese, as she gave Daniel little yellow tablets of laudanum for his diarrhea.

Then the two Wangs fulfilled their promise by introducing us to the Laurel Hill Restaurant across campus and never again did we eat at the Dining Hall for Foreign Experts. At first we were embarrassed to see the Dining Hall staff because we had rejected their work, but their continued friendliness suggested they were not insulted by our mealtime defection, which led us to suspect that they had never wanted to feed us in the first place; that the poor food was the result of intention rather than incompetence since they got paid whether they cooked for us or not.

Dining Out on Laurel Hill

Laurel Hill Restaurant was a great contrast to the Foreign Experts' Guest House Dining Hall. The food was delicious, abundant, varied, and one third the cost at the Dining Hall. And there was an unlimited supply of orange soda. The master of the restaurant, *Lao Ban* (Boss), an old man with no front teeth, always greeted us warmly. The first week he and his workers insisted we eat in a private dining room equipped with napkins and tablecloths and fans. After a few visits we refused this special attention and ate in the large room, sweating in the heat with everyone else. We were eager to adapt, eager to experience everything Chinese.

Sunnyside eggs, corn flakes and orange juice were not available at the Laurel Hill Restaurant. Our breakfasts began with a bowl of stir-fried noodles seasoned with hot chili sauce. We skipped the garlic cloves fried in sesame oil but learned to appreciate "oil sticks," a kind of sugarless cruller, the Dunkin' Donut of China. These twists of raised dough were deep fried at low temperatures so that large quantities of oil would be absorbed. They continued to drip oil after they were lifted from the frying vat and hung on skewers. We followed the local custom and dipped our oil sticks into bowls of warm, sweetened soy milk. Then we drank the remaining milk directly from the bowls, practicing the required slurping noises.

The limited range of choice for breakfast was unique to that meal. The restaurant menu for lunch and dinner boasted a huge selection of dishes, with more available on special request. The menu, which changed every day, was chalked on a large blackboard outside the building in stylized Chinese script that we could barely decode. When *Lao Ban* saw our plight he encouraged us to go into the kitchen and point to things we wanted. As we entered we noticed a sign over kitchen doorway: "Customers stay out."

In the kitchen we could examine the ingredients for each dish, already chopped and set out on plates, waiting for one of the chefs, often Lao Ban himself, to select and dump into a smoking puddle of oil. Steam and smoke rose from a row of huge woks that were heated by a coal-burning forge. Dishes of frying hot peppers sometimes drove us choking from the kitchen, but Lao Ban would merely blink his eyes as he stirred and tossed.

Along one wall of the kitchen, noodles and dumplings swam in huge vats of boiling water. In a room behind the kitchen, food was cleaned and chopped, fish were refrigerated, and chickens squawked as they were slaughtered. Outside the kitchen stood a large wooden barrel filled with steaming rice for self service.

Restaurant patrons included military officers from the nearby army post or the retirement village for Long March generals. Some students, members of the faculty and university workers who had extra money would occasionally forgo their government-subsidized meal tickets and treat themselves to a special meal at the Laurel Hill Restaurant. Bones were spat onto the tables and flies perched by the hundreds on customers' backs, but the food was delicious.

Every day we traveled across campus to the restaurant, sweating in our light summer clothing, marveling at students who donned vests and sweaters as soon as the temperature dropped below eighty. We greeted the old people selling orange soda and ice cream outside the restaurant and waved to giggling children who pointed at us, calling out, *"Waiguo ren! Waiguo ren!"* (Foreigner! Foreigner!).

With each meal we learned how to order a greater variety of dishes: the sausage and pepper omelet called "Fragrant-Intestine Fried Egg," the equivalent of Swedish meatballs called "Balls," stir-fried noodles with meat, whole sweet and sour fish, quail's eggs in a delicately sweet tomato sauce, egg drop soup, tofu soup, mushroom soup, several stir-fried pork dishes with names that translated into mundane labels like "fried meat pieces" or "fried meat strips" but in Chinese sounded as wonderful to us as they tasted. String beans, baby bok toy with mushrooms, cauliflower, and carrots spiced with soy, chives and a touch of vinegar. Eggs and vegetables cooked with lard, which provided delicious flavor but made us grateful that our serum cholesterol level had not been high before.

We always brought toilet paper to use as napkins and carried our own chopsticks, not fully trusting our artificially boosted immune systems to ward off disease. We learned to avoid menu items whose Chinese names contained the "moon" radical, a piece of ideograph warning that the dish was made from the internal organs of something—livers, stomachs, lungs, intestines.

We also learned to be wary of chicken. Chinese chickens ran free, eating whatever they wanted, living what must be a pretty good life for a chicken. Their meat was claimed to be more flavorful than the meat of American chickens who were imprisoned all their lives with nothing to do but grow chicken meat, but if chicken happiness produced richer taste, it also produced meat with much higher tensile strength and an abundance of gristle, fat, and bones.

When ordering we often made mistakes, misread the menu, mispronounced the tones and got something we didn't expect. The workers at the order desk would laugh as they saw us coming, anticipating our comic routine of faulty Chinese. Sometimes the result was a disaster, sometimes it was a treat we added to our regular list. As we spread the word about the good food, we were joined by foreigners from other universities and soon the Laurel Hill Restaurant became an expatriate meeting place, the center of news and gossip, and a place to make Chinese friends.

One of them was Xiao Han from the Foreign Affairs Office. When Golden Zhou disappeared from our lives, Xiao Han appeared as his replacement. He talked about Golden Zhou with an admiration that was almost reverence, and reinforced our belief about Zhou's mastery of the world. Unlike Zhou, Xiao Han was shy and deferential, but no less interested in our well being, and no less eager to teach us about China. With his own beliefs about the essentials of Chinese life, he introduced us to sautéed eel, convinced that its magnificent flavor would overcome our fear of its tiny bones. Golden Zhou had urged us to eat eel but we had countered his persuasive charm with our own laughing protests. Xiao Han's modest insistence was harder to resist, and unwilling to hurt his feelings, we took small bites, chewing gingerly, acknowledging the eel's good taste with grunts and nods as we tried to separate flesh from bones inside our mouths. We watched Xiao Han spit his bones into the table's ashtray and braced ourselves to ignore our cultural taboos and do the same. Xiao Han's discards were as clean as a museum display but even after many minutes of chewing and sucking, ours looked like road-kills, half scavenged clumps of bones and mangled flesh.

Xiao Han ordered a mountain of rice at each meal. As we practiced conveying food into our mouths with chopsticks, Xiao Han would lift his bowl to his chin and rake the rice into his mouth with his chopsticks, each load sucked in with a sharp inhalation. We tried it, discovering another advantage—the raised bowl also served to catch drips and sauce-slippery chunks that fell from our chopsticks. From then on we increased the size of our rice order and cradled the bowls under our mouths, using the rice as an edible bib.

Often we ate at the Laurel Hill restaurant with Daniel, with our tutor Li Meili, and with other teachers from the English Department. Li Meili was thirty years old, married but had not yet had a child. Her coworkers and family urged her to get pregnant and every year the pressure intensified. Li Meili's sister-in-law had twins and wanted Li Meili to raise one of them so they both could get the state benefits for one-child families. A family with twins was not eligible for the benefits and could even be fined for having more than one child.

Ah, we asked, since it was considered patriotic to have only one child, wouldn't it be even more patriotic not to have any children at all? Li Meili said her family would be very unhappy if she never had a child. In China, the one-child policy was a desperate compromise with four thousand years of tradition. More could not be expected.

With each meal at the Laurel Hill Restaurant our lessons in dining etiquette and family values continued. We met new people, exchanged gossip and, contrary to the warnings we had received, didn't lose any weight. Then cooking stoves were installed in the Guest House apartments. Our eating practices changed and we added a new activity, even more interesting than eating at a genuine Chinese restaurant, that of shopping in a Chinese market.

Cooking with Gas

When it came to cooking Chinese food, we considered ourselves Old China Hands. In graduate school, we had never remembered to start meals until we were too hungry to wait for the results of Western roasting and baking. Because Chinese cuisine has short cooking times, we usually chopped and stir-fried our dinners. We ate Chinese style and used chopsticks nearly every day for four years. That had been a long time ago, but like riding a bicycle, we knew we could do it again.

The kitchen in our Guest House apartment was about two meters long and barely a meter wide, with a cast stone sink and counter along one side. Our letter of invitation promised a stove, so we asked for one. Xiao Han said nervously that the Guest House Office was arranging to install gas pipes and we would get stoves as soon as the work was complete. "Gas pipes will be much safer than having a gas tank in your apartment, don't you agree?"

Three weeks later Xiao Han and Golden Zhou appeared at our door carrying a chrome-plated two-burner stove with piezo-electric ignition. "Where will the gas come from?" we asked, having seen no pipes installed. Golden Zhou smiled archly like a novice magician and asked us to "wait a small bit." They returned several minutes later, dragging a large gas tank between them. The tank itself, much larger than those connected to barbecue grills in the US, was too big to fit in the kitchen so it squatted, rusty and grim, in our living room, connected to our new stove by a long plastic tube.

During our year in China many projects in the Guest House were begun and some even completed, but the installation of gas lines was not one of them.

Cooking gas was subsidized and regulated in China; it was illegal to use it for any purpose except cooking. We had a little red booklet with official seals allowing us to exchange an empty gas tank for a full one at the "gas station" adjacent to campus. Xiao Han said we were very privileged to have these special gas cards because many faculty members couldn't get these cards and had to buy their gas at much higher prices from a station far away.

The full story turned out to be more complex. Ordinarily every teacher would be able to get a gas card, but the gas station and the university were feuding. The university refused to allow the heavy gas station trucks to drive on campus roads and the gas station retaliated by refusing to issue gas cards to university personnel. Of course Golden Zhou had managed to get them just for us, without bothering to explain what a feat he had performed.

Our Chinese kitchen freed us from many of the complexities of Western cooking. We didn't have to push the correct numbers on the microwave or set the oven thermostat and timer. We didn't have to measure ingredients or read recipes. But we did have to exchange our gas tank before it ran out, and determining when the tank was nearly empty was not easy. We learned to rock the tank to assess how much liquefied gas sloshed around, learned to be alert for subtle changes in the flame color. Our detective efforts were unique; others waited until the gas ran out, usually in the middle of cooking.

Many Chinese transported their gas tanks by strapping them to the back of their bicycles, outrigger style. Since a full tank weighed more than twenty kilograms, mounting and riding with such cargo required skill; the bicycle had to be tilted way over to one side to maintain balance. Robin tried it but the tank shifted suddenly, knocking him over and summoning a crowd of laughing Chinese. Humiliated and bruised, he decided one experience with this native custom was enough and next time we paid extra for home delivery—thirty cents.

A week after the stove was installed, Golden Zhou arranged to get refrigerators for all the foreigners. We might have valued an evening of his company more than the luxuries Zhou procured for us, but we expressed our gratitude for his gifts. In China a refrigerator was a badge of prosperity and most Chinese accorded it a place of honor in the living room, often leaving it unplugged to save electricity. After the workers left, we moved ours behind a door near our dining table, sacrificing status for convenience. People from the Guest House Office and the Foreign Affairs Office tried to persuade us to change its place to a more central location: "It would look better," they urged. "It's not safe to put a refrigerator in the corner." We remained unpersuaded.

With a new stove and refrigerator, food shopping was the next step. Unlike the empty grocery stores we saw as the Soviet Union collapsed, food in China was everywhere. Vegetables and meat and fruit were sold on the street wherever a stall or cloth on the ground would fit. Markets were filled with exotic smells and sights and fantastic confusion. Food on tables, food in baskets, food lying on the muddy ground, money tucked around and under the food, live chickens foraging among the customers, live fish flopping at our feet. Orange soda and ice cream were hawked from tables and pushcarts. There were noodle shops on every street and varieties of bread baked or steamed or fried or broiled in every imaginable form of pot, kettle, oven or metal drum. It was possible that some people somewhere in China had too little food, but we didn't find any in Wuhan.

Fruit was abundant: five or six varieties of apples—yellow and red and green, stumpy ripe bananas, pineapples, pomelos, litchis, persimmons, large crisp apple-pears we had never seen before, smaller pears, dates, figs, grapes the size of plums, tangerines, oranges of all shapes and sizes, greener and splotchier and tastier than the cosmetically improved varieties in the US.

The display of vegetables rivaled the best stocked groceries in New York or California. Carrots, turnips, lotus root, varieties of eggplant, cauliflower, broccoli, cucumbers, melons and summer squashes, Chinese winter melon and bitter melon. Chinese cabbage (bok toy), baby bok toy, nappa, spinach, a stalky lettuce, and heads of cabbage. Scallions, chives, ginger, garlic, yellow and red onions. Several varieties of potatoes and sweet potatoes, yams and jicamas. Leafy coleus-like vegetables with a tangy taste came in waves of reds and yellows and greens. Plants with purple stalks and yellow flowers, a good taste and a broccoli texture turned out to be the oil-producing rapeseed plants. Peppers of all varieties, bell and chili peppers in a rainbow of colors, many of them fiercely hot. Melons and squashes and beans and leafy vegetables we had never seen and which had no English names.

Rabbits were displayed skinned and dressed or still alive. Scrawny ducks and chickens, limp and plucked, floated in basins of cold water. Living poultry squawked as they were felt up by prospective executioners. Red eels, black eels, gray eels, wriggling eels, peaceful eels in water, eels spiked through the head as they were being split open, their blood shockingly red. Eels in pieces, chunks and slices. Yellow fish with bright scales, white fish, red fish, spotted fish and mottled fish, dark fish and flat fish, fat fish. Small fish and giant fish laid out on the market sidewalks, gills still pumping, tails beating against shoppers' feet. Little pale shrimps, turtles, soft-shell and hard-shell crabs, five of them trying to escape from one shopper's string bag. Hanging sides of pork, chunks of fatback, blobs of liver, brains and intestines. Mushrooms and other fungi, yellow, black, brown, curly, dried and shriveled, pouring out of burlap bags. Bags of peanuts shelled and unshelled, bags of long green seeds. Barrels and barrels of unknown condiments.

We ventured timidly into this profusion, missing the packaged meats back home that hid their provenance, cringing at the gore, uncomfortable at meeting living creatures soon to be devoured. The first time out we bought only eggs and tofu.

But even this was not easy. Chicken eggs came in various shades of brown, white and blue-green, as varied as the plumage of the chickens. There were also duck eggs, quail eggs, and hundred-year-old eggs that looked as if they had been laid by burning phoenixes. The eggs were neither refrigerated nor dated, and the sellers mixed the old eggs with the new ones. Three of our first five eggs were bad, the smell so strong we ate only peanut butter for that meal. After that experience we shook each egg we considered buying to find out if it rattled, holding it close to one ear and covering the other to dim the market noises. Our theory was that eggs that rattled had a gas-filled space in the shell, a sign they were more likely to be bad. The sellers giggled, amused by our way of choosing eggs. Chinese friends told us other ways to judge the quality of eggs, by color, mottling and shape, but our method seemed more reliable. In the fall only one egg out of every six we bought was spoiled, a better rate than other foreigners, but still pretty disappointing. Eventually we tried a Lower East Side shopping practice: "Please, you give us the best eggs," we said in Chinese. When the vendor selected eggs for us, they were nearly always good.

Tofu was also more difficult to buy than in the US. It came in dozens of varieties: brown tofu steeped in soy, "stinky" tofu (the aptly-named Chinese equivalent of limburger cheese) riddled with black mold, tofu in thin sheets of brown and white, tofu rolls that looked as if they had been hand squeezed. We limited our purchases to plain white bricks, one tenth the price of the packaged kind back home. Still, we found that impatient tofu makers often burned the soy milk, imparting a charred flavor that was hard to detect among the other overpowering market smells. To find good tofu we had to put our noses very close and inhale. The sellers laughed at our strange behavior but each one hoped their tofu would pass our test. Even after we had chosen, other sellers invited us to smell theirs.

Occasionally tofu that passed our smell test among the fish and pork carcasses in the public markets failed when brought home. After several disappointments, we decided to try another source.

Every day a man walked by the Guest House, metal pails hanging from a bamboo pole on his shoulder, crying "Dou-fu-uuu." Janice ran downstairs as the Dou-fu Man turned the corner of the building. A cook from the rejected Dining Hall saw Janice and called to the Dou-fu Man: "Foreigner wants to buy tofu." Janice caught up with him, chose two pieces of tofu and handed over a one yuan note. He slowly gave her change, pausing after each ten-fen note, looking up as if he expected or hoped she would abandon the rest of her change.

Unfortunately Janice forgot she had been using "Essential Balm," a Chinese panacea concocted of menthol, camphor, peppermint, eucalyptus, clove and cinnamon. It cured stuffy noses and was completely effective against foul odors. Back upstairs Robin smell-tested the tofu. Alas, it had the same burnt odor as in the market. Janice ran downstairs again, caught up with the Dou-fu Man, telling him that she wanted to return the tofu and get her money back. The Dou-fu Man backed away, astonished at the request, unwilling to give a refund. Janice dumped the burned tofu cakes back into his bucket and he ran off.

Marketing Skills
We didn't purchase living food at the markets because we were too squeamish to perform the necessary executions. Wang W and Xiao Han reminded us that live food was the freshest kind, that fish were easier to clean if we removed the scales while they were still flopping. We were not encouraged.

We tried to buy meat that other people had already killed but lost our resolve when we got close to the huge slabs of bloody pork hanging in the market stalls. The organ meats were displayed on trays like the aftermath of an autopsy. We backed away from the corpses of skinned rabbits and limp chickens and shivered at the dead frogs, peeled and gathered on strings, sold by slippery characters who moved around the edges of the market, watching for the police. Selling frogs in China was illegal because frogs were needed to keep down the mosquito population.

FOODSTUFF

Hearing about our failed shopping excursions, Li Meili offered us lessons in buying meat. Together we took the bus to the giant market at Big East Gate. At first we walked around to see everything that was for sale. The live meat section blended into the pet section; we couldn't find the border and maybe we didn't want to know. Exotic black and bright orange fish with air sacs under their eyes swam in washbasins next to their more appetizing cousins. Pigeons with iridescent green and pink necks paced in hexagonal wood and string cages and a colorful bird with a very long tail feather waited next to baby quails. Hundreds of parakeets and rows of bird cages, little birdseed crockery and loose birdseed seemed to signal that these were to be companions rather than cuisine. Kittens, some carried in burlap bags and exhibited surreptitiously, were sold next to dogs on leashes, most very skinny. Rabbits of all varieties and colors twitched and quivered in their cages. Spiny anteaters and small porcupines were neighbors to the cats. Li Meili explained that cats were very expensive because people from the countryside used them to control the mice in their silos. Ah, then all the animals in this area are pets, we suggested, with complicated feelings. Not necessarily, she answered. We walked on past rows and rows of small animals, wondering whether they would be petted or stir-fried.

As we moved away from the live animals to the pork displays, Li Meili explained that male pigs tasted better than female pigs so we should look for the "organ" of the pig before buying meat. We asked her whether the organ was still attached. No, she said, it would be on the counter next to the carcass. So how would we know it came from the pig being sold, we asked. She didn't answer.

As we got closer to the slabs of meat, Robin said, "Look. There it is. The pig penis."

Li Meili stopped in shock and then laughed and laughed. "I didn't know it was *that!*" she said. She had translated the English word "penis" into Chinese to realize for the first time what the pig's "organ" was.

"It doesn't look like one," Li Meili said, blushing.

"What is the Chinese word?" we asked.

She began to speak and stopped. Began again and stopped, "I can't say it."

We watched her bargain for meat, going from seller to seller, looking at each slab, rejecting some and asking the price for parts of others. Chinese usually bought meat with large amounts of fat but for us Li Meili chose a section of light pink meat with only a small rim of white. The seller, a scruffy man in an old blue jacket, smiled broadly and agreed to her offer of several *jiao* less than what he had asked. As the meat man cut our piece from the slab and weighed it on a hand scale, onlookers said to Li Meili, "Don't bargain for the foreigners. You are helping foreigners against us." She scolded back in local dialect. Then she turned to the meat man and fired a comment at him. He cut off another hunk of meat and added it to the piece in our plastic bag.

"Thank you," we said, surprised and happy at the bargain. "Why did he give us extra?" we asked Li Meili.

"I told him I *could* buy meat from the man down there whose scales are honest." She smiled triumphantly.

On our first solo run a week later, a fellow customer showed us that our meat was being weighed on a scale with a large slab of fat stuck, as if by accident, underneath the pan. The meat seller removed the fat from under the scale, smiling as if it were a game, giving no indication that he had done anything wrong or even embarrassing. Weights and Measures officers patrolled the market, ready to fine cheaters. But we were foreigners, people whose large noses proclaimed the size of their wallets. It must have been a great temptation to try to get something extra from us, even if only a few cents.

Bargaining for food became one of our major entertainments. Sides of pork, fresher than supermarket meat back home and, yes, government inspected, became objects of our studied contemplation even as we tried to ignore how much they resembled their donors. Backpacks already full of easier purchases—cauliflowers, apples, carrots, bananas and seller-picked eggs—we paced the rows of hanging meat, eyeing each piece, poking and squeezing and turning the slabs to see the back side, trying to look as if we knew what we were doing. Bloody-fingered and tough-minded, we declined all propositions: "Don't want. Don't want. We're still looking." After we examined every gory slab, we doubled back, asking some merchants, "How much money?" When we located the best piece, we accepted some fat with the lean and bargained down the price to only slightly more than a native shopper would have paid.

Before the meat was weighed, we checked the scale to see if it balanced empty. When it didn't, the seller smiled guilelessly and picked up another scale. No guilt, no apology, no defensiveness or hostility.

The meat men would help us assemble the purchase price from among the twelve different denominations of Chinese currency, counting them out slowly to show us that they had not taken more than the agreed upon cost. The notes differed in size and color as well as markings but the lower denominations got so dirty, faded and wrinkled that we had trouble distinguishing them. The sellers returned any extra if we gave them too much—diddling the scales was part of the game, but they didn't shortchange.

The local grapevine—which we called the "bamboo telegraph"—carried word that the Qingchuan Hotel had butter for sale, so we went there to buy some of the "cow-milk-oil." The hotel staff charged us twelve yuan for each *jin* (1.1 pounds), claiming the price was high because it was churned in Beijing. We didn't believe them, but we bought it anyhow.

When we returned to the hotel for more butter the hotel staff demanded twenty yuan a jin. We said *"tai guile!"* (too expensive!) and walked out, hoping they realized that greed had killed their golden goose. Besides, the hotel butter hadn't been very fresh and we had discovered margarine for sale at a little corner store.

We couldn't imagine wanting anything but Chinese food our first weeks in China, but a nostalgia for the old tastes slowly overtook us. One day we made crepes in our wok. We tried the local supermarket bread, a sweet white loaf that would have been rejected by any decent corned beef or salami but was great for French toast. We found cans of tomato sauce in the markets and added spicy Italian and Mexican foods to our repertoire. We ordered containers of parmesan cheese by mail from Hong Kong. We discovered oatmeal and powdered whole milk and bananas and raisins, and treated ourselves to "exotic" Western breakfasts. We convinced ourselves that we were not retreating to old habits, only welcoming a more international cuisine.

3
BUDDIES AND BANES

We hadn't planned to make Western friends in China. Not only did it seem a waste of time but we were easily embarrassed by the behavior of other Westerners. We felt superior to tourists and called them *"waiguo ren"* (foreigners) as the Chinese did. This made the Chinese laugh, but we were not entirely joking. We wanted to fit in, to adapt to the culture; we wanted to be Chinese.

By the end of September most of the apartments in the Foreign Experts' Guest House were occupied by Americans and Belgians. Back home, we would have had little in common with the other residents of the Foreign Experts' Guest House. But back home we would not have imagined that others so different from ourselves, just because they were foreigners like us, could share our wonder, our joy and frustration at things the Chinese took for granted. Soon we found ourselves closer neighbors than we ever expected, giving our little community of "foreigners" the coherence, loyalties and frictions of a family.

Goddaniel and Anti Bud
Daniel and Bud moved into their apartments on the first floor just before we arrived in Wuhan. Both were twenty-six years old and graduates of American universities that had exchange programs with Central China University. Bud was tall and muscular, Daniel short and slight, but to many Chinese they looked alike because they were both blond.

Daniel's effect on Chinese students became legend when he monitored an exam for us. As part of the exam, we had asked the students to describe him. They wrote:

It is a handsome boy with a suit of handsome clothes. For Daniel, if without the pleasant pale white jacket and match it with a red colour underwear, even he boasts the golden hair, white small face, and the short charming beard, he wouldn't be so attractive to girls as he is now to the girls in the class. All the girls from time to time look up from their papers and observe him carefully. I am sure all the girls will give a more vivid, clear picture of Daniel than I have done just now.

He's sitting still like a marble. I've suddenly found that he is improbably charming and handsome. He's neither tall nor short. His hair is golden and kursy, two big eyes are like two stars shining in the night sky. When he looks at you, his eyes are so gentle and attractive that you really don't want to move your eyes away from him. His face, nose and mouth are also very ideal. When he speaks, his voice is like a singing bird, a happy stream. Unfortunately, because he is sitting, I can't see too much about him. However, I'm completely sure that the other parts of his body are as lovely as his face. If I were a little bit prettier, I'd love him regardless of anything.

Oh, How lovely he is! He is as pretty as a girl. He has a high nose, which can put things. A small mouth, like a round letter "O". When he opens his mouth, it moves like a bird mouth. His eyes are very deep, at first of sight, they seems to be two wells. After a minute, his eyes give off amiable lights. His hair has been cut in "W" shape, and also are blonde. His jacket is very big, trousers are very small. In Chinese eyes, he is a clown. Overall, in my eyes, he is like a girl more than a boy.

With the running of the bell, comes in a blond-skinned young guy, who looks as so greenish that we may take him as the chicken coming out of the egg with the wet behind his ears and with the smoke of milk-smelling vapor. "Daniel, the monster to give you the test."

Daniel assured us these descriptions abused poetic license, but he didn't deny the compliments and laughed good naturedly at the insults. He had spent the previous summer in Wuhan and already had many Chinese friends. He studied Chinese martial arts with a *wu shu* master. David was also a born-again Christian and many Chinese were eager to accompany him to the only Christian church in town if only to discover why this religion so displeased the State.

Students often confided in Daniel their questions about Love and Romance. "What if you love someone and they don't want it?" they asked. Good question! The social system that discouraged romance in China also protected young people from rejection. No romance, no heartbreak. Daniel's students found it hard to understand why we foreigners so eagerly risked rejection and misery. How could we live with the pain of a broken heart? Daniel tried to explain that rejection was something that happened to nearly everyone in the West, just a part of romance. And besides, it gave us great music.

Rejection was not taken lightly in China and the sanctions for giving up the old ways were sometimes harsh. Breaking up with a boyfriend could subject a young woman to a lifetime of gossip. Daniel learned of a student who had dared to have two boyfriends, one a foreigner. She had invited Ethan, an American teacher, to meet her parents, but during the visit her Chinese boyfriend showed up. Her parents were scandalized and called the Public Security Bureau who escorted the American back to the university. The next day Public Security told Ethan that his girlfriend no longer cared for him so he should just forget her. Then *she* was brought in separately and told that *he* didn't want to see *her* anymore so she should telephone him right then and tell him that she didn't want to see him either. When this variant on the old police ruse somehow failed, Ethan was threatened with deportation for "disturbing social harmony."

Ethan had since left China, but Daniel was told he resembled this notorious unfortunate. Perhaps that was why Daniel was subjected to special scrutiny. The Public Security Bureau ordered one female student to stop visiting Daniel and told another to befriend him in order to report his activities and attitudes. Both young women told Daniel instead.

Daniel was insulted that anybody thought he might be exploiting or corrupting his students, and angry that officials were trying to control the people who visited him. He learned to say "*Guan ni pi shi*," a rude form of "Mind your own business" (literally, "tend to your own farts"), and waited for a chance to use this expression on someone from Public Security.

Back home we would have assumed that any young lady who spent a lot of time in a young man's apartment was likely to be sleeping with him. In China, we did not make the same assumption about Daniel's visitors, but night door wardens and Public Security officials did. Old Dong, the Guest House guard, shone a flashlight through Daniel's windows at night, checking to see if he was alone in bed. Old Dong gave stern lectures to Daniel's young women visitors, leaving some of them in tears. When Daniel objected, he was told that Old Dong used to work for Public Security and forgot he was no longer a policeman, as if that made his behavior acceptable. Chinese friends and visitors to our apartment did not get scrutinized or threatened in the same way because we were a couple; the possibility of a ménage à trois apparently did not occur to Old Dong.

Chinese are accustomed to giving advice and interfering in the private lives of people for whom they feel responsible; they feel a duty to help others do what is right. Students said everything they did, even if only rumored, was put in a dossier that followed them for life. These blots included sexual transgressions.

A young Chinese teacher was falsely accused of spending the night with Daniel. Although unsubstantiated, the accusation had a social function. The young teacher was an attractive woman who had rebuffed the affections of many an eligible male; she was being warned to get married and settle down. She did, knowing that her future depended on her regaining a good reputation.

BUDDIES AND BANES

Romantic misunderstandings continued to haunt Daniel. One student told her political adviser that Daniel had proposed marriage to her. Daniel hardly knew this student, remembering only that she had asked him to teach her to type and he had answered, "You can teach yourself." She tried his typewriter and reported to her friends that Daniel had taught her to type.

Was Daniel the victim of a student with a dislocated sense of reality, or was there another explanation? Our classmate from the US, the angelic blonde Ma Duona, wrote that she smiled at a stranger in Nanjing and received a proposal of marriage in return. Perhaps in China, where romance was new for college students, it was easy to imagine signals of love and romance where there were none, especially in the presence of blond foreigners.

Daniel had his own romantic interest. The previous summer he had met a pretty young teacher in the history department. She spoke no English and Daniel spoke little Chinese so their exchanges had to take place through intermediaries. This would have been a serious obstacle for any romance but it was not enough of a barrier to reassure the authorities, who decided with no warning to transfer the young woman to a teaching job in the remote countryside.

The young teacher wrote letters and poetry to Daniel, which Li Meili translated for him, parables about being wounded by gossip but not giving in. Then suddenly she wrote to Daniel that she was no longer interested in a romantic relationship with him. Daniel saw the puritan hand of the authorities behind the unexpected rejection, but Li Meili told him he might have been rejected because he was not manly enough, that he should gain weight, wear better clothes. Too bad he wasn't taller, she said. Daniel laughed at Li Meili's ambitions for remaking him and continued to eat as moderately and dress as informally as he had before.

Daniel's neighbor, Bud, exhibited all the macho and bravado that Daniel lacked. Bud mumbled like Marlon Brando and displayed his muscles like Sylvester Stallone. Bud seemed inspired by China to display his repertoire of foreign words, mainly *"Wunderbar"* and

"*Ciao*," baffling the Chinese who struggled to understand his English. He sang honky blues and reggae while riding his bike through campus. He played basketball and lifted weights and exhibited the results in sleeveless undershirts, his hands tucked in his armpits to make his biceps swell. Students called him the "Foreigner Who Wears Underwear on the Outside."

His refusal to temper his personality for the Chinese sense of propriety sometimes got Bud into trouble. One day in a burst of exuberance he ran up to Little Tao, a Guest House worker, lifted her up and whirled her around the lobby. Whether from a feeling of real offense, or to protect herself from gossip, she reported him to Public Security for making an Indecent Assault. As a result Bud had to endure a series of lectures about proper behavior. But he bore no grudge, continuing to care for the offended woman's baby daughter. We often saw him in the hallway, holding the little girl and soothing her with his mumbled English slang while she revenged her mother with indecent assaults on his hair.

Bud's mumbling and mispronounced foreign idioms contrasted with his fluency in American Sign Language. When he saw deaf people signing on a Wuhan street, he tried to sign with them. But Chinese Sign Language uses Chinese characters as a basis for the signs, so he was unable to communicate. Inspired to learn the differences, he asked the Foreign Affairs office to help him visit a school for the deaf. "There are no such things in China," he was told by someone who decided that disabled people were not to be shown to foreigners.

This rebuff confirmed Bud's view of the "Establishment." He refused to have anything to do with the Foreign Affairs Office, refused to attend the social functions they organized for us and ignored the university van they provided for us to go shopping on Saturday mornings.

In time Bud began to eat at the Laurel Hill Restaurant, sitting like a drifter in a seedy bar, wearing a sleeveless undershirt, his head hunched down between well-muscled shoulders, staring past a liter bottle of local beer, complaining about the muh-fuhin' authorities and their stranglehold on young Chinese. He wanted to be seen as a loner, the champion of the down-trodden against the corrupt and powerful.

Paradoxically, his role as street-champion of the underprivileged clashed with his need for someone to take care of *him*. He wanted someone to cook him good American food and do his laundry, someone to make sure he got enough protein and enough sleep, someone to repair his ailing bicycle and worry about him when he rode off into the countryside. We gave him food and tools and offered occasional moral support, but only laughed when he flaunted his helplessness. For a while, he paid the workers in the Guest House to do his laundry, even though he had a washing machine like the rest of us. The workers teased him about his helplessness, holding their noses as they picked up his socks.

When he began to hang out with Li Meili, we did not have the same faith in the integrity of his motives that we had with Daniel. We worried that a woman too shy to tell us the Chinese word for "penis" might be naive enough to succumb to Bud's blond muscularity.

When we saw them together at the Laurel Hill Restaurant, Li Meili ran over to greet us, taking Janice's arm in a gesture of intimate friendship. Had Li Meili gotten up a little too quickly? Why did Bud look disappointed to see us? Were the suspicions of Public Security influencing our judgment? And then as we joined them, and listened to Bud's complaints about food and laundry and life, we realized that he was not looking for a girlfriend, but for a mother. We had already turned down the role and Li Meili was merely his next candidate. A few days later Bud gave up on Li Meili and offered himself for adoption to Pierre and Jeanette, a Belgian couple who lived on the top floor.

Belgian Savvy
Pierre and Jeanette lived in the apartment at the end of the third floor corridor. Pierre taught physics at Central China University; Jeanette, also a physicist but without a Ph.D., taught French at Wu-

han University. Jeanette was very pretty, with blond hair and defined cheekbones highlighting her aristocratic face. Pierre had a European mustache and a way of half closing one eye as if to say "Aha! I knew it." He had come to teach in China as an alternative to serving in the Belgian Army. This was their second year.

When we first met them, Jeanette seemed aloof but Pierre more than made up for her reticence. He was eager to tell us what used to be wrong, what was still wrong, and what he was sure would go wrong with China. His criticisms were sharp and unforgiving and he was not shy about who heard them. When people from the Foreign Affairs Office saw Pierre in our room, we were embarrassed.

Pierre spent most of his time with the Particle Physics Research Group but he also served as a consultant to the university library in their cataloging project. In addition, he worked with students on computer programs analyzing China's economy. This provoked the suspicions of the Public Security Bureau: Why was a foreigner so interested in tracking the inflation rate? Why was he graphing the value of the *yuan* in relation to the US dollar? He was a physicist; he should not be interested in economic matters. We admired Pierre for the breadth of his intellectual interests, but Chinese authorities thought he was a spy.

His frequent criticisms about everything he found wrong with the country made people think he was hostile to China but Pierre proclaimed that, on the contrary, it would be hostile to China *not* to criticize, because that would be to assume China could not improve. Public Security officers did not see it that way; his mail was monitored, his guests were told he was not home when he was, and some of his friends were questioned about what they discussed with him. To add to the suspicion, the Girl-Who-Had-Two-Boyfriends studied French with Jeanette. While we admired the dedication of the student and the generosity of the teacher, to the authorities their association indicated a conspiracy.

Unlike the Americans, Pierre and Jeanette claimed no interest in learning Chinese, saying they wouldn't need the language once they returned to Europe. In fact they had no trouble with basic communication in Chinese, so we supposed their denial was based on a comparison with their fluency in other languages: French, German, Flemish, and, for Pierre at least, English. What they lacked in pronunciation of Chinese they made up for in their resourcefulness at pantomime and sound-effects. When Pierre wanted to buy a bus ticket to the river bank, he imitated a ferry captain pulling a steam whistle cord and called "Tooot, tooot." It worked.

We learned that Jeanette's quietness was not snobbery but shyness about her imperfect English. Robin's French turned out to be adequate as a bridge between Jeanette and the other foreigners when Pierre was not around, and Jeanette soon became the center of our lives, charming us with her continental gestures and good nature.

When we first saw their apartment, its terrazzo flooring was so much brighter and cleaner than our own stain-darkened floors we thought it was made of different materials. Jeanette assured us, "Nooo, zey ahr ahl ze sa-me." Their secret was that they didn't let the Chinese workers mop the floors with muddy water. We borrowed their Belgian scrub brush and discovered that Jeanette was right, underneath the stains our flooring was made of the same white stone as theirs, but we were never able to refuse the cleaning staff their right to mud-mop our apartment, so the sparkle of our floors did not survive.

Pierre and Jeanette's intolerance of dirt, incompetence and untruth combined in anomalous harmony with an uncritical generosity toward the other foreigners: They lent Daniel a bicycle nearly every day, fed Bud regularly, made soup for anyone who became ill, lent us supplies even though we didn't always return them, shopped for us, shared the fancy foods they brought back from Hong Kong, skipped parties and shows to baby-sit for friends.

They had been in China longer and they knew more about what was really going on than any other foreigner. Pierre and Jeanette told us about the political hierarchy in university departments, warned us about international mail being opened, and explained that sexual behavior and philandering was far more widespread in China than it appeared. It was they who first told us that the red-checked posters we saw on city walls announced the execution of criminals. The families of the criminals were required to pay for the bullet used by the executioner, as a symbol of their shame, responsibility and atonement.

They knew the city well and showed us where to buy cans of tomato paste and where to find rotini and other pasta. They taught us to look for food products with Western languages on the label because those were for export and usually of better quality. We learned from them the Chinese shoppers' maxim that products manufactured in Shanghai were best. They reminded us to buy large quantities of anything we liked because it could disappear from the markets and not return for months.

Jeanette showed us the European style of buying food at the public markets. She had grown up on a farm in Belgium so the required execution procedures were familiar to her. We watched her bargain, delighting in her *pffts* and gestures of refusal, but we never learned to match her skill and perseverance nor her courage to purchase live fish and chickens.

For all their help, perhaps their greatest contribution to our foreign community was the anger and impatience they expressed. They voiced our common complaints, and publicized the frustrations and injustices that befell us all. We accepted this service with some guilt, knowing their anguish kept our own tempers intact. When people from the Foreign Affairs Office complained about the Belgians' intolerance, we lacked the courage to admit that we often agreed with Pierre and Jeanette.

The Journalist and The Poet
Until the third week in September, we were the only residents of the second floor. Then two more Americans arrived: Nelson the Poet, an English professor from the University of Tennessee, and Helen the Journalist from Washington DC.

Nelson and Helen had toured Beijing with Xiao Han and then traveled eighteen hours in a "hard sleeper" train compartment to get to Wuhan. Xiao Han was not able to get them the soft sleeper berths the Golden Smoothie had gotten for us. To make their cramped quarters more comfortable they had checked their luggage in the baggage car but when they went to claim it, the luggage had disappeared. They believed it had been stolen. Xiao Han's reassurance didn't help: "Luggage is never stolen in China. It gets lost."

Several weeks after their arrival we heard loud noises in the hallway and opened our door to see Golden Zhou with a woman dressed and coiffured in Communist Party severity—stone gray hair and stone gray suit in straight no-nonsense lines. Next to her was a pile of luggage, one suitcase wrapped in cardboard and tape.

The stone gray woman came over to shake our hands and began to read aloud from a small piece of paper. Zhou interrupted her, explaining that we were the wrong people. Helen and Nelson were then fetched and introduced, and the official read her speech of apology. Zhou translated: Helen's and Nelson's luggage was not delivered sooner because one of Helen's bags had split open. The woman, an official from the railroad, explained that they had kept *all* the bags at the station, both Helen's and Nelson's, while they had meetings to decide what to do about the damage. After three weeks they had decided that Helen would be allowed to buy a new suitcase at their expense.

Before she arrived, Golden Zhou had told us that Helen was over sixty. He was impressed that a woman so old would come to China to teach. (Chinese retirement age was fifty-five.) We had imagined her to be a frail aging lady, so we were pleased to see she was a hearty, take-charge character who seemed immune to the inconveniences of life in China. She had volunteered to teach English to Chinese students just for the adventure. She told us about her connections in diplomatic circles and referred to Senators and Cabinet members by their first names. She had a son who wrote for the *Washington Post* and another who was an actor and film producer.

Helen's bulk surprised and amused the Chinese. Although China did have a number of chunky older people and some nearlyzaftig young women, what was an acceptable size for an older American woman was an astonishing excess in China. She collected large crowds wherever she went about in public. Onlookers exclaimed, "*Pangzi!*" ("A fatty!"). We didn't translate this for her.

For years Helen had been an older woman on her own, a single parent of four boys. She had learned survival techniques that did not always delight us. She was used to organizing her troops and assigning chores. At first we were happy to intervene with the Guest House staff, practicing our Chinese to get repairs and equipment for her, but we found ourselves being called on too regularly: "My radiators don't turn on. Could you help me with them?" and "Oh, you're going out shopping? Could you get me some . . .?" Our enthusiasm shriveled.

Helen was eager to do things in return for the missions she assigned, but the services she was willing to render were not always ones we wanted. We didn't want to spend hours or days making group travel plans and ticket arrangements. We didn't want the Foreign Affairs Office scolded because they did not do enough for us when we were ill. We didn't want people to be told that we were famous professors, or authors of "marvelous" books.

In addition, we worried that Helen imposed on the Chinese, issuing instructions they were too polite to refuse. She invited Chinese to dinner parties at which they did the cooking; she sent them on fetch-and-carry errands when we refused. We thought Helen's talk about her connections in Washington might lead some Chinese to believe she could arrange entry visas, jobs and university admissions in the US. Perhaps we should have worried more that the Chinese were trying to take advantage of our Helen, but we didn't. We felt responsible for her behavior—she was one of us, she represented us, and like family members watching a relative misbehave in public, we found ourselves wincing when she ordered people about.

The night Nelson the Poet arrived, he was tired and, we later learned, a little drunk. He started talking academic shop, describing what he wanted to teach. We recognized familiar academic words and the syntax was correct, but we didn't understand what he was saying. We looked attentive, we nodded, and tried to change the subject.

Nelson had round cheeks and a chin that folded up under his sparse beard. When he walked he pulled his shoulders closer together and set each foot down with a splat. Academics from the South usually try to suppress their accents, but Nelson played his up, enjoying the role of Good Ole Boy, drinking beer, lacing his language with profanity, wearing shabby clothes. Nelson's command of language was extraordinary, but alcohol would scramble his thesaurus. A certain expression of intense concentration indicated that he wasn't following what anyone was saying.

It was easy to be critical of Nelson because he did so much that embarrassed us. He drank too much at a banquet given by university officials and had to be helped upstairs. He lost his temper and shouted in public. He carried hundred yuan notes of FEC sticking out of his shirt pocket.

He was away from his wife for the year, lonely and horny as a result, he told us. The Chinese reserve and modesty about sex, their Victorian attitudes, challenged him, inspiring crude jokes, innuendoes and off-color remarks. We enjoyed Nelson's wit about his own helpless celibacy and his torment from unrequitable passions toward Chinese women, but, please, we thought, Not-In-Front-Of-The-Chinese. We hadn't yet realized that "The Chinese" were more entertained than shocked by our conversations and life style. We were foreigners, and no more expected to understand their moral standards than pandas mating in the public zoo.

Nelson developed a baroque passion for lovely Little Lin, the newest and youngest member of the Foreign Affairs office. Younger than his daughter, she flirted and teased and played up to his admiration. In the state we had learned to recognize as alcohol-induced, he would stare at her with an intensity that was Just-Not-Done in China. Little Lin, in return, giggled, mimicked his words, hid his possessions and invented stories to tease him.

"Everyone else has tickets to the performance, but there are no tickets left for you, Nelson," she told him.

And another time: "We can go to all the other stores today but we cannot go to the liquor store, Nelson."

Little Lin liked to tease about withholding something: "Airplane tickets? I don't have any for you. Maybe Xiao Han has them."

Nelson soon learned to react with astonishment or mock anger until he got more information: "What? No tickets for me? Tell Director Fang I want *his* tickets. He must give me his tickets."

Sometimes the stories of loss or inconvenience were true, but because Little Lin played these jokes so frequently, we didn't believe them until it was too late, until the driver really had bypassed the liquor store, or Nelson had to trek across campus late at night to find the person who had the missing tickets. In these cases Nelson's anger was likely to be real.

He would try to get his revenge in fantasy. Inhaling deeply a newly opened Almond Joy, he shouted in ecstasy, "Ahhhh. Little Lin's underpants!" He extolled her tight jeans and the crevices they created and revealed. "How I would like to die and return as those jeans!" he proclaimed, downing the rest of his martini.

One Saturday, when Nelson fell asleep in the van on the way home from shopping, Little Lin hid the box containing his new scroll painting. Nelson woke up and looked anxiously for his painting, which he valued because the artist had written Nelson's name on the scroll and signed it with a dedicatory poem. Trying to hint that Nelson was the victim of a joke and not an art theft, we exclaimed that we had never seen such a wondrous painting; it must have been the figment of a dream. Little Lin followed our tone and proclaimed that we had never been to the art store, that we had just come from the zoo where we saw pandas and giraffes. Nelson caught on and said that one of us must have his scroll; he would search Little Lin and *that* would be worth the price of the painting.

For a while, we thought Nelson believed he had a poet's license to say or do whatever he wanted, indifferent to the effect on other people. But we were mistaken. One evening, Xiao Han asked Nelson where he wanted to go for Spring Festival vacation.

Nelson said, "How about Hong Kong. I hear there's lots of sex and shit there."

Xiao Han laughed nervously. Janice said, "Xiao Han, please send Nelson to Hong Kong. Get him some sex and then maybe he will stop talking about it."

Helen jumped in: "That's right. You really overdo it, Nelson."

We all laughed and the topic changed. But the next morning there was a note on our door from Nelson. "I apologize if I offended. I did not mean to. I only intended to chide the Chinese about their overdone sense of propriety."

We looked forward to being with Nelson when his insightful wit was not diluted by alcohol, but he believed *in vino veritas*. He was determined to get us drunk to discover more about us. We disappointed him when the only effect of too much alcohol was that we grew inarticulate, laughed a lot, and staggered from his apartment to ours. No great secrets could be revealed by people whose tolerance for alcohol was so low. He thought we hadn't known each other long and were still honeymooning. We were delighted that we appeared so romantic after so many years together and found that his interest in us acted as an aphrodisiac. What he imagined we did, we in fact did, giggling at Nelson's effect on us and thankful that Chinese beds had no squeaking parts.

Hallowed Tradition

By the end of October, deprived of things Western for more than two months, we foreigners treated the upcoming Halloween as a major holiday, an excuse to introduce our Chinese friends to our bizarre costuming tradition. Nick, an American from a neighboring university hosted the giant party.

Nick dressed as an ancient Roman with a laurel wreath and bed-sheet toga. Americans from other universities came as ghouls, street punks, and costume-puns on *"Mei you,"* that frequently expressed "Don't have," pronounced like the deli slang for mayonnaise. Some African students came in their traditional native dress, and everyone brought music tapes.

We dressed up our tutors, one as an American Indian, the other as a pirate, using blankets, tempera paint and cardboard feathers. Robin became a Communist Party Leader— cap and Mao Jacket with a gold pen in the pocket and Janice became an Extra-Terrestrial— silvery mylar blanket and a second head made from a painted balloon.

Helen the Journalist became one of the ubiquitous Chinese thermos bottles— aluminum pot on her head as the cup, cork in her mouth, and a flowered sheet with a handle taped to it around her large body. Nelson decided at the last minute to come as a "well-hung man," donning a leather jacket, a bag over his head and a noose around his neck. We laughed at his pun but refused to explain it to the Chinese.

The reputation Bud sought as a unique character was established firmly by this event. Li Meili asked if we had seen him. "He is dressed as a woman and looks vomity." Bud had borrowed Helen's bathing suit and stuffed its bulges, shaved his new goatee and transformed his face with Helen's makeup. He modeled his costume by acting like a go-go dancer on the make, arms over his head, well-rouged face squeezed in passionate abstraction. One of Bud's (male) Chinese students and basketball partners remarked that "Bud is a very . . . uh . . . exciting man." Daniel said Bud's makeup job was too good, that we weren't seeing a costume but an alter-ego.

At first we saw our Western friends in simple terms, mere thumbnail sketches, but as the year went on they refused to conform to our stereotypes. We wondered whether it was China that brought out their complexity or had we merely overcome our need to simplify everyone and everything in order to make sense of this confusing world. It took us even longer to appreciate that some of our Chinese friends were no less complex, no less likely to surprise us.

4
FOREIGN AFFAIRS

Guardian Angles

It was not discouragement by government officials or local xenophobia that hindered our making Chinese friends. Our problem was much simpler and much more fundamental: Friendship requires communication, and communication requires a common language. We were handicapped—we could not express many of our thoughts and feelings in Chinese and the Chinese had trouble with our colloquial English. We were uncomfortable when we couldn't make ourselves understood, but to do so we had to speak slowly and clearly, avoiding idioms and obscure words. We had to sacrifice puns and culture-specific references. Even contractions were a problem—we had to say "cannot" instead of "can't" because the latter is almost indistinguishable from "can" to anyone but a native speaker. With all these restrictions on what we could say, we soon cherished the humor, the slang, the profanities and the sloppiness of American speech, things we had always taken for granted. Bud groaned with pleasure at Nelson's salty language, "I love it when you talk dirty." In fact, we all did.

But we did make Chinese friends. The language barrier was overcome by their kindness and concern. When we had a problem, they offered help with such enthusiasm we could not refuse. Their playfulness and good nature compensated us for having to forgo our wordplay and shortcut slang.

We came to rely on several Chinese for companionship, for information, and for emotional support. If they visited us, we felt loved; if they came to our building and didn't knock on our door, we were sad. If we were too easily embarrassed by our fellow foreigners, we compensated by being too forgiving and accepting of the Chinese. We tended to believe whatever they told us, even in the face of conflicting information.

The first Chinese we got to know, the ones we saw most often during the year, were those from the Foreign Affairs Office, the *Waiban*. Other universities had Waibans that acted as watchdogs and chaperones, making sure foreigners did not get into trouble or embarrass their hosts, but our Waiban officers were different, or so it seemed. They didn't restrict us; they protected us. They treated us as friends and invited us to their homes.

Eight people worked in the Waiban. Most of them had been appointed within the previous six months, including Golden Zhou and Director Fang. Everyone in the office, except Director Fang, asked us to address them by the title "*Xiao*" (Little) in front of their surname: Xiao Han, Xiao Lin, Xiao Li, Xiao Pu, Xiao Song, Xiao Zheng, and Xiao Zhou.

The Golden Smoothie
In Beijing, Golden Zhou awed us with his ability to negotiate, charmed us with his smile and disarmed us with his conversation. When we got to Wuhan we looked forward to seeing him but that happened rarely. It wasn't that he spent more time with other foreigners, just that he always seemed to be too busy with something else.

Unlike most people at the university, he lived with his wife and child in an apartment off-campus. He talked proudly about his wife, a computer scientist whom few people knew. It seemed as if they were very close but we rarely saw them together. Golden Zhou loved to dance, but he went to the university dances alone. We wondered if this caused gossip but the only gossip we heard about him was from someone, who heard from someone else, that Zhou once ran a special office which bought televisions at government discounts and then sold them to make money for the university.

This story was easy to believe. In China where the expressions *mei banfa* (no way) and *mei you* (don't have) are national jokes, Zhou knew how to work the system to get things done. It had been

Golden Zhou who got us stoves and refrigerators when the head of his department wanted us to eat in the Dining Hall; he got us travel documents when others said it was too late; he coordinated the jobs of several workers so we got hot water; later he came to our rescue in the hospital and at the Bureau of Public Security.

Not all the foreigners appreciated Golden Zhou. Some were suspicious of him because he *was* such a smoothie and they had learned to distrust such people. In particular, Bud's hatred of The Establishment focused on Zhou. When a young woman from another university said she could not eat lunch with Bud because Zhou had reported their noon meetings to Public Security, Bud knew who The Enemy was.

We heard a different story, that the woman's husband asked her not to eat with Bud because people were gossiping about them. Golden Zhou was too sophisticated to have been involved in something so petty, we thought, but Bud was sure his lonesome lunches were all Zhou's fault.

In October, when Zhou asked to speak with us privately, saying he had a problem he wanted to discuss, we agreed eagerly, happy to be his confidantes. Zhou's problem was that someone in the Foreign Affairs Office had told Bud he couldn't go to Beijing during the National Day holidays, that Beijing was "closed to foreigners" during that time. Bud had canceled his travel plans and later found out that other foreign teachers had gone to Beijing with no trouble.

We thought it was funny. Did someone think Bud couldn't take care of himself? Did they think he might embarrass the university and so should be kept home?

Zhou took it very seriously. "Who would tell Bud that the national capital would be closed on the national holiday? This was wrong." Zhou explained that foreigners were allowed to go anywhere except restricted areas like military bases. It was important to him that Bud know this was all a big mistake.

Golden Zhou was using the Chinese Indirect Approach, a style of problem-resolution in which all misunderstandings and delicate situations are handled through an intermediary. Since this was our first exposure to the Indirect Approach, it didn't occur to us that *we* were being asked to convey Zhou's personal and official regrets to Bud for missing his trip to Beijing. We treated the conversation as confidential and never mentioned it to Bud. Only later did we begin to understand this social custom.

Golden Zhou worked the Indirect Approach for our benefit, although we did not realize how smoothly our problem had been solved until weeks afterward. The Vice Chairman of the English Department, Wang Y, had asked us, "to give, you see, a public lecture for the, I should say, university."

"About what?"

"Anything, you see, you want to talk about," he said.

"Okay," we responded enthusiastically, "how about a talk on the problems of research fraud? We wrote a book about ethical problems in higher education, and we've lectured on this topic to general audiences before."

Wang Y hesitated. "Perhaps you could talk on something more interesting, something about university life in America, for example."

We thought our topic *was* about university life, but he clearly didn't want that. We felt constrained to talk about an area in which we had some expertise. We didn't understand that our job was to draw crowds and enhance Wang Y's reputation as a purveyor of foreign experts, that he wanted a topic with more pizzazz.

Realizing his hints were not working, Wang Y proposed we give a talk about Marriage in America. Waxing enthusiastic, he explained that we could talk about the Great Divorce Problem. "Chinese people, you see, think everyone in America gets, you see, divorced. It is a big problem. They would like to know, I should say, what to do about it, how to solve it."

Oh.

The next day Wang Y asked us to set a date for the talk. We stalled. What could we say about divorce in this puritanical country? We couldn't advocate premarital cohabitation. We couldn't recommend divorce to alleviate unhappy relationships. And we couldn't suggest that it might be normal for people who develop and change throughout their lives to grow apart. We went through a list of rhetorical questions, worrying and laughing at how outrageous our opinions might appear to the Chinese sense of morality. We even joked about giving a provocative talk in order to embarrass Wang Y. We regaled our friends, both foreigners and Chinese, with our dilemma.

Then the Golden Smoothie paid us a visit. We had not spoken to him about the talk, but he had heard about it, indirectly, of course.

"You do not have to give this such a talk. You can talk about anything you want."

Wang Y stopped asking us to set a date for our lecture; in fact he never mentioned it again. We decided that the Chinese Indirect Approach was a pretty good way of dealing with problems since one of ours had disappeared.

We adjusted to Golden Zhou's absence, content with his occasional visits for official purposes, accepting that our company was not as interesting to him as his was to us. Then one evening he showed up at our door, as warm and charming as he had been in Beijing. He began telling us about his past—the closing of schools during the Cultural Revolution, his train ride to see Mao Zedong in Beijing, his being denied university admission because his parents weren't really "peasanty" peasants. He explained that this turned out to be fortunate because students who went to university at that time were soon sent off to the countryside to do manual labor, whereas he was allowed to remain in Wuhan as a secondary school teacher. He began each anecdote with, "I am lucky." For Golden Zhou, "I am lucky" did not express inappropriate modesty. It expressed unbounded self-confidence that the world had favored him, that he was lucky and would always be, that everything would go well for him and his. Even if he was only trying to convince himself with his optimism, he certainly convinced us.

His self confidence inspired us to ask about the story of selling TV sets to make money for the university. We confessed we believed the story because we thought he had the skills to manage such a deal. Laughing, he said he would never do anything that violated the law, but this denial only convinced us that he had managed the deal so skillfully that no law had been broken.

Becoming more confidential, he told us that some years earlier he was not allowed to visit foreigners without another Chinese present. The rule had been made to prevent foreigners from learning state secrets. The government had since realized that most citizens didn't know any state secrets, but, he added, some people in power still believed the old ways were best.

Other people had told us they didn't visit us in the Guest House because they were afraid of reprisals when the winds of politics changed. Was Zhou also one of the wary ones? Was he giving us a message—that he didn't visit us more often because people would become suspicious of the time he spent with foreigners? We never would find out.

During this evening of confidences and life stories, Zhou punctuated his sentences with head-tossings and laughter and affectionate pats and touches for Robin that Chinese males give freely to other males. His occasional ungrammaticalities added to his charm. The visit seemed to be a renewal of friendship, but a month passed before we saw him again.

When Zhou visited again, he said right away, "I will be very frank with you because I cannot keep this thing—can I say?—in my heart." He put his hands over his heart, enhancing each phrase with a gesture as if to make up for shortcomings in his English. He was "sorry to tell us" but he had met with administrators from other universities whose foreign experts did more teaching than we did. He knew that we met our classes together and he was willing to count those as full courses in figuring our teaching hours, but he still wanted us to teach more.

Wang Y, the Vice-Chairman, had already tried to persuade us to take on more courses. We had flatly refused, pointing out that we were teaching over three hundred students, and any more hours would be too much. Then we had freely complained to Chinese and foreigners alike about Wang Y's wheedling. Golden Zhou was telling us that he had been behind Wang Y's request, pre-empting the gossip that he believed would get back to us.

We mobilized our joint defenses. Robin stressed the many hours required to prepare for the lecture courses and the large number of student papers we had to read. Janice showed Zhou one of the handouts we had prepared because no textbooks were available. He was immediately sympathetic. Instead of teaching more courses, we could continue to prepare these handouts, he said, because then the university could use them as class material in future years. We were disarmed, relieved, and parted the best of friends. Only later did we wonder what we had won. Preparing the handouts was no longer optional; we had just agreed to write a textbook for the university.

Director Fang Speaks
Our relationship with Director Fang had gotten off to a bad start when we abandoned the Guest House Dining Hall. Although the Dining Hall staff seemed happy to be rid of us, Director Fang considered it a personal failure. He frequently reminded us that shopping for food and cooking took a lot of time and trouble. But we enjoy shopping and cooking, we responded defensively.

Then we heard from Wang Y that Director Fang wanted to *require* all foreigners to eat at the Guest House Dining Hall. Our protests were not subtle. No doubt Wang Y conveyed our reactions to Director Fang according to the protocol of the Indirect Approach, because the policy was never mentioned again. It is possible that Director Fang asked Wang Y to sound us out so he would not lose face if we rejected his plan. More likely, we suspected, was that Wang Y leaked the story in order to make trouble for the Director.

As we walked to the restaurant across campus we sometimes met Director Fang. He would return our greeting, brush back his lock of hair and look very sad. "You are going to the restaurant?" he would ask in a tone that sounded as if we were on our way to court to testify against his mother. We would try to cheer him up by saying we could meet colleagues and students at the restaurant, something we thought he would appreciate. We refrained from pointing out that the restaurant offered a wider choice of much higher quality food, much lower prices and much better sanitary conditions than the Dining Hall.

Director Fang told us he had investigated the matter of our being served "old" food at the Dining Hall. He had questioned the staff and they admitted giving us food that had been served the day before, but they assured him it was not old. He repeated, "They did not give you *old* food. The Dining Hall is going to make a menu for the foreigners. Then, I am sure, conditions will be much improved."

To someone from a culture with a history of thousands of years, "old" may have had a stronger meaning than we intended. We were about to qualify our statement when Daniel said firmly, "We won't eat there anymore. We have all gotten sick from eating there."

Instead of surprise or disappointment, instead of sympathy or even denial, we got reassurance. "My office is working on solving this problem. When the Foreign Experts' Dining Hall has a menu, conditions will be much better for you."

Director Fang's resonant nasal voice pronounced each English word so perfectly and uttered well-formed sentences so slowly and carefully, yet often his responses were inappropriate, as if he were acting in a different play or had lost his place in the script.

We puzzled over the Director's conversational anomalies. Daniel suspected he might be hard of hearing. Robin suggested he didn't listen to us because he was too busy composing a fluent response to what he imagined we should have said. Janice believed he had spent his years in Washington studying how American politicians answered questions at press conferences. We made merciless fun of his English, ignoring our own inadequacies in Chinese.

Director Fang's conversation style bewildered Chinese as well as foreigners. At the English Department's year-end party—to which the General English Department teachers were not invited—Director Fang made a speech about new opportunities and exchange programs for study and work abroad. This seemed to be wonderful news because every Chinese scholar wanted to go abroad. Fang went on to say that university leaders were especially pleased with the progress made by students who were not English majors. There was a sudden hush in the room since the non-majors were all taught by the teachers who had not been invited to the party, teachers from the General English Department! It seemed that Director Fang was delivering an oblique criticism and those present had lost their chance to study abroad. We learned afterward that some of the older teachers had not worried. They knew Fang was trying to say something nice but hadn't remembered which department was which.

Director Fang decided to change the name of his "Foreign Affairs Office." His subordinates asked each foreigner, individually, which of two titles was better, "The Exchange Office of International Education" or "The Office of International Educational Exchange." We unanimously, if unenthusiastically, chose the second. Only then were we told that Director Fang had insisted on the first.

We had been exploited in a masterful example of the Chinese Indirect Approach. Fang's subordinates couldn't tell their boss that his English was flawed but they could report that the American foreign experts criticized his wording. Fang, believing that the foreigners didn't know whose wording they rejected, wouldn't lose face.

Director Fang's attraction to impressive wording had a history. His subordinates told us he used to edit all the English correspondence written in his office. Once he challenged the word "see" in a sentence, "'See' is not quite the right word. Use 'visualize' instead. Yes, 'visualize' would be better."

His young subordinates mocked Fang's wording, calling to each other: "We'll visualize you tomorrow." "Visualize you soon."

When we heard from someone at another university that the salaries of foreign experts and teachers would be raised, the rumor was soon confirmed by Director Fang who told Nelson that he would get a raise but he must keep it secret from the other foreigners. Fang implied that only Nelson would get a raise and that it was the direct result of Fang's intervention on his behalf. Nelson reported that Fang told him this on three separate occasions, apparently forgetting he had told him before. Then Chairman Wang Z and Vice-Chairman Wang Y of the English Department came separately to tell Nelson about the new raise, each implying they alone were responsible for the increase and Nelson would be the sole beneficiary. But thanks to Golden Zhou, we already knew the decision to give all foreign experts and teachers a raise had been made by the State Education Committee in Beijing.

In a country where trading favors was an essential currency, Fang and the two Wangs were trying to make national policy seem like a personal favor. Since Nelson had a voice in who would be chosen to go to the US on his university's exchange program, they were trying to build up credit with him.

The deception was so easily found out it seemed childishly inept but in China obvious lies were not taken seriously. We foreigners, however, felt insulted by the lies, as if we were assumed to be too stupid to know better. This was one cultural adjustment we never made, and even at the end of the year, when we should have known better, an obvious lie would still infuriate us.

Soldier Han
Xiao Han's full name was *Han Bing* ("Chinese Soldier"). He had a face of angled planes that deserved to be immortalized in sculpture, and thick beautiful hair that he wore long. When he wasn't worried or nervous about the foreigners in his care he had a very warm smile. He was easy to like, and not just because he shared our

opinion of Director Fang. Our attempts to speak Chinese pleased him and he taught us useful words such as those for ant, roach and electric fan. He also taught us how to ask for change, how to open a bank account and how to use the public buses.

The new economic prosperity in China encouraged people to dress as well as they could, to flaunt their new access to consumer goods. Construction workers wore suit jackets, or skirts and nylon stockings on the job. In this respect Xiao Han was unusual. Unlike Director Fang who wore white shirts and custom-tailored Mao jackets and unlike Golden Zhou who switched easily from the formality of Mao jackets to stylish Western clothes, Xiao Han nearly always wore casual clothes: jeans, T-shirt and a windbreaker.

It was not because he did not have fancier clothing that he dressed down. We found this out when Robin got a new Mao jacket for his birthday and Xiao Han wore his own Mao suit to Robin's party. Xiao Han's suit was the finest we had seen in China, better than Golden Zhou's or Director Fang's, but he never wore it again during the year.

We believed Xiao Han dressed to avoid standing out, to avoid calling attention to himself, a habit he must have learned during the Cultural Revolution. Our conclusion was reinforced because Xiao Han criticized others whose dress was too extreme for his taste. He would point out young women whose lipstick was too bright or who wore large earrings, young men with styled hair and flashy clothes. "I don't like this such person," he would say.

We learned about his past a little at a time, some directly from him, the rest from other people. Golden Zhou told it like a Horatio Alger story: Xiao Han was once a lowly worker at the university. He used to do odd jobs, electrical work and plumbing, and then became a service worker at the Foreign Expert's Guest House. He studied English on his own and went to night classes at the university. And then he was given a good job in the Waiban.

Xiao Han was the child of two academics who were banished to the countryside during the Cultural Revolution. He had spent his teenage years as a kind of indentured servant to a peasant. He was assigned to feed the pigs but there was not even enough food for the people. The pigs were too scrawny and he was always being criticized.

"What did you learn in the Cultural Revolution?" Pierre asked him.

"To eat rats and steal from the peasants," Xiao Han replied.

As we learned more of his story from others, we began to realize that it was also a story of stigma. Because he was doing farm work instead of going to school, Xiao Han did not learn enough to pass the entrance examination for university admission. His nightschool diploma branded him as second rate and everyone knew it. Moreover, his former coworkers in the Guest House resented his new job and called him *gou tuizi* (dog leg) for helping the foreigners. This insult had a pejorative force worse than "Uncle Tom," for the dog's leg belonged to the running dog of capitalism.

When we first moved into our apartment, Xiao Han asked us for a list of what needed to be repaired. We gave him a list much longer than he expected—missing window glass, no hot water, broken chair legs, broken air conditioner, broken shower hose, leaking faucets, roaches and ants, holes in the wall. He apologized for the condition of the apartment, apologized for the length of the list, apologized for all of China. Embarrassed to have brought on such apologies, we tried to lighten things up by adding to our list of needed repairs: "End the fighting in the Middle East," "Open a pizza restaurant nearby." Xiao Han began to loosen up. We told him our roaches had to be killed because they were very big and woke us up at night by knocking over the furniture. He laughed and relaxed. Then we offered to cover the dirt and holes in our walls with *da zi bao*, "big character posters" used during the Cultural Revolution to criticize and humiliate people. This time Xiao Han didn't laugh. We had joked about something that years later was still too painful a subject.

He apologized for China again when the Guest House failed to make repairs. We told him that landlords were the same all over the world; they were quick to take but not to give. We were playing on the Chinese stereotype of the pre-Revolutionary landlord. Only much later in the year did we admit to Chinese friends that while we were abroad we ourselves were landlords, renting our house to tenants.

As we got to know him better, Xiao Han's seriousness added to his charm. He worried about us and his emotions showed, so he seemed more genuine. He got upset when things went wrong, visibly angry at incompetence. When Daniel got a lingering cold, Xiao Han insisted that Daniel come to his house for every meal. "Oh, he looks so weak, I have to feed him." When Nelson lost his temper, Xiao Han excused him by explaining that poets had more emotion than other people. At one evening gathering Helen said pointedly, "I can't wait to start cooking." Xiao Han's smile disintegrated and he mumbled, "Stove," something he had promised but not yet succeeded in getting for Helen. Robin said, "Xiao Han, I want an airplane and I need it tonight." Xiao Han smiled weakly.

Xiao Han was easy to talk with and we confided in him almost as much as in our tutors. He was the first one we told of our discomfort about giving a lecture on The Great American Divorce Problem. We complained to him about the evasions of Wang Y. We told him stories we heard about American visitors changing money in the black market. We talked with him about "spiritual pollution," described how Robin was accosted by pimps in Thailand, joked with him that homosexuality would help solve China's population problem, and teased him about his closed-minded attitudes toward sex.

He in turn teased us about our closed-minded attitude about eating dog. "What do you like to eat? I will cook dog for you," he threatened, knowing our reaction.

We visited his apartment unannounced. "Now I know you are my real friends," he said.

When he invited us to his home for dinner, the food was wonderful, dish after dish of richly flavored meats and broths and vegetables. He and his wife shared the cooking, alternating dishes.

At the end, as we were about to burst, they brought out what they knew was a favorite, a delicately spiced, steamed Wuchang fish that cost them nearly three days wages.

Xiao Han was an enthusiastic consumer and owned a stereo system, color TV, electronic keyboard instrument, and refrigerator of very high quality. He bought these consumer products, he said, to enrich the life of his daughter, the round-faced cherub he held in his lap. Next month he was going to cover the concrete floor with decorative linoleum, an item heavily advertised on local television.

After dinner we sat in the two upholstered chairs while Xiao Han and his wife and daughter sat on the bed. The three-year old was coaxed to sing a song she had learned in school. She sang with her hands folded behind her back until she raised one hand to her mouth, made a biting gesture, pulled her hand away and then swung it in a throwing motion. Then both hands swept up and she jumped, crying "Poof!" Her father explained that she was singing "The Hand Grenade Song."

Both Xiao Han and his wife doted on their daughter, their one child, the focus of their emotional energy. Their own relationship came second; they were together as partners engaged in a common project, the love and care of their daughter. At parties Xiao Han would dance with his daughter, but not his wife. She didn't dance, he said indifferently.

Xiao Han told Nelson that weekends were boring, adding that most Chinese opposed the plan to reduce the work week from six to five days because work was more interesting than being at home.

"What about parties, visiting friends, going out?" we asked.

"Chinese people don't do that except on special occasions," he said.

"What about staying home and enjoying the company of your wife?" Nelson pressed, suggestively.

Xiao Han didn't think that would be very interesting.

When the discussion focused on Chinese marriage, Xiao Han said it was better for a man to marry a worker, as he did, than to marry a woman with a university education. He backed this up by describing a friend who had been miserable while he was engaged to a university teacher. When the girl left him for another man, he decided he would marry a worker and now his life was much happier. We wondered whether the story was autobiographical.

Xiao Han told us about a young woman who had broken up with one boyfriend and married another. He disapproved, saying such a person was coldhearted. We said the woman should not be obligated to continue a relationship if she didn't love the first boyfriend. Xiao Han disagreed—one should choose a spouse for suitability, not love. The girl's first boyfriend had been politically and economically more suitable than the second, so he should not have been rejected. Xiao Han didn't think doing without love was so bad; it was rejection that had to be avoided.

Little Imp Lin
If not standing out was the goal for wary adults, it was not their goal for children. And to Xiao Han and others in the Waiban, Lin Li (Forest Beauty), the Waiban's newest employee, was their "baby sister." Little Lin dressed in bright colors and used our Saturday trips downtown to shop for new clothes. Her pretty face and adult body made us forget that she was a child to the Chinese.

Little Lin, barely twenty years old, had been assigned to work in the Waiban just after we arrived in China. This was her first job and she knew almost nothing about its business. She was hired through *guanxi*, connections, as were most Chinese—her father was a professor at the university—and like many new college graduates, she had never worked, never been responsible for her own money, never had to take responsibility for herself. She lived with her protective father who did nearly everything for her. She talked about her father frequently but never mentioned her mother. When we asked, she said she and her mother did not like each other.

Little Lin's job was to help the foreigners with business dealings, but when it came to transactions at the Bank of China we found we knew more than she did. When we wanted to buy bicycles she took us to a store that didn't sell bicycles. She excused herself by saying that the store had sold bicycles the week before. Soon we learned that Little Lin preferred to give a wrong answer to a question than to admit she didn't know something. She covered lapses in understanding with smiles, pouts and bouquets of unrelated information. If confronted with the truth she would stamp her foot, dive-bomb her middle finger toward the floor and say, "I *knew* that!"

Our first impression of Little Lin was not positive, but we were not immune to her charm. She came to visit us one afternoon to tell us about her day. That morning she had waited to meet an important man from the Yale-China Association. She told us this man "cheated on" her.

"How?" we asked, tickled by the sexual image.

When they first met he didn't admit he was connected with the Yale-China Association. When she found out later in the day she confronted him with: "Good morning, Mr. Yale."

"So now you know I have been cheating on you," she reported his reply.

Despite our delight at the locution, academic integrity required us to ruin the story by teaching her to say "kidding" instead of "cheating on." Her eagerness to pick up English slang and to try out new phrases provided us with a continuing source of entertainment. Even Bud, who avoided everyone else from the Waiban, taught her to say "Bullshit," and then doubled over with laughter when Little Lin came out with her version, "Boo-leh-sheet." We warned her not to use this expression too freely, but this only encouraged her to say it more. Daniel worried that our commitment to pedagogy was going to wipe out her quaint locutions.

One morning Little Lin wore a new miniskirt, making Nelson ecstatic, but by afternoon, she had changed into jeans. She said she had been "criticized" for wearing the miniskirt. Apparently the miniskirt, which Chinese call a "carry-me-away skirt," was not childlike on her. She didn't like being criticized and wanted sympathy from us.

"Who told you not to wear it?" we asked.

"People in my office," she said.

"Why did they say that?"

"Perhaps because I am too fat."

"But you are not at all fat."

"They said Waiban people should not wear this such thing."

"Maybe they thought it was too sexy." We were not sure she knew what "sexy" meant, or if she did, that we should be talking about such things with her. We rephrased it cautiously:

"Maybe they thought it would make men have too many romantic thoughts about you and then it would be hard to do business."

"And women too," Robin added, always ready to promote a more enlightened view of sexuality.

"Shhhh," Janice said, not wanting to shock Little Lin, but we were all laughing so hard it did not matter what we said.

Little Lin accepted her colleagues' right to pass judgment on her clothing but she objected to her father's protectiveness. He always wanted to know what she had been doing and fussed when she came home late. If she expected sympathy from us, she got none. He was no different from an American parent, we told her. She continued to complain until she moved out of her father's apartment to room with Xiao Li, another member of the Waiban.

Little Lin and Xiao Li moved into their unheated quarters on the night of the winter's only snowfall. They were proud of their new home and invited all their friends to see it. Their apartment was in an unfinished building, accessible only by walking a plank that spanned a deep excavation. So new was it that residents had to go to another building to get water or to use the toilet. The hallways were blocked by piles of wood shavings and concrete rubble to which new residents contributed cabbage leaves, fish bones and rice pot scrapings. The smell, even in the winter, was very powerful and Little Lin and Xiao Li had to keep their door closed.

We offered to organize all the foreigners and the Waiban to help them clean up the mess in the hallways. "Oh no," Little Lin said, "It will just get dirty again. Someone else is supposed to clean it up." The residents of the new building lived with the terrible smell for weeks, until a clean-up worker was hired.

The two young women got their one-room apartment through special connections with the housing office. Little Lin proudly told us about their negotiations: Two apartments were available, numbers 23 and 21. They were assigned number 23 but since it was at the west end of the building, Little Lin thought it would be too hot in the summer. When Little Lin went to plead for number 21, the housing office didn't want to give it to her, so Little Lin told them that in the West the number 3 was an unlucky number and none of the foreigners would visit them if they lived in 23 and this would prevent her from doing her job well. Whether it was because numerology superstitions were still potent in China, or because Little Lin was so charming, she was given the key to apartment 21. When she and her roommate opened the door they found that one wall was still unfinished, an ugly, badly-mortared brick that hadn't been plastered or painted. They decided they didn't want number 21 after all; they would go back to number 23. "How to get?" they wondered, after they had given such a good reason for rejecting it. Little Lin went back to exchange 21 for 23.

The housing officer said, "You told us that 3 was unlucky for your foreigners. Why do you want 23 now?"

"Oh," said Little Lin, going into her carefully rehearsed explanation, "2 plus 1 equals 3, so 21 will be more unlucky than 23 because *both* numbers go to make the 3." He gave Little Lin the key to 23.

When Golden Zhou gave Little Lin assignments she didn't like, she would pout and refuse with a stamp of her foot. Zhou behaved like a parent rather than a boss toward her, sometimes stern, sometimes coaxing. This was not unusual. Chinese work relationships are shaped by the Iron Rice Bowl, the guaranteed job. In a system where most people stay in the same job for life, the work unit becomes an extended family, a supervisor becomes a parent, and co-workers have the right (and the responsibility) to meddle and criticize, as if they were close relatives.

When we wrote the Waiban a letter from Thailand, Golden Zhou took the letter to show it to the financial office, to brag about his foreigners who could write in Chinese. The people in the financial office saw the beautiful Thai postage stamps and asked to have them. Little Lin didn't want to give away the stamps and did a little dance of frustration at this news. Golden Zhou put his arm around her and said she could keep the stamps if she wanted to, because as the youngest member of the Waiban it was her right. However, the people in the Financial Office did her favors and she had to stay on good terms with them; if she didn't give them the stamps now, she might have trouble later when she wanted a favor. Of course it was all up to her, Zhou concluded. Little Lin decided to give up half the stamps.

Little Lin loved to ride in the university cars and tried to establish *guanxi* with the drivers. However, she did not always go about it correctly. One evening the university bus arrived to take us to a variety show where several people from our university were going to perform. The performers were on the bus, eager to get to the theater and change into their costumes. Old Dong, the Guest House night guard, climbed aboard and told Robin he was wanted on the telephone. It was Little Lin, calling from the university garage. Apparently she had gotten there late and the bus driver hadn't waited for her. She wanted him to come back to the garage to pick her up.

Why didn't she ride her bike over, Robin asked.

No, she would not ride over; Robin must tell the driver to pick her up.

Why didn't she speak to him directly, Robin asked. Did she think her Chinese wasn't good enough? Was that why she wanted Robin to give the driver her message?

No, she didn't want to talk to the driver; he should have waited for her. Robin must tell him that she had all the tickets so no one could get into the performance without her.

The driver, apparently compliant, drove to the garage and stopped the bus outside the gate. Little Lin stood inside the yard with a look of triumph on her face. She lounged back against a parked motorcycle and made an imperious gesture for the driver to bring the bus through the gate into the yard to pick her up. She was not going to move one step; he must go to her. When he saw her gesture, the driver gunned the engine and we zoomed off down the road.

In fact we had no trouble getting in without tickets. Little Lin's roommate, Xiao Li, was already there and showed us to our reserved seats. The performers from our university did arrive in time to prepare their costumes and we all had a lovely evening. Only Little Lin missed the performance. She had overplayed her hand and had to spend the evening at her father's house.

5
THE FOREIGN EXPERTS' GUEST HOUSE

The Foreign Experts' Guest House, our home for the year, stood on top of a hill at the south-east corner of the university campus. From the roof of our building we could see a Buddhist temple, an ancient stone wall, a crematorium, East Lake, South Lake, mountains through the haze of air pollution, and most of the rooftops on campus. On very clear days we could see all the way downtown to the landmarks of Wuhan: the Yellow Crane Pagoda and the TV tower with its rotating restaurant. Directly below us was a yard bordered by short palm trees and featuring a pair of stone picnic tables in a nest of long grass. Every day the workers strung clothesline across the yard and children played Ping-Pong on the picnic tables or kicked a soccer ball between the benches. Every few weeks the workers "cleaned" the yard by pulling up some of the grass.

Our usual route to the center of campus was a rocky dirt path that went behind the Guest House, under low-hanging electrical wires, past piles of coal and stacks of old furniture outside the carpentry shop. The path turned onto a narrow sidewalk between the university print shop and a rope-wrapped water pipe dripping into a concrete sump. After a sharp left around a blind corner, site of frequent collisions between pedestrians and cyclists, it became a dirt track between a swampy field and an abandoned nursery of flowering shrubs and then crossed a rutted dirt road bordered by brick and tarpaper shacks.

The residents of these shacks squatted outside, tending cooking fires or washing clothes in large basins. At first they stared at us open-mouthed but soon they returned our smiles and encouraged their children to wave. Our path slipped under the lines drying their brightly colored laundry and then divided, one route winding between the new mathematics building and a field piled with heavy construction equipment and steel girders, the other following a rutted dirt road past more shacks where chickens, dogs and children investigated the muddy puddle around a water spigot. Both routes ended on paved roads on the main part of campus, a sharp border between countryside and city.

As we rode our bikes to class, a thousand watts of theme music blasted from loudspeakers mounted throughout the campus, a vestige from earlier years when political slogans pealed like church bells. These days Western music was preferred—the theme from *Love Story* was a favorite, along with *Für Elise*, *Bolero*, and a disco version of the music from *Close Encounters of the Third Kind*. It made us feel as if we were in a movie, headed toward adventure.

Five times a day the university station broadcast its music, followed by announcements, directions, warnings.

"The movie tonight will be . . . . ."

"The following faculty members have been promoted . . . . ."

"A gas leak has been discovered on the west side of campus and all people are warned to stay away."

"Four students in the chemistry department were caught cheating. Their names are . . . . ."

Repairs and Adjustments
Before we arrived, we had worried about our living quarters. Would the rooms be dark and dismal, small and cramped? Would the walls be thin and the rooms noisy? Would we have any storage space? Back in the US when we asked Teacher Fong the Chinese word for closet, she couldn't think of one. Chinese homes don't have closets, she said.

In many ways our apartment was much better than we expected. The three rooms—living room, study and bedroom—were a decent size, each twelve to twenty square meters. The windows were large, and the interior walls very solid—plaster over concrete over brick. The bathroom had the promised Western style toilet, a sink, a medicine cabinet, and a tub with a telephone shower. There was a balcony large enough for a few chairs and bamboo poles to hang laundry on, and we even had a tiny kitchen. "The Chinese do have closets," we wrote home to Teacher Fong, "but they call them kitchens."

Our apartment came with furniture, two air conditioners, a color TV, a washing machine, mosquito netting and a spittoon. Everything but the TV looked worn and seedy, furnishings from a rural motel far from the interstate. Even the four-year old building looked ten times its age. When we first arrived we were so tired, hot and uncomfortable that we didn't realize we should have been praising our accommodations to our hosts. Far more luxurious living conditions, we were told many times, than the president of the university had.

Many things in the apartment needed repair. When we inquired about this we were introduced to the building "technician," a surly young man who wore fancy Western clothes and smoked cigarettes without removing them from his mouth. We learned his mechanical skill was exceeded by his skill at appearing too busy to do any work. When he did help, we were usually sorry we'd asked. He set about repairing our kitchen faucet by unscrewing the valve, and when confronted with the resulting geyser, tied a rag around the fitting while he went off to find a replacement washer and we mopped up his flood.

One of our air conditioners did not work, a serious problem because the Wuhan weather was tropical and our west-facing study became a furnace. We suggested trading our broken air conditioner for a working one from an unoccupied apartment. Xiao Han consulted with the technician and told us this could not be done. "Why not?" we asked.

Ah, the technician told Xiao Han, the air conditioner could not be traded until the broken one could be sent to the factory and the truck to take it to the factory wouldn't come until next month.

We were surprised that the illogic of this explanation did not bother Xiao Han. We offered to exchange the machine ourselves, but Xiao Han asked us to please be patient.

We waited, impatient, sweltering, the weather gradually tempering as the month elapsed. We reminded Xiao Han many times of the day our air conditioner was to be replaced. On that day the surly technician came to look at our air conditioner for the first time. We explained to him that the bottom of the evaporator frosted over, a sign that there wasn't enough *qi* (gas). He agreed as if he understood, and walked out. A few minutes later the technician and Xiao Han carried an air conditioner from one of the vacant rooms into our apartment. No repair truck ever arrived. No reference was ever made to the original story.

Later we discovered that the technician and other Guest House workers had used the vacant apartment for their midday naps. It was only when the weather got cooler that they were willing to give up the air conditioner.

As recent house renovators we were not used to accepting disrepair, so we repeated our requests for help until they were granted or until we were told such unbelievable stories that we knew nothing would be done. When a leak in our shower hose got so large that none of the water made it to the small holes in the shower, the technician pronounced it *shoubuliao,* "impossible to repair." We repaired it ourselves, showing off our success, not caring that the technician had lost face.

We stunned the Waiban and the Guest House staff by doing our own repairs. In China tenants did not make their own repairs, and academics, especially, did not do manual labor. When we offered to paint the pocked and stained walls of our apartment, the Guest House manager told us all the apartments were going to be painted before the end of October. Even Xiao Han did not believe that one but he begged us not to take any action until that deadline had passed.

Golden Zhou explained the administrative problem. The Waiban had no direct power over the Guest House staff or building, and the Guest House staff did not have to make repairs for us because taking care of foreigners was the Waiban's responsibility. In the US we might have thought that such an arrangement was deliberate, a clever way to avoid accountability. In China, we didn't assume the same sinister motivation; in China we thought this arrangement was merely the result of disorganization and bad planning.

We compromised by covering the worst parts of the wall with calendar pictures of Chinese fashion models. This wasn't our style of decor but it did allow us to do some impromptu research: We asked all our visitors to indicate their favorites. Most Chinese preferred the fairy princess type with the vacant smile; we foreigners liked the tough cutie who looked ready to take on the world.

When October ended we washed off some of the grime and painted the bedroom walls with blue and purple circles, giant polka-dots, balloons released to the sky, a magical galaxy of planets. Anticipating objections, we had worked out a justification for our actions: The former residents chose to decorate their walls with dead insects; we chose colored circles instead. The tempera paint would wash off so the next tenant could remove our decorations just as we washed off our predecessor's wall-kills.

Instead of hostility we got praise. "Like an art museum," the graduate students said. Encouraged, we painted a wide orange stripe diagonally around our living room. Again everyone approved. Then we painted a huge circle on the bedroom wall facing the living room, shading it to look three-dimensional. A trompe l'oeil. People came in to touch it. Even Director Fang applauded.

Our relationship with the Guest House workers improved when we posted both our Chinese and English names outside our door. The workers called us by our Chinese names, singing out *"Zhen Mei"* or *"Luo Bin"* whenever they saw us. Even tough Little Tao, who wore makeup and well-tailored Western-style clothes— the one who had reported Bud for embracing her and was said not to like foreigners—even she greeted us and smiled. As we rode to class each day we met Old Dong and Little Peng and the Guest

House manager (whom we called "The Dragon Lady") riding to work. Most people we passed smiled and greeted us, whether we'd seen them before or not. Only the surly technician rode by with head averted. Even when the Dragon Lady was unhappy with us, she would forget herself and return our greeting. Word got back to us that Guest House staff and people in the Foreign Affairs Office considered us "good people, nice people, but fussy." Golden Zhou had taught us well, we thought.

And each day something improved, looked better, got cleaner. Repairs to our apartment could have been made before we arrived—broken windows and furniture, dripping faucets. Yet, instead of being annoyed that this had not been done, each repair made us happy, perhaps happier than we would have been if the repairs had been anticipated. One day a flapping awning was silenced; next day we discovered the building vacuum cleaner did work once the filter was cleaned. Each day we got a chance to try our Chinese vocabulary and international pantomime on the Guest House workers.

They laughed at our attempts and most of the time we also laughed at their charm and eccentricity and orneriness, and at our own linguistic handicap. Not only did we have trouble understanding their local dialect, but we couldn't rely on the truth of what we did understand. And when we discovered a fib, no one was ever ashamed, no loss of face was evident. Everyone seemed to think it was tremendously funny.

"Tonight, hot water, no hot water?" Janice asked.

"No hot water." Big smile from Old Dong, the night desk man.

"How come?"

"Electricity broken."

"What?"

"Electricity broken," he repeated, pointing to the fluorescent light. But the light was on!

"Electricity not broken," Janice said, pointing to the light.

Old Dong looked up, astonished. He laughed. Janice laughed. She left saying, "No hot water. Waa Waa," pretending to cry. He laughed harder.

Perhaps we were denied hot water in order to entertain the Guest House workers with these exchanges. More likely, the people who were supposed to turn on the water, fire up the boiler and turn on the steam didn't think that hot water was very important. They didn't get hot water themselves so it was hard for them to understand why we wanted it so much.

Fuwuyuan

The Foreign Experts' Guest House had a staff of workers to clean our apartments, refill our thermoses, empty our garbage, wash our towels and sheets and guard the entrance. Service workers at the Guest House and elsewhere were called by a word so hard to pronounce that we had to practice over and over to say it correctly: *fuwuyuan*—Foo Woo You Enn.

Each floor of the building had its own *fuwuyuan*. Ours was Old Ma, a small, trim woman with traditional Dutch Boy haircut, a pleasant face and garlic breath. Xiao Han suggested we ask Old Ma to do some of the cleaning we were doing for ourselves. We tried to get her to use the vacuum cleaner but could not convince her to keep the nozzle against the floor. She wanted to use it as a broom and found its brooming ability unsatisfactory. She was very good-natured about the lesson but we knew we were defeated when she returned to using her branch broom with such energy that little dust devils swirled in the sunbeams.

Old Ma was curious about us. She often knocked on our door before we had eaten breakfast, wanting to come in and talk, or at least communicate, which was easier than it should have been given our mutual language deficiencies. Unlike many people we met, she was brave enough to risk insulting us by speaking Chinese as if we were toddlers, slowly and carefully, pointing and gesturing to make many words unnecessary. She could not write, but Little Peng, the third floor *fuwuyuan*, could, and between the two of them and our

Chinese-English dictionary, nearly anything that needed to be said could be.

Old Ma told us she had five children. The older four were workers who had gone without a university education but the youngest son was still in school. He was the family's only hope for a university graduate. Old Ma wanted us to tutor him in English. We offered to give him a lesson on Thursday night. Old Ma said Thursday would be *bu fang bian* (a term that covers a range from "impossible" to "inconvenient"), so we suggested Sunday. She said, okay, he would come on Thursday *and* Sunday. While we were still tottering on the logic of her reasoning she said her son would come every week on those evenings. She got Little Peng to write this down in Chinese to make sure there was no misunderstanding.

A few hours later our red velvet slipcovers reappeared, the ones we had thrown away because they were in such bad shape. Although they had been laundered and patched they still looked mangy. Old Ma and Little Peng stretched and sewed them back onto the chairs. We didn't have the heart to remove them again.

After dinner on Thursday Old Ma and son arrived for the English lesson. The boy knew about a dozen English words and most of the alphabet, but didn't understand that similar arrangements of letters, CAT and HAT, had similar sounds. Robin looked up "rhyme" in the English-Chinese dictionary, showed him the characters and the boy said he understood. His mother looked on, encouraging him, never correcting, never criticizing.

The next morning Old Ma came in while we were breakfasting to give us a set of four drinking glasses. The glasses matched the carafe that had come with the apartment, so she must have had them all along and only now deemed us worthy of receiving them. For beer and soda she explained, but with hot water would go "Poof!" Her hands sprang apart to demonstrate a shattering glass. She said her son learned a lot from us; his father said his pronunciation was very good, and that Teacher Luo and Teacher Zhen were very good teachers.

Jeanette told us that last year Old Ma's son had been tutored by an American who believed he had a learning disability and didn't have much hope for him. This teacher had given Old Ma's boy the name Greg. Old Ma was a long-time Party member and her husband was a veteran of the Korean War, called "The War Against United States Imperialism," so the family had a bit of local clout.

The following Sunday, before Robin had finished his shower, little Greg arrived alone, asking us to help him prepare for a big English exam on Monday. We went to work, but our high-pressure teaching soon wore Greg out. He tried to distract us from his lesson with questions about sports in America. Still, our stress on the letter-sound relationships seemed to be paying off. He now realized that the word "bed" ought to begin with the same letter as "bag" and "bike." We gave him candy as a reward and sent him off with our compliments.

"You are a very good student. You did very well tonight."

"Oh no. Not good. I'm not good," he said, smiling bashfully.

The next day Old Ma came in with two beautiful embroidered silk quilts, one for now and a heavier one for very cold weather. "Brrr" she said in explanation, hugging herself. The quilts were standard issue but we got ours well before other foreigners did. She also gave us candles for when the electricity failed.

Two days later, Old Ma came to tell us that Greg got a 95 on the exam and was moved up to the next level. The grades of the other students ranged from the 80s down to 40. We asked her for a few more clothes hangers, and she brought us ten, washed our sheets ahead of schedule and replaced our chipped washbasin with a new one.

The special favors continued. Our bedclothes were aired and washed more frequently. She gave us a teapot and little demitasse cups, a matching set. She gave us four yogurt bottles, the beginning of a collection we used as beer and soda glasses for parties. When we went away for a weekend, she found our dirty clothes and laundered them. We returned to discover them all on hangers drying in the doorways.

We were getting used to being spoiled. We had not fully appreciated the effects of the *guanxi* system. It was more than using connections, more than trading favors; it was nice to receive special goodies regularly. We wondered what would happen if little Greg did poorly on the next exam. We wrote home a detailed description of Old Ma and Little Greg.

For breakfast on Midautumn Festival Day Old Ma gave us mooncakes, oblate pastries with a sweet filling. She told us how grateful she was to us for teaching Greg, how much she liked "English" people, how she had enjoyed working in the Guest House for seven years, how much she liked us, how polite we were, especially to her, and how she felt for us. She sat close while she talked and despite her garlic breath we enjoyed her company.

Then one week later Old Ma was abruptly transferred to another part of the university. Another *fuwuyuan* from the building was also transferred, one from the first floor whom Daniel and Bud particularly liked, the only one who was beginning to learn English. No one would tell us why Old Ma was transferred but we recalled Pierre's warnings about mail surveillance and wondered if our letter describing the exchange of favors might have had something to do with it.

Pierre, Xiao Han and others assured us that Old Ma was a treacherous person, that she would eventually have gossiped us into trouble, that we were well rid of her. They said she searched our apartments and spread stories about people. They convinced us not to fight for her return, but we still missed her. Greg continued to come for lessons, although we sensed that if he'd had his way he would not be spending his Sunday evenings studying English with us.

Old Ma's replacement was a pretty, young *fuwuyuan* who could speak and write standard Chinese and knew a little English. We began to get fond of her when she too vanished. Finally we got Old Min, a woman who was about the same age as Old Ma but so deferential that she wouldn't come into our apartment while we were home. Days went by without her finding a time when we were both out. We began to clean up after ourselves. Then she timidly knocked on our door, accompanied by Little Peng, who did the talking. "Could we please come in and clean?" said Little Peng in Chinese as Old Min illustrated with sweeping motions.

We told Old Min and Little Peng to come into our apartment any time, and they both nodded enthusiastically, but Old Min never came in without being invited. "Please," we said, "help us. It is so dirty." Old Min apparently was doing something right because she didn't get transferred.

The Murine Invasion

While everything was going well for us, elsewhere in the building there were problems. We met Jeanette carrying mousetraps upstairs. She looked very discouraged until Robin cried, "*Mort à la souris!*" to cheer her up. Then she told us of Pierre's fight with a rat in the bathroom.

"He, how to say, *blessé* the rat . . . .."

Robin: "*Blessé* . . . um . . . wounded."

". . . wounded the rat and it was, uh, bleed all over. It run around the room and it jump on Pierre's shoulder. It was horreebl."

We accompanied her upstairs to see the war hero. Pierre described how Xiao Han chased another rat into their bedroom and jumped on it with both feet. When Xiao Han saw the rat still struggling he ground his feet against the floor to finish it off. Pierre jumped and ground his sandals on the floor in imitation.

Pierre and Jeanette told us there was a bounty on rats in China: one *jiao* (ten Chinese cents) per rat tail. One American took a rat tail to the health clinic, but they wouldn't give him any money, refusing to admit the bounty existed, for that would be admitting to foreigners that China had a problem with rats. The American then gave his rat tail to a little kid who collected the money with no difficulty. There was even a man at the university who made his living from the rat bounty; people hired him with the understanding that his pay would be the tails of the rats he caught.

We weren't as disturbed by the rodents as some of the other foreigners. A graduate degree in psychology guaranteed familiarity with rats and mice. Pedigree laboratory rats to be sure, but pointy-nosed, bewhiskered, rat-tailed creatures all the same.

Yet we all became extraordinarily sensitive to small blurs of motion and would spring to action, hurling shoes and books. We tried to coax and cajole the Foreign Affairs Office into doing something. "We have a small problem," we said with a smile. "And it has a tail." In the spirit of Saturday morning cartoons, we dropped firecrackers and boiling water into their entrance holes. When that didn't work, we sealed the holes with newspapers and mortar. Still they came.

One day after a particularly fierce battle with the rodents, Pierre and Jeanette met Xiao Pu, a prim young man from the Waiban. He said, "How are you?" not anticipating the consequences of his greeting.

Pierre said, "Oh fine. I have just killed another mouse."

Xiao Pu said, "Oh, you have mice?"

Pierre, who had been complaining to the Waiban for weeks, said sardonically, "Yes. We have mice. They are ruining our food. We have killed four in the past week."

Xiao Pu didn't like to hear unpleasant news. He smiled uncomfortably, then laughed as if Pierre had just told a joke: "Oh, the mice come because you have food. I don't have any mice because I don't have any food."

Pierre thought he was being criticized for eating, or was being told that mice were natural and there was nothing one could do about them, so he answered irritably, "I don't see why the Waiban or the Guest House don't buy traps or poison to get rid of the rats and mice."

Xiao Pu hesitated. He said, "Poison? You mean for the rats?"

Pierre said, "Yes, of course for the rats."

Xiao Pu: "But poison is very dangerous. Dogs or chickens or horses could eat it and die."

Pierre did not say that if these creatures entered his apartment they deserved to die. Instead he said, in a pained, exasperated, talking-to-a-two-year-old voice, "But there *are* no dogs or chickens or horses inside the building."

Xiao Pu: "But what about the birds?"

Pierre then lost his barely controlled temper. He shouted, "You ... you ... you are the stupidest person I ever met."

As Jeanette and Pierre told us this story, Jeanette, pink with blushing for Pierre, put her hands on the sides of her face, rocking it back and forth with an "Ooo la la," and told us she had to drag Pierre away. Pierre was ashamed he had lost his temper. We did our best to cheer them up, understanding Pierre's exasperation in confronting an illogical, stupid argument. We were benefiting, cathartically if in no other way, from Pierre's willingness to get upset.

Meanwhile the rodent invasion continued.

Helen was awakened by a noise and saw a dark shape on the top of her mosquito net directly over her head. She sat up and scrambled to one corner of the bed. Her movement shook the frame and the rat ran around in frenzied circles on top of the netting. Helen got out of bed and threw things at the rat until it jumped into her open dresser drawer and began to scamper through her underwear. She slammed the drawer shut, trapping it. In the morning Helen delivered an ultimatum to the Waiban: Get rid of the rats or I go home.

The next day the Waiban delivered wire cages with trip doors and Xiao Han demonstrated how to bait them. Helen's rat was caught that same day. The Guest House technician, cigarette in mouth, took the cage outside, followed by an audience of female *fuwuyuan*. He pulled off one of the legs of the captured rat with his pliers. Then he and two cooks from the Dining Hall kicked the maimed rat as it struggled and squealed. Finally they smashed it on the concrete walk. Our *fuwuyuan* wasn't there, but pretty, anti-foreigner Little Tao was, and so was Little Peng, sweet, pigtailed, white-socked Little Peng, laughing with the rest of them.

Two months after rages and coaxings and pleadings and boiling water and firecrackers, after Helen's ultimatum, after our apartments had been moderately rat-proofed with wooden strips along the doors, after rats began eating students' clothing in the dormitories and mating in their bathrooms, Beijing launched a nationwide campaign against rodent pests, using warfarin-treated grain. Signs went up all over China announcing the event. Xiao Han composed a sign in English for the Guest House saying that soon there would be "good food for rats" put in all the living quarters.

We went to the Waiban Office during lunchtime and left a note on the door for Xiao Han, written in very tiny Chinese characters:

> You think we can't read English but we are very smart. We know all about the 'good food' and we are laughing at you.
> (Signed,) The Rats.

Xiao Han told us later that when Director Fang saw our note he got very worried that we foreigners hadn't understood Xiao Han's sign and that we might eat the poisoned grain ourselves. Director Fang had to be told our note was a joke. "Poor Little Fang," we said and Xiao Han laughed at our daring to call his boss "Little."

Weeks later two *fuwuyuan* and a ceremonial official entered our apartment to distribute the treated grain in spoonfuls at the feet of our furniture. We saw similar piles in department stores, offices, restaurant stairwells. The entire nation had mobilized against the rodents. Within a week they were gone. Gone from the building, gone from the Laurel Hill Restaurant, gone from the streets and drainage ditches. And the rats did not return. We saw one rat in a drain gutter nine months later, the only one.

In and Out of Hot Water

While other foreigners found the rats intolerable, our boiling point was brought on by the absence of hot water. One day, after being assured of hot water for the evening, we went out jogging. When we returned, nothing came out of the hot water tap. We checked with Nelson and found him already heating water on his stove. Downstairs Xiao Pu was watching television with Old Dong, the night desk guard. The television was Nelson's, who had given it up to discourage Xiao Pu's nightly visits to Nelson's apartment. We said to them in Chinese, "No have hot water."

Old Dong said, "Have."

We repeated, "No have."

He insisted, "Have."

Xiao Pu said in English, "You have hot water."

This could have gone on all night so Janice said, more testily than she had planned, "Would you like to try ours?" Robin nudged her to calm down.

Xiao Pu and Old Dong reluctantly abandoned the television set. They were going to show us there was hot water. Old Dong looked through drawers for keys—many drawers opened and closed while we waited. He found a key in the back of the seventh drawer and led us to a vacant apartment on the first floor. He opened the apartment, went into the bathroom and turned on the tap. A few drops came out. Then nothing. Xiao Pu told us to feel the spigot. "See. It is warm!" he said triumphantly.

"But there is no *water* coming out," we said, astonished that we were explaining this. We were tempted to say, "You are the stupidest person we ever met," but Pierre had done this for us already.

"Perhaps there is something wrong with the pipe," Xiao Pu said, confident, self-satisfied, smug.

"Let's go look," we proposed, when neither of them made this suggestion. Old Dong got a flashlight and slowly led the way to the third floor and then up the narrow bamboo ladder to the roof where the water tank was located.

"Yes, there is hot water." Xiao Pu said.

"But no one has turned it *on*," Robin pointed out.

Old Dong turned the valve so the hot water could flow into our pipes. We thanked him as if he had done a wonderful thing.

Xiao Pu said arrogantly, "See, there was hot water." We were ready to wring his neck.

After many such encounters we took our problem to Golden Zhou who explained how many different workers were needed for hot water production: Coal stokers at the steam plant, boiler tenders, valve turners, water pumpers. Never had we seen a system that required so much human intervention and depended on such elaborate coordination. Zhou finally managed to cajole and convince them all to work together. Old Dong at the front desk was assigned to call each unit at certain hours of the day to make sure they had done their job in the proper sequence.

We got hot water for a week before it stopped again. The next day we saw the cooks from the Dining Hall next door shutting off the valve to our building in order to redirect the steam to their own. Prompted secretly by Xiao Han, we wrote to the university Vice President.

It was a scandal: The foreigners accused the Dining Hall cooks of stealing the hot water! Emergency meetings were called to take care of the crisis and restore face. The Vice President assured us we would have hot water regularly in the future, but, Golden Zhou told us, officially it was agreed that the foreigners must have turned their own valve the wrong way.

When the weather got cold, an inspection of the heating system, which Golden Zhou had been urging for months, uncovered a massive leak in the incoming steam pipe. Most of the steam had been escaping under the building, forming a cavern and making the rooms on the ground floor uncomfortably warm. The steam boiler was shut down immediately. It was Christmas Eve.

The Christmas Eve *jiaozi* dumpling party was in our apartment. Waiban people, students and tutors arrived to help us celebrate. Director Fang brought a bottle of Chinese brandy. In a fit of good will we made special vegetarian jiaozi for Xiao Pu who was Muslim and didn't eat pork. Jackets came off, sleeves were rolled up and everyone pitched in to make the jiaozi.

Slabs of pork were turned into a good imitation of ground meat by going at them with big cleavers, one in each hand, thunking alternately into the meat. Du-donk, du-donk, du-donk. Vegetables were slivered, squeezed in a cloth to remove excess liquid and combined with the meat, eggs and seasonings. Flour and water were mixed in a large washbasin, guests kneading the dough in turns before it was rolled into snakes from which little disks were cut. Using a slim rolling pin that tapered toward the ends, the experts rotated the pancake with one hand, palming the rolling pin back and forth to turn each disk into a little pancake. This all happened at blazing speed; an experienced jiaozi maker could turn out a finished jiaozi wrapper every four or five seconds. Li Meili could even roll out three little pancakes at once.

Nearly everyone helped assemble the jiaozi. With a wrapper in our left hands, we used chopsticks to place a dollop of filling in the center of the wrapper and then brought the rim together to seal it. The simplest shape was a half-moon with scalloped edges, but skillful chefs turned out a variety of patterns—fish and ducks and pigs and boats and hats.

Chopping, mixing, kneading, rolling, laughing—thirty working bodies made the apartment so warm we opened the windows. After a day of crawling among underground pipes to encourage the workers, Golden Zhou arrived and took over the cooking. The good spirit of the party made us forget about hot water.

Then, after the Chinese bicycled home, and the rest of us were sitting around the remains of the jiaozi, we heard it—the unmistakable clank-clank of steam entering the water tank. The plumbers had worked into the night for the foreigners on their "special day," so we would have our hot water. We were so moved, so touched, that we wrote a letter to the Waiban thanking them and the workers. Golden Zhou got our letter translated and put into the campus newspaper as a testimonial to the workers of China.

Martinis and Building Construction
In November the tiles and roof structure of the neighboring building were dismantled, beginning a renovation that was to house foreign guests the following year. The inside was gutted and the debris thrown out the windows. Sand, cement and aggregate were mixed on the roads and walkways around our building. Soon our Guest House was surrounded by rubble and construction materials; puddles of mud, slurries of mortar and hillocks of scrap materials reshaped the terrain, making every bicycle ride to central campus a challenge. Helen, who didn't ride a bicycle, waded through everything in her Bill Blass raincoat, never complaining.

Each day we foreigners watched the progress of the renovation as if it were a football game or soap opera on TV. We played sidewalk engineers from our heated apartments, cheering the energy and skill of workers out in the cold, jeering the primitive equipment and construction methods as we sipped our Wuhan beers and dry martinis. Nelson took this opportunity to condemn the Chinese for ruining good martinis by preserving their olives in sugar.

We worried about the workers. Men and women formed human conveyor belts to move bricks, stones and buckets of mortar up flimsy scaffolds. Carpenters worked at power saws and plumbers used high-speed cutting wheels with no eye protection. Masons dodged falling debris with no hard hats. Welders lifted their masks to strike electric arcs. Nelson saw one man carried off the field "with a face like a pizza." We asked the workers what had happened but our expressions of concern were rebuffed. No one acknowledged that an accident had occurred.

So much concrete was used that a brick building the size of a double garage had to be built to store the dry cement. Caravans of trucks lined up to blow dry cement into the shed. There was no exit for the trucks so they U-turned, missing our building, our bicycles and sometimes us by centimeters. Truckloads of white aggregate for the stucco were unloaded against our building. A power elevator was installed to carry bricks and mortar to the fourth floor of the construction.

A huge mixing machine was installed outside our windows and we listened to the kung-fu shouts of the workers, often just young boys, who ran up a makeshift ramp with barrows of cement, stones and sand. Ha-YAAAAAH! Workers hustled bricks from one place to another, trotting with wheelbarrows, jogging around the site, resting far less than construction workers in the US. Of course the supervisors compensated for this energy; they did nothing but watch.

The huge concrete mixer began to churn heavy aggregate with sand and cement, working late into the night, a giant clothes dryer filled with rocks. Ka-CHUNK. Ka-chunk. Ka-CHUNK. Saturdays. Sundays. It never stopped. In any room facing the cement mixer we had to shout to be heard. We two could stay in our living room whose windows were on the other side of the building. Daniel, Bud, Nelson, and Helen were not so lucky; all of their windows faced the mixer.

On the night of Helen's Chinese lesson she could not hear her tutor. As the cement mixer ka-chunked away she came to our living room, the only room in which she could be heard, to express her outrage. She could no longer live like this. She could not think. To us it was one more major inconvenience, another bad joke on us, but to Helen this was the last straw. She was going home.

Helen's previous threat of repatriating was, we thought, a bluff to get some action on the rats, but this time she was serious. She really wanted to leave. We asked the Foreign Affairs Office how long the noise would continue, and Director Fang, proud of the new construction, said "Until March. And then next year all the foreigners' living conditions will be much improved," as if he thought we should be happy about sacrificing for our successors.

Nelson worried about Helen. They had spent a lot of time together, and he had gotten the story of her life. "She really doesn't have anything to go home to, from what I can see," he told us. None of us wanted her to go. So what if she said "Gorgeous" and

"Marvelous" too often; she added character to our lives. We had settled into a social equilibrium that would be disrupted if she left. Her departure would be a defeat for all of us, evidence we couldn't help each other survive in this new environment.

Golden Zhou was sent to intercede. He called on Helen, working his charm, offering her any of the three empty apartments on the other side of the building. As usual he was successful. She chose the one at the end of our hall, then mobilized her students, people from the Foreign Affairs Office and us to move her things. She spent the next day decorating and fixing up her larger and quieter apartment.

Golden Zhou's job wasn't over. Social customs in China required that jealousy be taken into account. In a country where there are relatively minor differences in salary, housing and other perks, small differences can cause large antagonisms. Chinese might be no more susceptible to jealousy than anyone else, but they are more alert to its dangers. So Golden Zhou came to visit each of the rest of us, very formally, to offer apologies for giving Helen a better apartment, worried that we other foreigners would be jealous or angry. We explained that we had all been anxious for Helen and now we were happy her problem had been solved. We felt proud that we had nobler feelings than were expected.

In high spirits, Helen went to Director Fang to thank him for arranging the new apartment. Director Fang did not say, "We wanted to make you happy," or "We are glad you like it." Instead he said, "That's all right. We all know you are old." We joined Helen in laughter and dubbed the concrete mixer "Helen's Bane." It was the holiday season and we were all happy again.

By the Spring, despite our hostility toward the endless ka-chunking of Helen's Bane and the piercing skree of wheelbarrow skids on the pavement, we had become invested in the deadline being met to finish the building. The renovation had become a symbol of the new China, the new incentive system, the new vitality, and we wanted it to succeed.

On Easter Sunday the building was nearly finished and Nelson, Daniel and we decided to "inspect" it. The workers were cleaning up rubble, carting off bricks and sweeping the road with branch brooms. Some were still building landscaping walls. Others were looking at us from the windows. No one seemed to mind us invading their job site, something we couldn't have done in the US.

Alas, construction methods had not changed much since our Guest House had been built. Like our building, the wiring and plumbing ran on the surface instead of inside the walls, and the window screens were splattered with paint. Workers still installed cracked and broken tiles along with the good ones and left smears of hardened grouting on the surface. Wallpaper had been put up before the woodwork had been installed or painted and it was now stained and torn. The Western toilets leaked and all but one bathroom floor was flooded.

We had imagined that the new building would be dramatically better than our present quarters but the construction was slipshod and the structure already looked worn and derelict. Director Fang, who had come to check on the building, did not share our dismay. He was delighted at everything: tiled floors, wallpaper, Western toilets, blond furniture. "Next year the living conditions of the foreigners will be much improved," he told us happily.

We walked back to our building, to our own walls, gouged and stained in familiar patterns, our own grout-smeared tiles and gurgling toilets. We liked our building better; after all, it was our home.

6
TEACHING IN A DIFFERENT WORLD

Overseeing and Oversights

Central China University is a national "key" university, one of few administered directly by the State Education Committee in Beijing. Its undergraduate students are from the top one percent of high school graduates, equivalent to an American college with a minimum SAT score of 1480. The graduate students are selected from among the top one or two percent of those already highly selected students.

We were enthusiastic about teaching such gifted students. Before we arrived we tried to find out what courses we were going to teach, how many students would be in each class and their educational background. We sent a detailed outline of each course we were prepared to offer. The responses from Vice Chairman Wang Y were vague and changed from one letter to the next. We arrived in China, knowing our classes would begin in a few days but not knowing what courses we would be teaching.

American universities hold orientation sessions for new faculty members to learn about campus traditions, research facilities, and whom to see about what. In China we were left to discover all this on our own. At Central China University, new courses could start at any time and students could be assigned or reassigned to classes all during the year. Most classes had already started before we arrived but this didn't seem to matter, especially since the other two Foreign Experts wouldn't arrive for another month. There was no fixed schedule that we could discover. "The cart will arrive at the other side of the mountain when it gets there," we kept reminding ourselves. Our classes would begin when they began.

Although we were anxious to get started, our department leaders decided we should rest for a week before we began teaching. This "rest" included daily tours of local sights and long evening banquets, so that even if we had known what courses to plan for, there would have been no time.

After a week of touring and banquets, Vice Chairman Wang Y came to our apartment to give us our teaching assignments. He was a pleasant looking man about forty-five years old with a 1940's American hair style. He had spent two years at Georgetown University in Washington, DC. Students told us he went there to study linguistics but was so mystified by the subject that he switched to literature and never got the intended Master's Degree. Yet Wang Y's English was fluent, in fact too fluent, his speech oiled by a few phrases, "You see," and "I should say," that he used so frequently they become his trademark. Nelson had only to say: "I am supposed to, I should say, go to Jingzhou next Saturday," and we knew who had arranged his trip.

We were eager to find out our schedules and we waited as Wang Y began slowly, amiably, ingratiatingly. After asking how we were adjusting to China, how we found the food, how we found our living conditions, he eased into business:

"I would like, you see, for you to teach two courses in linguistics to the graduate students. Maybe one in, I should say, linguistics and one in, you see, philosophy and, you see, psychology of language. You could, in point of fact, teach them, you see, together."

This arrangement sounded good to us. We had frequently given lectures together but never a whole course. He told us there would be about twenty graduate students. A good size for a class, we thought.

Slowly Wang Y introduced the next course. "I would like, you see, for you to teach, in point of fact, one other linguistics course to the upper-level undergraduates, you see."

He paused long enough for us to assume the subject of our teaching was closed. We had three courses that we would be teaching together. We went on to ask about secretarial services, course materials, supplies, offices, desks, keys. The discussion continued on other matters.

Quite a bit later in the evening, Wang Y said: "You see, you can also, you see, teach something else. I would like you to teach English composition. To the juniors, you see."

This was an unpleasant surprise. A composition course meant reading and grading an unending flood of student papers. His letters had hinted we might be asked to offer a course in English literature. We thought this wouldn't be too bad since Nineteenth Century literature was a hobby of ours. But a composition class meant hackwork.

"You see, there is no way out, someone must, you see, teach this course. Only a native speaker can, you see, really judge, you see, the essays of the advanced students."

We looked at each other, exchanging a signal of resigned co-operation.

"That is, I should say, one composition course each."

Two composition courses?

"You see, I have no way out. So, you see, I must ask you to do this."

And so on.

Business that could have been done in fifteen minutes took more than two hours, probably because Wang Y believed that a good administrator's work required a lot of time. The course load he proposed was not so terrible. If we had been assigned these courses originally, we would have been content, but after undergoing such lengthy titration we felt conned. In *The Hobbit,* Gandalf the Wizard coached the thirteen dwarves to arrive at Bilbo Baggins' house two or three at a time so Bilbo would let them in, which he surely would not have done had they arrived all at once. We felt we had been Bilboed by Wang Y, and it was not a good feeling. Nor would this be the last time.

TEACHING IN A DIFFERENT WORLD

On the evening *after* our first class meeting, Wang Y came to our apartment to tell us when the classes would meet. He began with the good news, that we would have Fridays off, that our three-hour graduate classes would be in the afternoon. Then he told us about the early morning courses, and that "maybe, you see, the undergraduate linguistics course will have more than seventy-five students, maybe, you see, one hundred." He went on about other things and seemed prepared to spend the night. Finally he gave us a paper listing our course schedules and we noticed that we were assigned to teach not two, but three composition courses.

Most university teachers in the US spend between six and nine hours in class each week. Each class hour might require several hours of lecture preparation and grading. We knew that Chinese students had almost twice as many class hours as their American counterparts so perhaps Chinese instructors taught twice as many hours as we did back home. Could we object to the added course if our Chinese colleagues did so much more work? Much later we found out that many Chinese teachers taught only *four* hours a week.

"Fourteen hours are too many for us," we said, mustering our arguments. "We need to prepare the lectures, grade thirty to forty papers each week, and do research. We won't be able to do a conscientious job."

"Oh, I should say, you don't have to, you see, grade all the papers. You can give an assignment, but, you see, only grade a few of the papers."

Again Wang Y told us there was no way out for him, no way out for us. Again we yielded.

When we met our classes we found we had been Bilboed again. The "seventy-five, maybe one hundred" students in undergraduate linguistics turned out to be 250; the twenty graduate students were forty; the composition courses were fifty percent larger than Wang Y's estimate.

The Best Late Plans
In China most things seemed to be "planned" at the last minute. There were sudden changes, canceled classes, and arbitrary reschedulings. A few weeks after he began teaching, Nelson found his classroom empty and the door locked. He went back the following week and there was no class. Mystified but conscientious, he returned a week later. Again no students. Eventually Wang Y told him his course had been canceled.

Halfway through the term, we too found our classroom door locked. When we returned home, Helen told us her classroom had been locked too. A student told her the class meeting times had been changed. Since Helen had spent more than a half hour walking through mud and puddles back and forth to an empty classroom, she refused to meet her classes until she received official notification of the new schedule.

At first we believed our university was unique in its disorganization, and that Wang Y was to blame, but Western friends at other universities reported schedules just as chaotic. When students told us that most Chinese professors did not prepare for classes, we were not surprised. If class meetings and even an entire term's course could be canceled without warning, motivation to prepare for what might never take place could not be very strong. This changing of our plans bothered us in a way that most other Chinese customs did not.

Accustomed to the long-range plans made at home, we didn't understand how serious scholarship could take place in an environment with such haphazard organization. We tried to lighten up, to look at it from the other side and laugh at our own outrage. Perhaps Chinese academics wondered how serious scholarship could take place in the US, where so much time was spent on endless meetings and compulsive planning.

So what was really bothering us? Two things. One was that when a change was known in advance, nobody thought to tell *us* about it. The second was that people were changing *our* plans without consulting us. Chinese might get mildly annoyed at the inconveniences of a changed plan, but they didn't see these last minute changes as an abuse of power. Chinese were used to others interfering in their personal plans. Understanding Wang Y's behavior didn't help us to like it.

Wang Y canceled a meeting we had scheduled with another teacher because he wanted us to attend an English Day celebration at a local high school. We went, resentful and hostile, and had a wonderful time despite our expectations.

Wang Y "invited" Janice to the Department's year-end party by ordering her composition students to tell her when she arrived to teach that she was not to hold class because she must go to the party.

When the Waiban planned a trip for all the foreigners, Wang Y decided at the last minute that the English Department would manage the outing and that all the English Department's foreigners must go, but the foreigners in the General English Department were excluded. This time we got so angry we boycotted the outing and it was canceled.

Although Wang Y acted without consulting us, he got upset when Nelson visited another university without consulting him. Other schools and agencies were supposed to get Wang Y's permission to see us, even though our own permission was not required. If the other university had arranged for Nelson's visit through Wang Y, they would have owed Wang Y a favor. Now they owed him nothing. We continued to resent that we could be lent out at Wang Y's pleasure and that our own plans were ignored.

Wang Y might have been exercising his normal prerogatives, but we now saw him as the culprit whenever anything went wrong. The desks, paper, office supplies and class lists he promised us never materialized. Unfortunately, no one else had the authority to grant our requests. According to Pierre, Wang Y's position was a political appointment, the Communist Party leader within the department. The Chairman (often translated as "Dean") of the English Department was another man, Wang Z. But whenever we asked

Wang Z for something that required an executive decision, he always referred us to Wang Y.

We thought Chairman Wang Z must have been in poor health. He was extremely thin with a face like a skull, his legs shook, he sweated, he seemed distracted or in pain. When we watched him trying to change a word in an English document, his pen circled the spot for long seconds and his hands shook so much we offered to write it for him.

When we asked students and colleagues about him they said it was not Wang Z's health that was weak but his knowledge of English. What we had taken for physical frailty was really mental terror—he was afraid of using English in front of us, afraid of making a mistake. In contrast to Wang Z, Wang Y had no such fears. We wished he had.

We learned that Wang Y disliked linguistics, our field. Perhaps his linguistics courses at Georgetown University turned him off, but we heard other reasons for his aversion. The linguistics scholars in the department were more widely published than he. One of them had written two books on linguistics that were used throughout China. When this man came up for promotion, Wang Y (and Wang Z) voted against him. Wang Y opposed the promotion because the linguist was younger than he by several months. The university president recommended the linguist for promotion anyhow. Our Chinese informants thought this kind of career jealousy was unique to Chinese universities. We knew better.

Classroom Compensations
We taught in the Foreign Language Building, located near the library at the center of campus. Its three stories of red brick overlooked a flower garden surrounding a fountain that played over a cluster of pitted volcanic rocks. Panes of glass in some of the windows were broken, giving the building a derelict appearance, a sharp contrast to the battery of shiny microwave antennas on the roof. Laundry was hung to dry on lines strung between trees in front of the building. In good weather, bicycles lined the approach

to the main doorway but when it rained, the laundry and bikes moved inside to fill the entrance hall. Just inside the door was a large mural in the stairwell depicting in socialist realism a blond woman and some other non-Chinese types over the inscription: WELCOME ___ FOREIGN FRIENDS. It used to say WELCOME YOU FOREIGN FRIENDS, reflecting Chinese syntax, but two foreign teachers sneaked in one night and painted out the YOU.

Peasants would come to the Foreign Language Building with truckloads of produce to sell to teachers and students at bargain rates. The sidewalk outside the building was sometimes lined with twitching fish from the university farm, sometimes bordered with books for sale. Along the walkways China's new entrepreneurs arrayed themselves with sewing machines, watch repair equipment, and eyeglass displays. During lunch time and at four o'clock, nets and ropes were strung between the trees and lampposts outside the building, and volleyballs and badminton shuttlecocks flew through the air, the players crowding the lawns and sidewalks. We cheered as we wove around them on our bicycles.

Our very first class in China was the linguistics lecture for undergraduates. Wang Wei, the man who had invited us to China, was there to show us to the large lecture room on the ground floor. As we entered we heard the sound of uncountable voices, as if from a giant party or the floor of a busy stock exchange. Half a thousand eyes fixed on us as we mounted the platform in front of the room. The level of sound dropped to a hush as we looked at each other, sharing the stage fright that never went away, even after twenty years of teaching.

It was late August and the tropical sun rose to shine through the large windows onto the podium. As Robin lectured, the sweat formed on his face so fast it ran off his nose and chin in a continuous stream. His shirt was saturated; his trousers stuck to his legs. We pictured ourselves as Humphrey Bogart and Katherine Hepburn in *The African Queen.*

We took turns addressing the class, and as we went back and forth we became aware of a growing attention in the audience.

Janice said, "And now Luo Bin will say something about . . . .." Before she could finish, the class thundered with laughter and cheers. Never had a Carnegie Hall audience been more appreciative. We knew we were doing something right although we didn't know what it was. Later Wang Wei explained the popular form of comedy in China called "Crosstalk," something like the old Abbott and Costello routines. To our students, who never heard two professors share a lecture, we were delivering an academic "Crosstalk."

Once classes began, students visited our apartment at all hours. Many came for special favors, asking us to correct their manuscripts, to lend them English books, to help them with translations for other classes. At Christmas time, delegations of students came to deliver presents and we held an impromptu party. Among the gifts was a statue of two Dutch children kissing, a symbol, the graduate class monitor explained, of our relationship.

One of our regular visitors was Jeannie Sun, whose features made her face a Slavic variant of Chinese. Admitted to the university for her athletic ability, Jeannie's English was not as good as that of most of her classmates, but she wanted to be the best in the class so she worked harder and longer than anyone else. She was the most self-confident, forthright student we'd ever met.

She volunteered to collect assignments from our class of 250 students and to distribute the handouts we prepared for them. She came to our apartment with a present of apples when Janice was ill. Her intellectual interests were broad and bold: She was determined to solve the mind-body problem discussed by Western philosophers and she wanted to know all about political parties in the US, surprised that anyone could belong to our political parties, that membership required no admission screening and no work. In comparing political systems we explained that in the US the word "Communist" was just like the phrase "Bourgeois Liberal" in China; many people were still afraid of communism without even knowing what it was. We asked her if anyone in her grade belonged to the Communist Party and she said "No, not yet. But maybe one will be soon."

"Who?" we asked.

"Me!" she laughed, "Are you afraid of me?"

Write and Wrong

Undergraduates at Central China University, like undergraduates in the US, ranged from determined hard workers to lazy unmotivated goof-offs. Some didn't come to class, some cheated or plagiarized, some offered a few minutes' effort as their weekly assignment. But many, including some who were not the best students, delighted us with their originality, their charm, their curiosity and their treatment of us.

When we asked them to write on current issues, we learned what they thought about the protest marches, about the rat problem, about the government's anti-smoking campaign. We learned even more when we asked them to write children's stories, to argue the pros and cons of having children, to evaluate the policy restricting disabled people from attending universities.

Until recently all undergraduates had been prohibited from having romantic attachments. Students thought this unfair because after college they were likely to be assigned to a work unit with few eligible marriage partners. University authorities had released the seniors from the prohibition, but our juniors were officially still under the ban. Although premature interest in romance and love was considered the result of "spiritual pollution" from the West, students were fascinated with the *idea* of romance, even more fascinated than their American counterparts.

Gratuitous references to sex and romance appeared in their compositions, no matter what the assigned topic. Many of the students wrote about having romantic partners. In his essay on smoking, Leonard, a delicate boy, wrote, "Whenever I smoke, my girlfriend is always preventing me from smoking." Larry, who sat next to Leonard, began his essay on not having children, "When I sit down to rest, my boring wife Leonard . . . . ."

For his Christmas story, Freddie wrote what appeared to be an attempt at pornography: Mr. Jones and Mrs. Green, who was married to somebody else, went into a hotel room together. Mrs. Green undressed and got into bed. "When he saw her he couldn't help but wait a minute. Mr. Jones take off his clothes as possible as quickly. Mr. Jones jump on Mrs. Green until they have their fill."

For the assignment on China's rat problem, Jim wrote a story instead of an essay:

Dating Rats

It was the birthday of my girlfriend. I spend the whole afternoon in searching almost all the shops for a gift to her, a delicate cat sculpture.

At the night, I brought her to a garden in the soft moonlight, with the cat in my pocket. She was so eager to know what the gift was, and I said leisurely that I wouldn't show her that before a kiss. When I was drawing her near, I suddenly found that some paces away two rats was kissing under a small tree. It was such a awful sight that made me lose the interest in kissing. I took her to another place, and arranged a chair. But when we were about to sit down, another couple of mice appeared to be dating under a chair in front of us. Obviously, they were imitating us! I was so angry that I took out an object from my pocket and shot it at the couple. The mice rushed away, leaving my "cat" lying convulsively on the ground, with a leg broken.

Although much stricter than Western arbiters of morality, Chinese officials shared one Western value: The Double Standard. Girls were watched over more closely and criticized more readily if they were too "modern," a euphemism that covered a broad range from "improper thinking" to overt sexual activity. Girls were no less interested in love than the boys, but they were more concerned with the consequences, and this showed in their writing. For example, Melissa's response to an assignment to "describe a strange thing about the US:"

A Strange Thing About the United States

It is known that Love Story is a famous American film, and I have been moved into tears by the heartbreaking ending and the true love of the couple. Anyhow, I find afterwards a strange thing about the United States: a couple can live together freely.

It is strange because such thing would never happen in a Chinese university without the interferences of the authority. The students are not allowed to date let alone living together freely. However, since more and more college students begin to date after they enter the college one or two years, the authorities of the college just warn us that dating is not encouraged and that they will break up these couples in the job assignment on graduation. There are also some brave young couples, influence by movies or novels, secretly live together. Unfortunately, their names will be enlisted on a large paper if they are found. Moreover some of them cannot get their bachelorship. Living in such atmosphere, naturally we think that phenomenon is strange.

The undergraduates and even some of the graduate students were in many ways less mature than American college students. To themselves, and to us, the undergraduates were girls and boys, not women and men. They giggled and cut up in class, more like junior high school students than college juniors. For many, their interest in sex was at the same level, a giggly fascination with something taboo. Yet their childishness was charming; they were more relaxed and more playful, without the affected cynicism of American students. Unlike their US counterparts, they did not have the pressure to be sexually adult, to act "cool" and mature.

Their parents and the state made many of their decisions for them as well as providing their support. The state paid for much of their education, including food and clothing subsidies, and many students continued to get money from their parents, even after they graduated. Summer jobs and part-time jobs for college students were extremely rare, not only because jobs were scarce in China, but because students were unwilling to work beneath their station. Oddly, when Chinese students go to the US for study, this snobbery disappears; most work hard at nearly any job they can get.

In China, university education is considered job training, requiring students to study only what would be useful for their future jobs. Our undergraduates entered Central China University as English majors and they took courses almost exclusively in English. Physics majors studied only physics and the necessary mathematics; economics majors studied only economics.

After being assigned a major field of study, it was very difficult for a student to change. When one of our English majors passed the examination for graduate school in economics, he was denied permission to go. The English Department told him, "We didn't train you for four years to become something else."

As a result of this early specialization, students learned relatively little beyond their own fields. We saw an example of this on the evening of the Mid-autumn Festival as we were sitting outside, eating mooncakes and drinking beer. The night was clear, the moon and stars overwhelming, with the strings of colored lanterns reminding us of the rooftop restaurant in Beijing. Our Chinese companions worked in the Waiban of the neighboring geography university, a school famous for its analyses of data from earth satellites. They had been English majors and their command of our language was excellent.

"What is the Chinese name of that?" we asked them, pointing to the brilliant flare of the planet Venus.

They didn't know the answer. They consulted among themselves and then asked us: "What is its name in English?"

Only after we told them were they able to tell us the Chinese name: "Venus is '*Jin Xing*,' the Gold Star."

They knew the Chinese name for the planet Venus and they knew its English name. Like a computer translation program, they knew the corresponding words in the two languages, but they didn't know the names referred to the brightest nonlunar object in the night sky. They knew the syntax and etymology of the word "Venus" and even where in Shakespeare it was mentioned, but their specialized education gave them no information about the connection between the word and the world around them.

Surprisingly, this narrow education, this preplanned life, this lack of independent study, did not produce people all with the same beliefs, the same attitudes, the same personalities. Instead it seemed to foster greater variety in personality and personal expression. Perhaps it was just that they didn't have to dress a certain way or act a certain way to be accepted, didn't have to worry about belonging. They were accepted. They did belong. They couldn't get away from it. This gave them a certain freedom that many American young people lack. We were surprised at our students' willingness to say nutty things and write wild stories. We tried to come up with a theory:

Each culture views conformity and individuality in a certain way. In our culture, individuality is celebrated, but conformity is considered the norm. Conformity is what happens if we are passive. It takes effort to be different, to do something unusual, to stand out in the world, effort that should be made, but effort nonetheless. We believe that if we relax, get too comfortable and don't pay attention, we will fall into a pattern of sameness and fail to live up to the American ideal of individuality. If we don't make an effort we'll be just like everyone else.

In China the view is reversed. They believe that the natural tendency, the default condition, is individuality. What takes effort is conformity. That is why friends, family and teachers have to warn people who go astray. This monitoring, this (to Western eyes) interference, is believed necessary, because without it, people, especially young people, would behave in nonstandard ways, become individualists who don't fit into society. In China, individualism is considered a kind of natural disintegration that happens if things are left alone. Social entropy.

According to our theory, Chinese students took for granted that without discipline and monitoring, they would fall into individuality and become deviants. Since we as foreign teachers didn't exert Chinese social pressure, our students relaxed into their individual characters, quirky and charmingly bizarre, behaving "naturally."

One of our favorites was a student we dubbed "Adjective Boy." He was the one who described Daniel as "the chicken coming out of the egg with the wet behind his ears and with the smoke of milk-smelling vapor." Adjective Boy, like many students, hoped to better his life by taking the examination for graduate school. He was eager, enthusiastic and obsessed with learning English, practicing it whenever he could.

One of our class assignments, inspired by Li Meili's questions about having children, was to argue the merits of having no children at all. The female students had no trouble with the assignment, assuming roles of professional dancers or great scholars who could not pursue their careers or help the country if they had children. Several of the males, however, could not bring themselves to defend this position. Some wrote about the advantages of having one child. Some argued against the one-child limit. One tried to escape the issue by writing that he should not have any children because he had AIDS. Adjective Boy also refused to follow the assignment, offering instead to write an essay to convince Janice that she should have children. Janice agreed, warning him that since he refused the original assignment, she would grade his paper more stringently. His essay filled many pages, much of it so flowery it was incomprehensible, his mixture of American slang with Chinese values producing a unique writing style:

> Dear, respectable, human, female, married, post-middleaged and anti-child Professor Janice:
> I have to gather all my courage and take the challenge to defend the children after your counter-child speech in class. In order to assure us of the future and soon-coming fruitful life with child, first I'll make the

best of my ability to persuade you and convince you in two ways: One is showing the necessities of child-raising. The other is to whip your back, curse you, call you various names and arouse your lost consciouseness. If these are not effective or successful, I'll manage to have a contact with Robin or get touch with the Chinese KKK members to hold up you whenerver you go out. Keep it in mind! OK? Let's get down to the topic. That's the swelt part of a carrot.

. . . It is beneficial for the intelligensia esp. a woman linguist to feed children. Scientifically and technically speaking, the intelligence of language will embed in the newly-created brain and pass innate ability through heritance. It is also quite compensating when you show your love and care for them, your children will show their love for you and pay for your assistance with their free and gay giggles or simple sneeze if you are ready to forgive their lack of vocabulary. . ..

When you are tired of life and prepare to go in the long, and twilight sleep in the bed of passing ages, a glimpse of retrospection of your youthful and energetic child, a smile of the young will surely light the dim light of your survival. How amuzing! How fantastic to see a kid, who belongs to you, and loves you badly . . . Through the mirror, you certainly catch the reflections and long vanished flush of your cheek. "How meaningful the life is!" you may stipulate. A child symbolizes love, youth and energy. Hurry up or it's too late to catch the last train of attaining a child paradise . . . A child will provide you with a Christmas card or a bunch of lilies on Mother's Day, or simply a pumpkin for Robin on Father's Day. He is watering at that, as you know. With satisfaction and ease, you will recall the old days, the burdens you bore shoulder by shoulder, the hardship you overcame hand-in-hand, even the inharmoniousness splashed with the fission of gaiety. "Do mother a kid" is my best suggestion and your best policy . . .

Can you imagine you parents yell out before you Are you a selfish ant or a lazy pidgeon who don't want to contribute to the states with a single baby? Are you a irresponsible and crazy hippie or yuppies. Aren't you afraid of breaking your class heritage line? Are you willing to be a lonely thing shrieking and trembling in the public medical center? Futhermore in the western world, fewer and fewer children are born each year, don't you care about a aging-future and old hemisphere.

We have prepared a basket of suggestion and a package of proposals for you. First, pull help from your kins or a maiden, who are fond of bringing up kids, as well they are surely good at this task. Then have a talk with your Robin dear . . . ..

Wish you well

Faithful and fearful

Adjective Boy's enthusiasm for Americanisms was shared by others. Phrases, styles and popular heroes from the US were valued and romanticized in China much the way French things once were in the US. English words were so popular on sports clothing that we could only find T-shirts bearing Chinese characters at tourist shops. "Rose" and "Rider Fellow" were in vogue for a while. Mickey Mouse pictures had replaced Mao's, although Mao was making a comeback. Michael Jackson and Madonna had become to the Chinese what Brigitte Bardot and Maurice Chevalier were once to us—more attractive because of their nationality than any homegrown stars.

Students incorporated aspects of American style in their clothing, adding their own Chinese variations. The boys copied the American collegiate fashion of sport jackets over blue jeans, or athletic warm-up suits, but they assembled their wardrobe over high-heeled sandals. Adjective Boy wore a costume-jewelry flower pinned to his crew-necked sweater. Some girls wore lipstick, but then so did some boys, at least for parties. Since Chinese lipstick came in bright greens and purples that turned to pink when applied, lipstick might have been more toy than cosmetic.

Hair styles were almost as varied as those seen in Venice Beach, California. There were curly permanents for both males and females, punk styles with short sides and long spiky tops. In the Spring several boys had their heads shaved; "Buddhist style" they called it.

At first the class of two hundred fifty Chinese faces were strange, or at least exotic. We had expected this because Chinese who had come to the US had told us it took them months to get used to Western faces, especially the light blue eyes and curly lashes that in China existed only on dolls or paintings of demons. With familiarity we learned that our students' faces were as varied as those from our own melting-pot land. After several months their faces no longer looked merely Chinese; instead they seemed to map onto all the other nationalities we had known. Martin Zhang looked Puerto Rican, Henry Liu looked Italian, some of Daniel's students with wide-set eyes, rosy cheeks and dimpled smiles looked Irish.

Unlike their Western counterparts our Chinese students did not come in all shapes and sizes. Most were willowy and delicate, a few were solid. None were obese, none were emaciated, and very few were tall. The tallest, one graduate student, was only as tall as Robin, a little over five-ten. Height was a sensitive topic among young males—high-heeled sandals were not just whimsical fashion. Li Meili explained that one attribute required of a "suitable" husband was tallness. Her sister-in-law married a short man and the family considered the marriage a failure. Students told us in China there were "five kinds of disabled—the blind, the deaf, the motorically disabled and the mentally disabled. And then there were males under five feet six."

The Chinese chalk in our classrooms was so soft that writing on the blackboard released an avalanche of white dust. At the end of each class our throats ached and our clothing was splotched with white powder. Chalk dust and coal soot settled on the chairs and desks and floors. Before sitting, students used cloths to wipe off their chairs and desks. When they wrote on the blackboard they kept their jackets and skirts from touching the dirty walls. Miraculously they returned to their seats free of the chalk dust that covered us.

Staying clean in dirty environments was not unique to students; we saw it all over China. People remained fastidiously clean while surrounded by mud and refuse. Trolley drivers in white dresses made emergency repairs to their vehicles without getting grease or dirt on their clothing. At the end of the day, street sweepers in tailored suits looked as if they had just gotten dressed.

Chinese make a sharper distinction between themselves and their environment than we do. They keep themselves and their clothing clean but they have more tolerance for dirt around them—food scraps dumped on restaurant floors, fruit peels and food wrappings dropped in the street, trash thrown from windows of vehicles and apartments. We, who looked in vain for public trash cans and carefully deposited our tea leaves in the sink instead of throwing them out windows, were magnets for food stains, mud and chalk dust.

In the wintertime the slim bodies of both sexes were disguised by layers of knit "sweater pants," shirts and sweaters and jackets. The students sat in the unheated classroom, blowing on their hands and shivering in their seats as we walked up and down in front to stay warm. Between classes they danced in the hallways to generate heat but during class the most effective method was cuddling together. Hugging and fondling of same-sex companions could occur in any situation, but in the winter it seemed that our audience resembled gay and lesbian couples watching a romantic movie more than students attending a linguistics lecture. We were charmed by this cultural difference, but not by another:

The students spat in class, right on the floor! The very first time it happened, when a beautiful girl dressed like an angel cleared her lovely throat and released a big gob onto the floor, we couldn't speak for long seconds. Regularly we heard the warning sound, a throaty rasp, and watched our dear students jettison globs of mucus past their well-tailored clothes onto the floor. Out of politeness, they rubbed it into the dust using a twisting motion of the foot.

We asked the students not to spit in the classroom but compliance was short lived. At Guest House social gatherings we joked about the spitting and schemed how to do away with it. We tried to desensitize ourselves by practicing phlegm-mustering hawks. Nelson, probably because he had lived so long in tobacco-chewing country, was the master hawker.

In the spring Robin showed his composition class a printed "notice" he claimed to have received in his mailbox. He criticized the notice for its complex wording and gave it to the class to revise into simpler, better English. It was April Fool's Day, but he did not remind his class of the date.

> By order of the joint committee appointed by the Ministry of Health and the State Education Committee the regulation against spitting inside any building of a university or institute governed by the State Education Committee shall be enforceable by a fine of 50 fen (5 jiao) for each offense. Every teacher is required to levy the fine against any student who spits in the classroom, whereupon a receipt shall be given to the student and the moneys collected remitted to the university or institute's accounting office.

Robin never told them it was a joke. Only two spits occurred in his class the rest of the term, a statistic envied by the other foreigners.

Unplanned Lessons
After Christmas and before the end of the first term, after parties and presents and steady hot water, after a term of brilliant graduate students and amusing undergraduate essays, we were delighted, almost euphoric, about teaching in China. We were not prepared

for what happened during the final examination for our undergraduate linguistics course.

We gave a multiple-choice exam to our more than two hundred students, the only kind we could possible grade in time. We warned against cheating, against talking or communicating during the exam, clarified some questions on the exam and watched our students work, thinking fondly about them all. We told two giggling girls not to talk, assuming their conversation was innocent.

As the papers were being turned in, we were distracted by departing students who came up to say good-bye. Then we saw several students flagrantly cheating, even exchanging papers.

Janice grabbed the paper of a girl who was copying from the boy next to her, arguing with him about the answers. The girl tried to grab her paper back. When Janice held it out of reach, the girl flailed and punched at Janice, desperate to retrieve her paper. Robin snatched the papers of two other students who had just exchanged them. At least ten papers were confiscated, more had gotten away. We were upset and angry, disappointed, heartbroken.

Within minutes of returning to the Guest House, students were at our door. Some of the cheaters came to plead for lenience. Some sent their political advisers, their friends and special character witnesses from their home towns. It went on all day. We had no time to eat, no time to bathe. We made a sign for our door in Chinese characters saying "We are very busy" but still they came. They badgered our tutors to intercede for them. Please don't tell Wang Y, please don't tell the Vice Chairman, they begged. They were afraid they would be expelled, shamed for life. Their names would be read out as cheaters on the university loudspeakers. Please spare them. Have mercy.

We received letters of "self-criticism," a form of contrition and self-humiliation left over from the Cultural Revolution:

> Respected Professor Moulton and Professor Robinson,
> Before I came here I was a teacher of English in a middle school in a little town. It's in Xuanzhou county, a backward place very far from here. There are few people

who know English in my town. I became a teacher of English only because I know a little English and English must be taught in schools in China . . .

Last summer I came to the Central China University for my further study. How delighted I was when I was told that I would have two American Professors teaching us Linguistics: Dr. Moulton and Dr. Robinson. It is the first time for me to have lectures given by foreign teachers. I went to your lectures every week and I appreciated them very much. But due to the poor ability of my English listening, I have much trouble with understanding the lectures. I couldn't follow your words and take the notes. So I have to work hard with the help of the materials given by you. Sometimes I didn't go to bed until midnight, trying to consult the new words in the dictionary, trying to understand the materials sentence by sentence.

Last Tuesday morning, I had been working hard during the examination. But I still didn't know many of the questions. When the time left us about ten minutes, I had not finished a few questions in the paper yet. I was extremely worried. I didn't know what to do. The fear that I would fail in the examination came across my mind. What a humiliation! On the spur of the moment, took the answer sheet of my classmate beside me. Oh, it's very, very bad! It's a blunder of mine! On the other hand, you did right to take my papers away.

As guests of Chinese people, you've been doing very well in carrying out your duties. You've been working hard to help us with our English learning. That's why the students like you so much. I'm so sorry and feel guilty to have made you so angry. As a matter of fact, I didn't mean to cheat you. At that moment, I did so only because of the fear. Now, I have realized it's a good lesson for me. And I'll remember and never forget it for the rest of my life.

Professor Robinson and Professor Moulton, now I have only a request. Please forgive me and give a chance to be your student again. I'll work much harder next

term, trying to be a good student. Please give me a chance of making up for the exam next term. I'll review the lessons during the winter vacation. Well, I think this scandal is all because of me. I'm to be blamed. It was I who took the sheet of my classmate. It's none of his business. I hope you will forgive him and give him a mark. I would like to accept punishment in any form if you insist on it.
Yours truly,
Lin Guojin

As we graded papers and looked up the names on student lists, we found that all the cheaters were from one particular group. Like Lin Guojin, they were high school teachers from the countryside who had been brought back to study at Central China University. Older than the other students in the class, their education had been disrupted during the Cultural Revolution and they were stuck teaching a subject they hardly knew. They had been summoned to the university to improve their education and assigned to classes along with younger, better-educated students. Some of them thought this remedial study was a wonderful opportunity. Others resented being called away from their homes and families, forced to undergo a re-education they were not prepared for.

Self-criticism was a special Chinese way of importuning us but other culprits used more universal methods. The girl who punched Janice came to see her several times, pleading, whining, crying until we let her in. She claimed she hadn't cheated, she was merely "checking" her answers. Without thinking clearly Janice said that she could prove she hadn't cheated by getting the student she had been "checking" with to come forward. If his paper was different from hers, we would excuse her. If his was the same, they would both be punished.

The next evening she returned with a young man we didn't recognize. He told us his name and we compared his paper with hers. The two papers were identical! Why had she come back?

What had she expected? She didn't know, she said. She didn't want to be punished. She would have done anything.

The boy she brought to our apartment was not the student she had been arguing with at the end of the exam. This boy had left early in the exam but she stayed on to check the answers she had copied from him with another student. We caught her only because she had been arguing with the second student over the answers that didn't agree with those from her first source.

One of Janice's brightest students from the composition class, Jim of the "Dating Rats," came to speak with her. He had heard that she was very upset about the cheating and he spoke quietly, intimately.

"Yes," she told him, "because it was so open, so rude and unfair to students like you who worked honestly and so hard."

"One of the cheaters is a girl named Li Hongli," he said.

"Right," Janice confirmed, "She and her friend talked and giggled in class and continued to copy answers even after I warned them."

"Well," he said shyly, "she is my girlfriend."

Janice had not expected this. The culprit was older, brash, certainly not his type. We had never seen them together, but of course, given the forbidden status of student romance, the more intimate the couple, the less they would appear together in public.

He pleaded with Janice not to go to the Vice Chairman. He put his hand over hers in supplication. Or was it flirtation? When Janice refused to yield, he left. But her faith in his intelligence was justified, because he convinced his girlfriend and her co-conspirator to go to Vice Chairman Wang Y and confess *before* we reported them.

Wang Y came to us. His inclination, after hearing from the two girls, was to forget the whole thing. By this time we suspected that cheating was pretty widespread and Wang Y was used to it. Officially, cheating was a serious offense and the punishment could be severe, but we suspected many students saw it as no more than cooperating with friends, and many teachers ignored it. Wang Y convinced us to allow the cheaters, if they were first offenders, to take a make-up exam at the beginning of the next term. He told us we would have to write a make-up exam for people who failed the exam anyway.

Despite our sternness toward the cheaters, we were considered heroes in the end. Either Wang Y tried to protect us—an unlikely possibility—or else he wanted to appear stern and powerful himself. He told the cheaters *he* wanted to punish them but we interceded on their behalf; because of us their names would not be made public. One week later cheaters in other departments were denounced by loudspeaker.

Of the eleven students accused of cheating, one was excused, the boy brought to us by the girl who was merely "checking" her answers with his. He was profoundly grateful to us for not prosecuting him. Six others quit school out of shame. Only Jim's girlfriend, the young man who shared his answers with her, and the self-criticizers repeated the exam.

A month after the makeup examination, Janice talked to Jim at a class party. All the students except Jim's girlfriend had come to find out their grades. Jim said his girlfriend had quit school and married someone else.

"Ha!" Janice thought, but tried not to let her feelings show.

"It is a secret," he said. "Li Hongli used to have a boyfriend in her home town. And they once loved each other very deeply. Very very deeply." His accompanying look suggested that "very very deeply" was the Chinese way of saying they had not practiced premarital celibacy.

"But that love changed, and she did not love him anymore. Then she came to the university and we began to love each other. But her old boyfriend wanted her to marry him. He insisted, and in China she has no choice, she has to marry him. Because in China even if you are no longer in love, you must do this. She had no way out.

"I am very sad and want to cry all the time. But I try to study hard instead so I won't think about it. And I stay with my classmates and do things with them so I won't cry. She still writes to me. She has written two letters and says she still loves me."

Janice blurted out, "Oh no. She shouldn't write to you. That is very bad. You'll get into serious trouble. Now that she's married she shouldn't be writing to you. You can't write to her. That's too dangerous. For her sake and your sake, don't write to her."

Jim lowered his head in thought. Then he said, "Since you tell me not to, and you are my teacher, I will not do this. Thank you for telling me."

At his age, we would never have taken a teacher's advice about affairs of the heart. In the US we would not offer such advice. In China, it is different: a teacher is not just a dispenser of academic subject matter, a teacher is a counselor about all of life. And we had accepted that role.

7
CHINESE LESSONS

Puns and Confusions

We went to China with fantasies that our teaching would win over one quarter of the earth's population to our view of linguistics. We had ambitious plans for research programs on Chinese grammar to test theories developed in the West. We did learn much more Chinese than we knew before we came, but we also learned how much more there was to learn, how much the language depended on the culture, how rich the dialect variations, how ubiquitous the puns.

For people familiar with European languages, Chinese is shockingly different. European languages share cognates and roots and words whose meaning we can guess. When Pierre wanted to encourage Jeanette to use English, he told her she only had to mispronounce French. In reprisal, we insisted that "bureau" and "buffet" and "banquet" were words their language had stolen from ours. If we opened a French dictionary to any page we were likely to see a list of French words that were also English words: exploit, exploration, explosion, exponential, exportable, exposé, and so on. So close were the two languages that we could understand when Pierre talked about technical subjects in French. A change in stress in *L'intelligence artificiel* or *le désarmement nucléaire*, and they were as clear as in our own language. Not so with Chinese.

Not only did our English give us no hint of the meaning of a Chinese phrase, but many Chinese words sounded alike to us. The 50,000 written characters in Chinese share only 1,277 different sounds, making for enormous ambiguity. Even worse—for us— those 1,277 sounds are distinguished by four "tones," variants in pitch that our years of speaking English had trained us not to hear. Without the tones there are only 400 different sounds.

For example, in English the meaning of "when" is the same no matter what the tone, but not so for *wen* in Chinese. *Wen* (fourth tone, falling pitch) means "question," but *wen* (low third tone) means "kiss." A polite way of asking for information begins: *Qing wen* . . . (Please, may I ask . . .). When Robin used the wrong tone trying to ask for directions, he asked for a kiss instead. With his foreign face this produced only a laugh and not an arrest for indecent advances.

In order to give Westerners a way of pronouncing and printing the sounds of Chinese, alphabetic renderings for Chinese sounds have been devised. The first widely known of these "romanizations" of the Chinese language, the Wade-Giles system, was a disaster. Chinese has sounds that are very like Western **B**s and **P**s, but Wade and/or Giles decided to render them in a peculiar way. The **P** sound (a bit more breathy in Chinese) was represented by **P**-plus-apostrophe, thus: **P'**. The **B** sound was represented by plain **P**. They did the same for the other voiced/unvoiced pairs, **T** and **D, K** and **G**. Since *"Peking"* doesn't have an apostrophe after the **P** or the **K**, it is supposed to be pronounced with the **P** sounding like a **B** and the **K** as a **J** (soft **G**) sound: *Beijing*.

Thanks to Wade and Giles, every Westerner who didn't know the secret apostrophe code learned to mispronounce Chinese. It wasn't until the Chinese invented their own system for international use, *Pinyin*—using the sounds and spelling of Portuguese, that Westerners learned how to pronounce the capital city.

Our struggle with Chinese was compounded by difficulties we had with the unique version of English spoken by our Chinese friends. Learned almost entirely from other Chinese and from books, they called it "Chinglish," a dialect of English that combines Chinese syntax with Nineteenth Century slang and a set of unique pronunciations. Many Chinglish phrases were so universal we found ourselves saying "wait-a-bit," "have-a-look," "study-the-matter" and "cannot-be-repair-ed" as if they were the common run-together terms they are in Chinese.

The Chinese use of one sound, *ta*, to represent "he," "she" and "it" confused and delighted us when carried over into English: "My boyfriend cooks for herself." "He can juggle the soccer ball with her foot."

Our problem was increased because natives of Wuhan didn't distinguish the sounds for **N** and **L**. It took us a while to understand that "lice labors" referred to a considerate family living nearby.

And, of course, much could be lost in translation, even the simple meaning of "maybe."

"Are you coming with us, Little Lin?"

"Maybe yes."

"When will you know for certain?"

"Maybe I am coming with you."

"Does Director Fang want you to do something else?"

"Maybe not."

"Do you know or not?"

"Maybe yes."

"How can we find out? Should we talk to him?"

"No no no. Maybe yes, I am coming."

From conversations like this, we concluded that the Chinese word for "maybe" is used as a polite softener as well as to express uncertainty, so that in Chinese, "Maybe not" means "No" and "Maybe yes" means "Yes." Maybe.

The subtleties of other phrases were revealed by their unexpected use. If we asked whether we were going to the Bank of China, Xiao Han might say, "Of course," which seemed like a rebuke, as if to say "How could we ask such a question?" When Helen asked Golden Zhou if he would dance with her, he said, "Why not?" conveying a lack of enthusiasm we assumed was unintended. We learned to ignore subtle differences in English forms of consent and agreement.

Xiao Han often expressed agreement using a repeated "Okay Okay Okay," which sounded very impatient to us, but was only his translation of *"Hao Hao Hao"* ("Good Good Good"). In Chinese a single *"Hao"* sounds abrupt and rude; it is usually reduplicated three or more times to express continued agreement. We heard multiple *hao*'s so often that Helen wrote special Guest House lyrics for "Deck the Halls":

> Deck the walls with Chinese posters
> Hao-hao hao-hao-hao, hao hao, hao hao.
> Improvise with woks for toasters
> Hao-hao hao-hao-hao, hao hao, hao hao.

Some aspects of Chinese grew on us. The Chinese language is very relaxed about sentence boundaries, showing an indifference to demarking "complete thoughts" with capitals and periods, something we at first deplored in our composition students and later found very convenient to do ourselves, continuing a line of thought without having to break it up with needless punctuation or abrupt capitalizations, until we finished whatever we wanted to say. See?

With only 1,277 spoken syllables to express 50,000 Chinese characters, puns both for humor and serious innuendo are an essential part of Chinese culture. For example, *yanjiu* is the word for study. With a slight difference in tone, it is also the word for bribe (literally "cigarette-liquor," the commonest of small gratuities). When officials hesitate to make a decision, as they often do, claiming they wish to study the matter (*yanjiu*), people laugh and say, "Oh, yes, we know what you mean—bribe (*yanjiu*)."

Another frequent pun is based on the similarity between the words for hen-pecked ("controlled by wife") and bronchitis ("airpipe inflammation"), *qi guan yan*. "Why do you have to go home so early?" "Oh, I have a touch of bronchitis," the punster would say to make people laugh.

In China, where direct criticism of government leaders is usually unacceptable, indirect criticism using puns is an art form. For example, student demonstrators in Tiananmen Square expressed their hostility to government leader Deng Xiaoping by smashing small bottles, since "small bottle" in Chinese is pronounced *xiao ping*.

Ambiguity is not the only source of humor in Chinese. The language has a wealth of four-syllable phrases that delighted us. The phrase for "extremely urgent" is, literally "set eyebrows on fire;" the phrase for "superfluous" translates directly as "draw snake, add feet."

Chinese culture also differs from ours in body language. Personal space is smaller than we are used to, and Chinese stand just a bit closer than Americans usually do. It was not enough to surprise us, and not enough for us to back off. Instead it gave us a feeling of greater friendship and intimacy when Chinese moved closer to us than we expected.

But there are hazards to the proximity. The Chinese consonants that linguists called "plosives," such as **P**s, **T**s and **K**s, are more plosive than their English equivalents and so more likely to be ejected with a spray of saliva. And the bit closer that Chinese prefer to stand makes the difference between whether that saliva falls to earth or lands on the listener's face. Many Chinese guard against this transfer of spittle by holding one hand in front of their mouths. The gesture has the additional advantage of deflecting the breath to the side, in case the speaker had fried garlic cloves for breakfast.

We had heard a story about Pearl Buck's travels in the Chinese countryside. Ms. Buck, who spoke Chinese fluently, visited a small town that never before had a foreign visitor. When she stopped with her guide at a tea shop, the owner brought them tea, honored to have such guests. When Pearl Buck spoke to him in Chinese, he was so startled he dropped the tea cups. As he hurried to clean up, the guide asked him, "Ah, were you very surprised?" "Oh yes," replied the shop owner, "I was amazed that I could understand Foreign Speech because I have never studied it."

The reactions to our attempts to speak Chinese were occasionally as dramatic. Sometimes one sentence from us, however badly pronounced and ungrammatical, convinced people that we were completely fluent. Crowds gathered to witness the miracle of foreigners who could speak real language. People then talked all at once, at full speed, trying to get more responses from us.

Some people, recognizing that one sentence did not a speaker make, treated us as babies and tried to teach us new words. The peasants in the food market held up their products and asked us to name them, rewarding us with laughter and thumbs-up signs whenever we got it right.

Each of us foreigners had a different approach to learning Chinese. Helen stuck labels with Chinese characters and Pinyin spellings on most of the furniture and fixtures in her apartment. "Kitchen," "Pot," "Cloth," "Floor," her signs said in Chinese.

Daniel became our local expert on Chinese epithets and epigrams. Through him we learned how to say, "That's life," "It's all in a day's work," "It's the thought that counts," as well as "Bad egg!" "Get lost!" and "Mind your own business!" in both polite and crude versions.

Bud had a series of tutors who gave up on him, saying he couldn't detect tone differences, but he seemed to overcome his handicap and by the end of the year he surprised us all with how well he could communicate. When we complimented his ability, he mumbled self-deprecation, Chinese style.

With the wisdom of a seasoned traveler, Nelson started by learning the words for numbers so he could talk about prices, train schedules, time and dates. At first he claimed that the Chinese pretended not to understand him, confident he had pronounced everything correctly. When he got a lesson on the different tones, he began correcting Little Lin's tones for English.

"Hi," she said in a tentative first tone greeting.

"Wrong!" Nelson said. "It's fourth tone. Hi! Hi!"

Tutors' Lives and Fates
Determined to improve our Chinese we arranged for regular language lessons. We had two tutors, Julie (Zhu Li, "Pearl Beauty") and Li Meili.

At our first meeting Julie wore stockings, high-heeled sandals and a light blue jumper over a white blouse. She looked very demure and feminine, very dressed up. She had horn-rimmed glasses reminiscent of old movies where the hero encourages the heroine to remove her glasses and says, "Why, Miss Jones, you *are* beautiful." Fortunately Julie was not forced to make a choice between looking good and seeing well, since fashionable glasses in all shapes, sizes and tints had arrived in China. When her old glasses broke she got a large-lensed pair with rose-colored rims that flattered her face and turned her, with her lovely smile and demure ways, into a very attractive young woman.

Julie was the Chinese ideal of a young lady: charming, optimistic, always good-natured and cheerful. She was part of a new generation, undamaged by the Cultural Revolution, uninvolved in department intrigues and innocent about treachery. She was the same generation as the students who went to Tiananmen Square, believing they could change the government with their dreams, unable to imagine they might be hurt.

She became very important to us during our year in China, listening sympathetically to our troubles with devious administrators and cheating students. When we told her about the problems we had with Vice Chairman Wang Y, her good-nature soon changed our anger into laughter as we called him names in Chinese: bad egg, foreign devil, highway robber, poison person, vomit head.

As we spent more time with our shy young tutor, she became more comfortable with us. She would splutter with laughter at the inadvertent puns arising from our mispronounced tones. She entertained us with imitations of foreigners speaking Chinese, the tones exaggerated and syllables shouted in second or fourth tone, up and down in a random singsong.

Humor and social commentary brightened the relatively drab exercises in our textbook and extended our vocabulary.

"Where is my book?" Julie asked, to help us practice answering questions.

"Oh, so sorry. I learned one can sell anything now in China. I sold it in the market and I will give you half the money."

"Where is the letter I received yesterday?" Julie asked.

"Oh, so sorry. Government officials came yesterday and read your letter. They said you are a bad person and they are coming back today to take you away."

After each lesson the three of us usually went to lunch at Laurel Hill Restaurant where Julie taught us new characters from the menu. She stood next to us at the order window in a conspiracy of silent laughter with the cashier while hungry patrons squirmed and clamored behind us as we struggled to pronounce our order.

Gradually we learned more about her. She grew up in a northern province, the youngest of four girls born to a peasant family. Julie had many names at home: As the fourth child she was called "Little Four;" sometimes the family called her "Little Thief" because she always wanted to take things from the family household to bring back with her to school; she was also called "Ugly Duck" because her older sisters, Big Older Sister, Older Sister Two and Older Sister Three, were all beautiful and married. However, Julie was the only one in her family to go to university. Her family would tease her by chanting, "We have an ugly duck who goes to the university."

On campus Julie lived with three other teachers in a dark dormitory room just long enough for bunk beds and a desk against each wall, just wide enough to walk between the beds. When we visited, the roommates and the boyfriend of one of them sat on the lower berth of one bed, we on the other, sharing the space with all Julie's belongings: one radio, several pictures, and a plastic bank in the shape of a smiling baby's head.

Julie's room was directly across from the toilet room. Every time the door opened a terrible smell filled the room. Indoor plumbing in China rarely came with proper flushing mechanisms, gas traps or vent stacks, so human waste plummeted to ground level through vertical pipes, drain water hesitated and burbled, and noxious sewer gases returned as receipts for these deposits. Despite the smell, Julie's current living conditions were better than when she was a student living with seven roommates. At the end of the year she would become twenty-two and be allowed to marry her boyfriend. His parents were important officials in the city and had lots of *guanxi*, so they might even get an apartment of their own. Her future kept her cheerful in conditions that would have made us cry.

Between people over forty who were wary of associating with us, and the young teachers and students who were openly friendly, fearing no reprisals, there was a third group, people who had been children or teenagers during the Cultural Revolution.

Golden Zhou belonged to this middle group as did our other tutor, Li Meili. The Cultural Revolution had shaped her bittersweet, maverick-intellectual character as surely as its absence permitted Julie's innocence. Although it did not leave Li Meili as fearful as some of the older teachers, the Cultural Revolution had deprived her of opportunities and education, and made her feel she had to work harder for less reward and recognition than others.

Li Meili didn't have a regular undergraduate degree because many schools and universities were closed, or essentially nonfunctioning, during a good part of the Cultural Revolution. Her parents had been early supporters of Mao and were therefore honored, until people found out her grandparents had not been poor peasants and then her family was disgraced. Friends no longer talked to them and she was shunned at school. At sixteen she was sent to be a worker, building railroad tunnels instead of going to school. As political fortunes reversed, Li Meili, along with other workers, peasants and soldiers, was sent to the university, while educators and intellectuals were sent out to the countryside to learn physical labor.

When universities returned to making appointments on academic rather than political merit, the status of *Worker-Peasant-Soldier* student turned from honor to stigma. Like Li Meili, many of the teachers in the General English Department were W-P-S appointments and segregating them was one of the reasons the Foreign Language Department split into two English departments. And, Li Meili admitted, the English language skills of many W-P-S teachers did show the effects of their inferior education. Government and university policies started discriminating against all W-P-S teachers, gerrymandering the requirements for educational and employment opportunities to exclude them.

While Julie was initially intimidated by foreigners, Li Meili was fascinated by them. She looked at our round-eyed, big-nosed faces and said over and over, "How beautiful."

"Oh no, we have big noses." Janice said, adapting the Chinese style of denying a compliment, knowing "Big Nose" was an insulting term for a Westerner.

"It's not a big nose, it's a 'high' nose," Li Meili explained. High noses are good. Chinese infants are praised by saying they have high noses; One of Li Meili's classmates even had cosmetic surgery to increase the bridge of her nose.

Li Meili also admired Janice's eyelashes. "Do all Western people have curling eyelashes?" We told her about eyelash curlers as evidence that not all Westerners have curly lashes, or at least not as curly as they want to have. The folds ubiquitous in Western eyelids are also objects of admiration to the millions of Chinese women and men who have had surgery to create folds in their own eyelids.

Li Meili watched Janice's newly washed hair slowly dry into curls and supposed that all Westerners had curly hair. We could not condemn her mistake since we once thought all Asians had perfectly straight black hair until we saw Chinese with wavy hair, thin hair, reddish and brown hair—sometimes on the very young or very old or very poor, suggesting that curls and light color were not always the result of cosmetic intervention.

Robin's beard was a special curiosity. Many Chinese men grow so few facial hairs they remove them with tweezers. Li Meili asked Janice what it was like to kiss a bearded man, and Janice invited her to find out for herself. Li Meili paused, as if to consider it, and then laughed. "I didn't mean that," she said.

"Go ahead, I won't be jealous," Janice said.

"No, no, no."

We had called her bluff. She would have liked to have been entirely liberated, to rise above what she thought of as her cultural inhibitions, but she couldn't do it. When we shared a glass of soda she tried to get us to drink at the same time in order to see us kiss in public. We refused. Finally she asked, hesitantly, "How do foreigners kiss? In the movies foreigners always turn their heads when they kiss. Do they have to turn their heads because their noses are so big?" We were not the only targets of her curiosity; we heard her ask a Japanese man whether it was true that all Japanese men were oversexed.

Li Meili's forthright questions may have taught us more about China, and how our culture differed from hers than what she learned from us about the West. When she asked how we could be good friends with Daniel who was two decades our junior, we learned that in China older people commanded so much respect as to prevent the equality required for close friendship. Li Meili was surprised to find out that we didn't know the exact ages of most of our American friends. In China our age was often the first thing people wanted to know about us—it was as important as gender in social dealings.

Daniel was the first to meet Li Meili's husband, Ming Yong. Li Meili told Daniel their pet names for each other were "Cat" and "Dog" because they fought like cats and dogs. Daniel assured us that they really liked each other, that the fighting was only banter.

Ming Yong was tall, not one of the "fifth kind of handicapped." But he had thick lips, Li Meili told us, and Chinese people don't like thick lips.

"Westerners think people with big lips are better to kiss," Robin explained, to defend Janice and also to make Li Meili giggle.

We told her that many Western fashion models have collagen injections to make their lips fuller.

Ming Yong had just been promoted to head the translation and interpretation department for the Research Institute of the Wuhan Iron and Steel Company, one of the largest industrial concerns in China. He lived on the other side of the city, in the Hankou district, while Li Meili had an apartment here on campus, on the Wuchang side of the Yangtze River. The trip could easily take three hours each way so they saw each other only on weekends.

Daniel and we were invited to Li Meili's apartment for dinner. She had three small rooms, plus a bathroom and kitchen shared with another family. Her apartment walls were covered with baby calendars and posters of blond babies, crawling babies, diapered babies. The hallway was open to the outside so the fumes could escape from the coal brazier used for cooking. It was winter and their building, like most buildings south of the Yangtze River, had no heat. We wore winter coats and hats during the meal.

Li Meili's husband did the cooking and the food was magnificent, a huge variety, with a special selection of unusual dishes. Li Meili criticized every dish as it was put on the table—one was too dry, one was overcooked, another needed more salt. Ming Yong said "Yes, I know. I am a terrible cook." He smiled as he watched his guests take second helpings. Li Meili's criticisms continued throughout the meal as each dish arrived and we applauded its taste, its texture, its arrangement. Li Meili said *she* could make these dishes better. Ming Yong said he didn't see anybody eating her dishes but they were eating *his*. The dialogue was partly competition, partly concern that we got the best possible meal, and partly the discomforting spouse-deprecation game that Americans also play.

Li Meili was so direct with us that Robin decided we should speak to her about criticizing Ming Yong in public. It was a bad idea, we explained, because it embarrassed Ming Yong in front of other people and made her seem disloyal. If she didn't like something he did, she should discuss it with him in private.

What we had done was very Chinese: interfering in the private lives of other people, giving them advice about how they ought to behave. Perhaps what was even more Chinese was that Li Meili followed our advice.

She told Ming Yong what we said. He agreed with us, but at first she was not sure she wanted to give up her public criticisms. Wife berating husband is a part of Chinese culture; we saw it on the street, in traditional Peking Opera and in contemporary comedy routines. A few weeks later Li Meili told us that we had been right; it was much better to discuss her dissatisfactions with Ming Yong in private, yet a few minutes later a criticism began to slip out and she clapped her hand over her mouth, smiling at us sheepishly.

As a result of our interference Ming Yong and Li Meili felt close to us, often visiting us on weekends, discussing their hopes and dreams and disagreements. They argued about what kind of automatic washing machine to buy. Li Meili wanted to buy a good Japanese machine, which cost nearly a year's salary, but Ming Yong wanted to spend less and be patriotic by getting a Chinese machine. They finally bought the Chinese machine, but after the first week the light went out and the dial stopped working.

Teachers' salaries were lagging behind the cost of living. The government raised teachers' salaries but allowed prices to go up even more. On hearing this complaint, we proposed a way for Li Meili and Ming Yong to supplement their income: Since people liked to stare at us, we would sit inside a large box with a peep hole and a sign: "30 *Fen* to See the Foreigner." Perhaps we might charge more to look at Daniel because he was blond. We needed a Chinese in front to collect the money, because if one of us did it, people wouldn't have to pay to see a foreigner. This would be a "joint-venture" enterprise, like the tourist hotels in China backed by Hong Kong capitalists.

Then we got another idea, one that we convinced Ming Yong and Li Meili to try: It had become trendy to use English on product labels, whether for export or not. Unfortunately, the labelers were not skilled in this exotic language: A liquor was touted as "outmoded" instead of the intended "old-fashioned;" a box of biscuits claimed to be both "new style" and "traditional." We proposed that the four of us form a company and write to manufacturers offering our services to help them with the English text on their packaging. We needed a license to form a company, Ming Yong said, so we formed a "group," calling ourselves the "English Language Consultant Group" and wrote letters in both English and Chinese to several manufacturers whose products were labeled incorrectly.

Each letter began with praise for the product followed by the bad news that the label contained errors of grammar, spelling and style. We suggested that potential buyers would judge the quality of the contents by the quality of the package. We warned that purchasing agents for foreign importers and the domestic customers who read English would be discouraged from selecting their product. This was followed by a patriotic reminder that every export product was a representative of China and every manufacturer should strive to make a good impression. Then we gave them a free sample of how to correct one of their errors, listed our credentials and assured them of our eagerness to help—for a modest fee.

One letter came back because the address was wrong but that was the only response. We wrote more letters. Still no response. We began to realize what we all should have known before, that in China we needed connections, *guanxi*, to initiate a business arrangement. No one was going to pay attention to us unless they knew us personally or knew a friend who would vouch for us.

We tried one last time, writing to a company selling "Fried Peanuts" in packages covered with cartoons and comments in faulty English. We told the company that "Roasted" was a better word for peanuts than "Fried" and that we could offer fourteen more improvements on their package wording. We never heard from them either, but several weeks later Li Meili came to us with their new label—the name of the product had been changed to "Roasted Peanuts."

8
CONSPICUOUS CONSUMPTION

Free Marketeers

Official publications proclaimed that China was firmly committed to the "socialist road" but Marxist-Leninist-Mao Zedong Thought is very flexible in guiding the economy of modern China. The Communist principle, "From each according to ability and to each according to need," was being modified to add, "And to each according to *results*." Superimposed on the state-controlled socialist economy was a "personal responsibility system" that functioned at all levels, from individual worker to the largest industrial concern. Committees in Beijing still made the rules and set priorities for the rapidly growing economy, yet when we looked at Chinese commerce from street level it looked just like Western style free-enterprise capitalism.

Even departments within universities were developing entrepreneurial sidelines in order to bring in extra money. The English Departments sold journals and books and offered expensive cram courses for students trying to pass examinations for study abroad. The university carpenter shop free-lanced by building crates and furniture for individuals.

The new economy had spawned entrepreneurial middle-people of all kinds: factors, brokers, promoters, advertising agents, consultants and accountants. Advertisements were everywhere: billboards, street banners, train placards, newspapers, television. China's new millionaires were celebrated as heroes of the revolution. There was a stock market, a Great Wall credit card, a national lottery, even a student loan program. *China Daily* reported that government-owned apartments in Beijing were turning condo with salary deduction arrangements that functioned just like mortgages.

CONSPICUOUS CONSUMPTION

There were new income taxes and new government bonds. Insurance companies were growing rapidly.

Reality and rhetoric had diverged. "Oh no, we do not have capitalism in China," our students assured us; "Capitalists exploit the workers."

Because many consumer products were new, there were few conventions about where they should be sold. From the largest department stores to the smallest street peddler's fold-up display, goods were proffered in strange combinations. Near the Bank of China one shop sold only truck tires and peanut butter. The shop next door sold firecrackers, pottery and string. Down the street was a store that sold only hardware and musical tapes. The Hubei Antique store sold ceramic statues, displayed in glass cases along with cheap garden trowels. A clothing stall sold raisins and hot sauce along with tailored skirts.

There seemed to be no feeling that certain things belonged together, that a person who sold canned mushrooms should not also sell hammers or arc welders. You sold whatever you had the *guanxi*, the connections, to get. In one department store, volleyballs were displayed at the same counter as air mail envelopes; vitamin pills stacked next to shoelaces. In another store, bicycles were sold next to socks and gloves but bicycle parts were on the other side of the store, next to the hand lotion counter, and food products were duplicated in three different sections of the store. The kaleidoscopic arrangement of goods challenged the ingenuity of the customers who had to figure out where things were.

In this juxtaposition of unlike wares, new display categories appeared each time we went shopping. At the Zhongnan Department Store cooking utensils were first sold all at one counter, next to medical supplies. A week later the defining category seemed to be "stainless steel products" because stainless steel cooking utensils were placed with drafting equipment and shelving brackets, while aluminum cookware and enameled bowls were displayed in another part of the store.

The collection and handling of money was also strange to us. Calculations were done on an abacus in the computer section of a department store but on a programmable electronic calculator at our favorite fruit stall. Money was usually unsorted, the bills crumpled or wadded into balls. Bargaining was frequent but restrained, probably because China had a tradition of price controls and penalties against price-gouging. Unlike other countries where vendors might settle for a quarter or even a tenth of their original asking price, the Chinese independent merchant yielded only token discounts to bargainers. Jeanette, whose bargaining skills buckled the knees of Belgian street vendors, first expected to halve the quoted price and work from there. But sellers in China didn't play that way. Bargaining was more of a social ritual than a major economic force, the seller yielding only to signal a favored relationship with the customer. It was *guanxi*, not money that governed the marketplace.

Because Xiao Han warned us about evil merchants who cheated innocent rich foreigners, we were careful, waiting for a Chinese customer to ask the price of an item before we showed interest ourselves. But our vigilance against cheaters was unnecessary—sellers quoted the same prices to us as to Chinese customers and even surprised us by returning more change than we expected, refusing the high denomination notes we handed them by mistake and reaching into our piles for smaller bills.

We met a few attempts to overcharge but the amounts in question were so modest. One of the egg sellers on Jade Lion Road, a rosy cheeked lass with a big smile, once tried to get a little extra from us. The price of eggs had just settled at 1.8 yuan a jin. We asked Rosy Cheeks, "These eggs, how much money?"

She said, "Two yuan a jin."

"Two yuan? Really? Last week they were 1.8 yuan." (The difference was a few cents per pound.)

"This week they are two yuan."

"Too expensive." We moved on to the next seller, and asked her how much.

"1.8 yuan a jin."

This was better. We tried to bargain, "Two jin, 3.5 yuan. How about?"

"Okay-Okay."

We turned back to Rosy Cheeks.

"You are a naughty bad egg. Two yuan a jin is too much."

She laughed.

In the capitalist world we were used to, Rosy Cheeks would be free to ask two yuan a jin even if her neighbor would sell for less. If she could convince us to buy from her because her eggs were fresher or because she was prettier or more trustworthy, then her extra profit would be considered fair gain. But in China there was an official ceiling on egg prices and what she had tried was price gouging, even if it amounted to only a tiny nick.

In the broader sense, we *were* frequently overcharged in China because foreigners pay a large premium for many things. Sometimes the differential was official. For example, as foreign experts we got a discount from the prices paid by foreign tourists, but we still had to pay more for air travel than did Chinese. Other services used by tourists, such as hotels, excursion boats and museums, usually charge foreigners much higher rates. The rationale is that the transportation industry is subsidized by the government so only citizens should benefit from the subsidies. However, foreigners of Chinese ancestry are exempt from the premium rates, suggesting the discrimination is based on race rather than citizenship.

At the State Market off *Luo Yu* Road, where prices were set by the government and no bargaining was permitted, the supply of food often ran out early in the day. Across *Luo Yu* Road was the Free Market where bargaining was allowed. Farmers delivered their quotas to the State Market and then grew more, extra, or better for the Free Market. At the Free Market the prices were higher, food displays were cruder and there was no roof. But there were more customers.

The unbounded entrepreneurial spirit otherwise praised in China was moderated when it came to selling food. Xiao Han told us that some people lined up at five in the morning to buy eggs at the State Market and then sold those same eggs for a higher price later in the day at the Free Market. The State Market limited the number of eggs that could be bought during one transaction, so these entrepreneurs and their family members had to enter the egg line several times. Xiao Han was angry at people who bought eggs for one price and then sold them at a higher price. "I do not like this such person," he told us.

Bargaining and Bicycles
Some of China's new Free Market entrepreneurs had trouble figuring out how to handle the idea of competition. Adjacent shops or stalls sold the very same goods—row after row of the same thermos bottles, the same plastic containers and basins, the same straw hats. All the egg sellers set up next to each other, providing no obvious reason to buy from one instead of another. At the free market only the butchers had a different ethic, trying to attract customers away from their competition by calling out offers of better meat or lower prices.

In State-run stores the only competition was among customers who had to attract the attention of the salesclerks. The job responsibilities of salesclerks included displaying and organizing their wares, counting money and talking with each other. Dealing with customers and selling things appeared to have a lower priority. This indifference to customers might have been a holdover from the days when goods were scarce. Whatever it was, these workers, like novices in a team sport, didn't have any "field sense;" they didn't see themselves as players in a larger enterprise, positioned and alert for the sake of profit.

According to stories from friends and reports in the press, Beijing salesclerks were sullen and rude to foreign and domestic customers alike. In contrast, despite the reputed bellicosity of Wuhanese, we foreigners, with our strange faces and potential for distributing FEC, got immediate attention from the clerks. Chinese customers moved aside to let us buy, no matter how strongly we objected to this favoritism. They were as curious about us as the clerks, gathering around to watch and help, forgetting their own errands. Everything we touched was enhanced. Even the shoes and sweaters and fabric we rejected were grabbed up and bought. So dramatically would we boost sales that we joked about hiring ourselves out as shills.

We had spent so much of our lives shopping in stores that trained their cashiers to smile and say, "thank you" that we were used to doing the same. When we said "thank you" in Chinese, people were confused. Even Xiao Han admonished us: "Don't say that. She is only doing his job, his duty." At the Free Market we became known as the "Thank-You People" and were pointed out when we showed up. The surly technician at the Guest House replaced a fluorescent tube in our apartment and complained to Old Min, "Now they are going to say 'thank you.'" At the Zhongnan Department Store, salesclerks giggled at our inappropriate gratitude. We explained to salesclerks that Americans always said "thank you," that it was our way.

In China, as in the US, the most salient aspect of consumerism was advertising—billboards lined the intersection of Victory Road and Sun Yat Sen Boulevard, many using English or pictures of glamorous Western women gesturing toward the products. Again, the juxtaposition of ads was as haphazard as the products they touted: a billboard featuring cosmetics might share a scaffold with ads for gears, bearings and hydraulic presses—industrial goods competing with skin cream for public attention.

During a single year, television ads underwent a transformation that had taken twenty years in the US. At first the ads were amateurish, sometimes just posters announcing any product, from wine to construction girders. It seemed to be advertising for its own sake, the brainchild of an overeager work-unit director with no clear purpose or audience in mind.

As the year went on, more and more consumer products appeared on television commercials. High-tech computer graphics replaced hand-painted display cards, actors presented the products in clever skits set to music. Glamour and romance were used to enhance the appeal. Young women in miniskirts pointed out the features of home appliances. A certain wine sealed the engagement of two lovers dining out. A ginseng tonic cured all ills. An educator type suggested to parents that their child might be intellectually and culturally handicapped if they didn't buy an electronic keyboard instrument. Handsome young people used the recommended toothpaste and when they saw each other's teeth it became love at first sight. The music swelled as they moved closer, leaning into a kiss. At the last second the toothpaste tube appeared between them and they kissed that.

The most noticeable of all consumer products was the bicycle, the equivalent of the American family car. People hauled everything on bikes. We saw bikes carrying triplets, propane gas tanks, a studio couch, a pig, bamboo poles ten meters long, a refrigerator, sheets of plywood much larger than a door, sixteen live chickens. Once we even saw twelve adults riding on one bicycle, but they were professional acrobats. On the street a family of three on one bike was common.

People washed and polished their bicycles on sunny days, decorated them with macramé fringes, ribbons and decals, fancy seat covers, handlebar streamers and chrome plated add-ons. Bicycles had their own lanes in busy streets. Bicycle parking attendants, usually elderly people on retirement pensions, charged a few *fen* to mind a bike at shopping areas. Bicycle mechanics set up shop on the street, displaying their tools on a cloth.

Eager to be part of this high-rolling street scene, we went with the other foreigners to buy bicycles. Pierre and Jeanette warned us to check every part and tighten every bolt before trying to ride a new bike. As we looked over the assortment at the Zhongnan Department Store, we were dismayed at their quality. The bicycles were heavy, rusting, gearless, cumbersome and poorly assembled, with missing bolts and spokes. Where were the light-weight, double-butted frame, alloy-wheel, multi-speed bikes we were used to?

We had trouble finding two usable bikes among the hundreds on the showroom floor. The only ones that fit Janice were the "Long March" brand, shiny green models with fancy hub brakes, but none of them had a full complement of working parts. With the help of the salesclerks, she found three from which to cannibalize parts to make one relatively intact bike. The best that Robin could find was a sturdy black farm-bike with a crooked wheel, a "Sea Lion" brand. Robin thought he could replace the missing spokes and adjust them to true up the wheel at home. Only later did we discover that Janice's bike had a skewed crank so we couldn't adjust the pedals to make them opposite each other and Robin's wheel had no holes in the hub to accept the missing spokes. Bud, refusing to believe that a new bike could need repair, learned a lesson when his bicycle fell apart as he rode home. Other foreigners had pedals that seized, locks that jammed, and in one case a bike frame so warped the rear wheel could not be made to point straight ahead.

How could a country that depended on bicycles have so many badly made ones? The answer was simple. The demand for bicycles was so great in China that manufacturers didn't have to turn out quality products to sell them. In the US if bicycles were so shoddily made nobody would buy them.

A little cross-cultural comparison calmed our indignation. We thought about American cars when they had little competition, and how *Consumer Reports* had described a new car with *eighteen* defects, including a major transmission fault, as having *fewer* problems than most. States had enacted "lemon laws" to help a buyer whose new car had so many things broken that it was unusable for more than three months. Some two-car families kept one car in reserve for when the other was in the shop. Bolts and parts missing? Faulty brake mechanisms? Wheels out of alignment? This sounded familiar. Chinese bicycles were just like American cars.

And just like car buyers in the US, we bought our bicycles in a mood of acquisitive joy, with fantasies of pedaling through the countryside, the wind in our hair, the world at our feet. And just like cars in the US, when we got them home we found the headaches of ownership were more than we anticipated.

In this new consumer society, the policy of "returns accepted, no questions asked," which once helped Sears Roebuck become the world's largest retailer, was replaced by *caveat emptor*. Buy a product in China and it's yours for better or for worse. There were no refunds, no exchanges, no credit toward another purchase, virtually no warranties.

However, *if* you were a foreigner, and *if* you had a Waiban behind you or a friend with the clout of Golden Zhou, then you had recourse. Our Waiban called the Zhongnan Department Store to negotiate about the broken bicycles, hinting that Sino-American relations depended on a happy resolution of the problems. Two young men came to the Guest House with a supply of spare parts and spent the day working on our bicycles. The Waiban gave the two mechanics a small banquet, paid their day's wages, and everyone was happy.

Now we were ready to hit the street in style, to join the hordes of cyclists weaving in and out of traffic, bells a-ringing, challenging trucks for the right-of-way, sailing along in the wake of tandem buses, passing human-powered carts, smiling at the people who stared at our foreign faces, coasting along in the rightmost of twelve lanes on Luo Yu Road, passing markets with hanging meat, apples, bananas, fish, eels, eggs, greens, finally reaching the turn to the Zhongnan Department Store, where a barrier separated the motorized vehicles from the wheeled masses.

There were rules of the road for bicycles, perhaps more than for cars. Bicycles were supposed to be licensed and traffic police would fine those whose plates had expired. It was forbidden to carry a passenger on a city street. People were supposed to dismount when crossing busy streets and when entering work-unit compounds. Bikes had to be walked down hills, a recognition of the enormous loads and unreliable brakes. Chinese complied with the dismounting rules the way many American motorists honor stop signs. Cyclists would swing one leg over the bar to stand on the left pedal and coast past the "must dismount" sign, hopping off only if they saw a traffic officer. Pierre refused to dismount, claiming with a grin that he couldn't read the signs and therefore couldn't be expected to obey them. The two of us, proud of our ability to read the traffic signs, obeyed the laws more often than the natives did.

Our first bicycle trip was to buy a bolt to replace the one missing from Janice's bicycle seat. The word for bolt had not been in our lessons, so Robin pantomimed our need with a twisting thrust of index finger through the circled fingers of the other hand, hoping the obscene symbolism of his gesture was not universal. The clerk, who recognized us from his repair visit to our Guest House, removed a bolt from another bicycle seat, gave it to us and refused payment.

We went across the store to the bicycle parts section and managed to buy a spoke wrench by pointing to some spoke nuts on display and making screwing motions. Then we went on a scenic tour of Chinese consumer products, wandering past electric drills and accessories, table saws, plumber's wrenches, pliers of all shapes, metric combination wrenches, some heavy equipment with the brand name "Robin," cans of paint, brushes, scrapers, electric light bulbs in much greater variety than we ever saw in the US.

We bought a pair of socks from a charming clerk who surprised us by answering our clumsy Chinese with excellent English. We checked out toilet paper, tissues, detergent, bars of soap, shampoo, stainless steel pots. Upstairs we passed rows and rows of fabric, towels, curtains, art supplies. The bright tempera paints inspired us to buy three jars: purple, blue and orange.

The "education" section of the store had a hundred forms of paper, loose and bound in many sizes, a display of pens and pencils larger than any stationery or art store we had ever seen, calendars, abacuses of many sizes and colors next to domestic (cheap) and imported (expensive) calculators and a Japanese computer. IBM computers were displayed upstairs.

The store carried a surprising range of products: lace bikini underpants, revolving colored light machines for dance clubs, iron-on decals of dragons and eagles, electric meters for apartment houses, Communist Party membership cards, sexy pinup calendars, pneumatic drills, hypodermic syringes, office safes, walkie-talkies, artificial flowers, motorcycles, candy. Expensive electronic pianos made by Casio and Sharp were displayed next to sports apparel. They were so popular we could not break through the crowds around the instruments to look at running suits. We wondered whether sports apparel and keyboard instruments were together by accident or whether a category of "False Needs" or "Nouveau Bourgeois Accouterments" determined their proximity.

Before we came to China we had been given a lot of advice about what would be scarce or unavailable. We had been told that tampons were nearly impossible to find so Janice had better take a year's supply. As evidence, our informant told us the story of a customs official who opened a tampon, convinced it was a storage compartment for microfilm, and was terribly embarrassed when the tourist explained its purpose. But there in the Zhongnan Department Store was a big sign advertising OB tampons, with instructions in Chinese. We also saw them advertised on television. Following similar but equally outdated advice, we had carried halfway around the world: plastic bags, antihistamines, solder, electrical tape, vinyl and acrylic cement—only to find all these things available.

We went up to the third floor specialty shops that displayed their wares in separate storefront windows like a movie set for Smalltown, USA circa 1950—no fancy glitter or sexy mannequins. We passed a film developing shop, the technician at work on the huge automatic developing and printing machine, a dishware store with real china (downstairs all the dishes were enameled steel), a store with electronics components displayed in small cut-glass dessert dishes. Transistors, diodes, capacitors, integrated circuits, pilot lamps, resistors, picture-tube yokes—a high-tech smorgasbord set out on rows of imitation Waterford crystal.

We strolled past a shop that specialized in sewing and knitting machines. Nearby was an area with children's amusement rides—a slide, see-saw and double rocking chair. Then we entered one of the most popular areas of the building, one that was always crowded—consumer electronics and electrical appliances. Chinese popular music, the style reminiscent of "She Wore an Itsy Bitsy Teeny Weeny Yellow Polka Dot Bikini," blasted out from the counter with the displays of audio tapes, boom boxes and high fidelity audio components. We heard a song with lyrics in Chinese except for one line in English sung by the female vocalist: "Boys, come up and sleep with me tonight."

Onward past posters of popular singers, microphones of all types, colors and sizes, television antennae with sci-fi designs worthy of Captain Video, tape recorders, radios, earphones. The television section was so crowded that we didn't even try to get to the counter.

As we went down the stairs, we passed a shrunken person who looked like Yoda's mother sitting on a step talking to herself. At the base of the stairs was a spittoon overflowing with apple cores and food wrappers. A man coming up the stairs tried to toss an apple core into it and missed. He didn't bother to pick it up. A woman carried her baby over to the corner, spread its legs, and aimed its split-pants bottom at the wall over the spittoon.

Many features of advanced consumerism were still absent. Credit cards were honored only in hotels and stores catering to foreigners (although the Bank of China would give cash advances on MasterCard and American Express). Check cashing was extremely rare, except at a bank, and even then, as Helen and Nelson found out, only with a letter from the head of their work unit attesting to their honesty.

Store hours and holidays were rarely posted, nor were they predictable. Many stores closed for one day near the end of each month but the day was never announced in advance. The Zhongnan

Department Store would put up a sign on its front door, "Today we are closed." Chinese customers would go up to the door, read the sign and leave, undisturbed. We were the only customers who seemed frustrated by the wasted trip.

The Zhongnan Department Store was the largest, or second largest, department store in a city twice the size of Chicago. Yet once a week, usually on Tuesdays but sometimes on Fridays, the electricity to the entire store was shut off. At such times, clerks lit candles, stuck them on the display cases and shopping continued by candlelight.

But progress was marching on. One day we found the central staircase in the Zhongnan Department Store blocked off. The next week large holes appeared in the second floor. They were not covered over; a distracted customer could plummet six meters onto the display counters below. Huge crates full of machinery appeared the following week. On our next visit we found an escalator had been installed. The line to ride it was so long we gave up and used the stairs. People were getting off at the top and walking down just to ride up again. For more than a month it was an amusement park ride, clearly the store's main attraction.

Every Saturday morning, a university van came to the Guest House to take us across the Yangtze and the Han Rivers to shop in the Hankou district of the city. We looked forward to these trips, which had the spirit of a summer camp excursion. On the bus Pierre and Jeanette would share their eighteen months of China experience with us, explaining government policies, pointing out the bomb shelters built during the Cultural Revolution and now used as shopping malls, the beggars whose existence was officially denied in China, the black marketeers and posters with red checks announcing the execution of criminals. Daniel would tell us the latest news about student life and loves. Helen would describe her plans for purchases and entertainments while Nelson rolled his eyes at her and at Little Lin, conveying very different messages. Sometimes in an expansive mood Nelson would turn the conversation to an analysis of Chinese social customs or report the effect of his Jack Daniels on Vice Chairman Wang Y or Director Fang.

We usually had one of two drivers. Driver Fu was a skinny man with a bad temper who yelled at the other traffic and blasted his horn a lot. Nelson called him "Old Crabby." Once Driver Fu leaned out of his window cursing a clumsy bicyclist and chased him across the road with the van, shouting profanities. Little Lin told us that he had been in a traffic accident in which someone was killed, that he had been banned from driving for a year, and now he had to drive the oldest, bumpiest van as a punishment.

The other driver, Driver Li, was friendly and easy going. He had a small boy whom he picked up at the end of our shopping trips. When we were late getting back, which was often, the little boy was waiting for him at the garage. We always greeted the little boy and he greeted us.

Drivers in China commanded their vehicles like airline pilots rather than chauffeurs. Each Saturday Little Lin would ask us which stores or shopping areas we wanted to visit, every week we reached a compromise with the driver about a manageable number of stops and nearly every week our plans were changed mid-trip. Little Lin would tell us the driver said the department store was closed for inventory, that a street was blocked off, that there would be no place to park today, that the driver had to get back early for lunch, that the bank was impossible to visit today because no left turns were allowed . . ..

We couldn't understand these lame excuses. We couldn't understand why the drivers, who in other situations turned out to be friendly and helpful, would give us such trouble. Even crabby Driver Fu greeted us warmly when we met him at a dance. It was one of the mysteries of China, but one of the few that we would solve before the end of the year.

"Change Money" People and the Black Market
We discovered many things that China would have preferred we not know about. As in our own country, China had pornography,

prostitution, corruption, illegal drugs. We saw homeless beggars and crazies wandering the streets, drinking from puddles, talking to invisible companions, but these unfortunates were rare enough to surprise us, and unlike other disturbances, they did not draw crowds.

A woman, hair matted and wild, clothes ragged and splattered, face dirty but surprisingly young and rosy cheeked, walked past us hugging an enamel cup. She sat down under a bush and began eating from the cup, which contained string instead of noodles, making faces, talking to herself. "Don't look at her. She's a crazy," people in the market told us. No one disturbed her, no one chased her away.

Pierre pointed out the beggars and crazies as if they were scandalous. "But there are so many more in the US," we told him, wondering if Europe had none of these unfortunates. Pierre explained why he directed our attention: "Yes, we have them too, but the Chinese don't admit they exist."

On the ferry across the Yangtze a man walked among the passengers singing Beijing Opera and holding out a tin can into which people dropped coins. On the return trip, a skinny, poorly dressed woman tried to collect money without providing an entertainment. A well-dressed man spoke to her sharply and shooed her away. He pointed to us. She shouldn't let the foreigners see what she was doing, he said. She was a disgrace. He struck her with his umbrella, driving her away. We thought his behavior more disgraceful than hers.

Having been raised in New York City, the street crazies, beggars, drug deals, prostitution, even three-card monte, which we saw hustled atop a mountain in Guilin, did not surprise us. But there was one street activity common in China that we didn't have in the US—the illegal exchange of foreign currency. In every tourist city, foreigners were accosted by the "Change Money" people.

"Hello. Change money?" they called, over and over. Even small children learned this phrase, perhaps their only foreign vocabulary. The going rate on the black market varied between 1.4

and 1.7 *renminbi* for each yuan of Foreign Exchange Certificates. A few years earlier it had been illegal for ordinary Chinese to possess FEC, but the law had changed, so anyone could purchase the imported goods that only FEC could buy.

In Guilin the black market was very open; not even the presence of uniformed police officers affected business. Outside every tourist hotel the black marketeers, nearly all women, stood in groups, calling to foreigners:

"Hello. Change money?"

"Change money? Change money?"

We smiled. We declined. They continued to pester. Finally Robin said in Chinese.

"Oh, you want to change money?"

One woman nodded eagerly, approaching closer.

"I will change money," Robin said. "I have *renminbi*. Will you give me FEC?"

"No, no, no, no!" The woman shook her head. Oh, such stupid foreigners. She began to explain that she wanted FEC, not *renminbi*. Then she saw our grins and caught on. "All right," she said with a laugh, "I will give you FEC. The rate is ten to one." Now we were the ones who shook our heads and refused. But the joke had solved one problem. No longer were we besieged whenever we left and entered the hotel. The change-money woman had become our friend, laughing and pointing us out to her colleagues as we passed.

In Guangzhou it was mostly men who stood in the streets and called, "Change money! Change money!" Here it sounded more like an announcement of goods for sale than a question. We walked from the railroad station to a chorus of these calls. On this trip Robin tried a different response. At the next "Change money!" he turned around and said sternly in Chinese, "I am a police officer!" The man jumped, looked at Robin's foreign face and burst out laughing. He laughed and laughed, delighted with the joke.

As Foreign Experts we could have really profited from the Black Market because we were allowed to convert seventy percent of our salaries to FEC, and we had special cards that entitled us to use *renminbi*. So we could have taken FEC to the Change Money people and increased our purchasing power about sixty percent. However our salaries were already so generous that we were no more tempted to risk trouble in the black market than an American millionaire would be tempted to hold up a convenience store.

American friends came to visit us after traveling to Guilin, Chongqing and Guangzhou, following the "backpacking crowd," as they called them. They watched the backpackers change money for profit to buy marijuana. They were shown maps of China with obscure cities circled. "Those must be the cities with interesting national minorities," we suggested when they mentioned Dali and Yangzhou.

"Those are the cities with dope," they told us.

In Guilin our friends had run short of money and decided to use the black market to get more cash. The next time they were approached by a Change Money Lady, they agreed to a rate of 1.5 even though the backpacking crowd advised them to hold out for 1.6. They expected to be led into a dark alley where the exchange could be made furtively, but the Change Money Lady led them to a woman selling souvenirs in the bright sunshine on the main street. The Change Money Lady's friend took out a package of *renminbi*, new ten yuan banknotes, numbered consecutively, banded in packages of fifty. The package was broken open and spread out on the sidewalk for them to count. Other Change Money vendors gathered around, watching them count, offering further deals, talking all at once. They hesitated, looking around furtively, wondering if this were a sting operation, then hastily counted the pile of notes and handed over their FEC. The Change Money Ladies looked at these innocent blue-eyed clients and threw one more ten yuan note on the pile, the way the vegetable sellers would give us an extra carrot or a few more stalks of greens, as a gesture of good will.

Our friends found that their successful criminal activity brought them problems. While the Change Money Ladies converted FEC to *renminbi* freely outside the hotels, the hotels themselves refused to accept *renminbi* from tourists, insisting our friends pay with FEC. Changing FEC on the black market was illegal, but the hotel's insistence on getting FEC from tourists was not.

In Shanghai's Bank of China we met two pretty American students who were interested in changing money to boost their purchasing power. It was late afternoon and the streets were crowded, but they were afraid. They asked us to come along to make sure nothing happened to them. We were right behind when a small boy fell into step with them.

"Change money?"

The boy was fair skinned with wide brown eyes, about twelve years old. The taller woman said, "What? You aren't Chinese. What do you want?"

"Change money?" he repeated, "100/145."

"One hundred/one fifty," said the tall woman.

The boy dropped back and bumped into an older man walking near the gutter. We saw a wad of *renminbi* appear in the boy's hand just before the older man disappeared into the crowd. The boy caught up to the two women and pushed the wad of notes into the hand of the tall blonde. She took it, believing that her friend had already handed over the hundred yuan FEC note. Counting, she saw there was a five yuan note at the bottom of the wad instead of a ten. She objected and the boy reached out and took it back. Now there were only fourteen ten-yuan notes.

"Not enough," the tall one said. The boy gave her back the five yuan note. "Okay . . ." she said approvingly, expecting another five, but her friend took this as a signal to hand over their hundred yuan FEC note. The boy palmed it, cut away to a different older man who sped up and faded into the crowd. Mystery Boy returned to them, and the tall woman objected, "You owe us five more." He indicated he had no money.

With a three-person team, the police couldn't catch any one person with incriminating evidence. One man carried the *renminbi* in bundles of 145 yuan. The other man received the FEC. Mystery Boy made the contact and the pass and stayed with the customers until the older men were clear. If the police closed in, the trio would split up. The only person who talked to the foreigners had no money at all except for very short periods, and then he never had the two currencies at the same time. And if he were caught, he was so young he would be punished less severely than his partners.

The two women filled us in on details that we missed. The taller one said, "I can't believe we *did* it. Did you see how they worked it? I was so scared. Let's do it again."

We went with them to the Peace Hotel restaurant where we could use *renminbi* with our special cards. They insisted on paying for our sodas with their new cash. We were their bodyguards, they said.

The next day we saw the mystery boy. He was glassy-eyed, but when he saw us looking at him, he came over, "Change money?"

"No, you cheated our friends. You are a bad egg," we told him.

"Tomorrow?" he asked.

Changing money had to be Big Business since an enormous amount of liquid capital was involved. Many of these Change-Money people were carrying the equivalent of a year's worth of income. Those neat bundles of sequentially numbered banknotes in Guilin must have been obtained directly from the Bank of China.

What happened to the FEC that the Change-Money people took in? Was it used only for trading back to people who wanted to buy foreign televisions, or was it part of a larger enterprise? The Change-Money dealers themselves did not look rich. They didn't ride around in expensive Japanese cars, they didn't wear Nike sneakers or Western clothes. Surely Mystery Boy and his team were not spending all that FEC on imported cigarettes for themselves and their friends. An operation that large had to be doing more than supplying the smart set with imported luxuries.

All over China were imported cars and many other foreign products—machinery, steel, equipment—that the country couldn't do without. Work units needing these foreign imports had to pay

FEC, supplied either by the government or some other way. The government had an interest in limiting the amount of money that left the country: If Chinese citizens and corporations could buy foreign goods as easily as they could buy Chinese, they might send too much money out of the country, hurting the balance of trade. Since only FEC could be converted to foreign currencies, the money spent on foreign products was limited to the money brought into the country via FEC. And the black market exchange ratio raised the effective cost of FEC, serving as a kind of tariff on imported goods.

Still, the government regularly announced the discovery and prosecution of black market rings. Perhaps the crackdowns were needed to slow down the flow of FEC and illegal money changing, because if all foreigners changed money illegally, the tariff effect would be undermined by this unofficial devaluation of Chinese currency. To the extent that the government limited the black market, it limited the devaluation of Chinese currency.

The occasional arrest and execution of black marketeers in the interest of economic management must have had an effect on Mystery Boy and his friends, encouraging them to find a different law to violate. Like other entrepreneurs, they had diversified. When we rejected the offer of "Change money?" Mystery Boy changed his pitch to "Smoke? Smoke?" imitating the characteristic inhaling of marijuana. In front of the Shanghai branch of the Bank of China, the aroma of burning cannabis was strong and we heard that opium was available again in some neighborhoods.

9

NUMBER TWO UNIVERSITY RESEARCH HOSPITAL

Bad Qi

We had planned to stay healthy in China. We had gotten shots for typhoid, polio, hepatitis A, hepatitis B, and Japanese encephalitis—all optional for travel to China. We brought a year's supply of vitamin pills, anti-malaria medicine, anti-diarrhea medicine, antibiotics, and a stock of drugs to reduce the symptoms of colds. We drank only boiled water, cooked our food at high temperatures and peeled all fruit, even grapes. We washed our dishes in detergent laced with iodine. We even brought our *Merck Manual*, the physicians' handbook that we do-it-yourselfers use to check the advice of medical experts.

When we went with Daniel to the doctor, we had seen the conditions of the university clinic, the floors inside no cleaner than the sidewalk outside, the whitewashed walls scarred and splattered, the wooden furniture old and worn. No gleaming chrome, no sparkling tiles and Formica. We had been surprised but not put off, realizing the high-tech glitter of US medical care came with high-tech prices. In China they didn't have the money to be fancy—the clinic fee was only thirty Chinese cents. Yet the things that counted seemed sanitary and reliable—tongue depressors saturated with iodine, instruments wrapped and autoclaved. And most important, Doctor Ming seemed efficient and knowledgeable. An American who taught at the local medical school said the main difference between the university clinic and what we were used to back home was that the "zone of sterility" was much smaller in China. Right. Anyhow, it had been Daniel who'd been sick.

We did try Chinese herbal medicine, a nostrum recommended for the sore throats that teachers in China routinely got from lecturing in chalk dust. So good was this medicine, one teacher said, that we could take it even when our throats were not sore! Our tutor, Julie, brought us some, a handful of shriveled black nuts. When we put one in a cup of hot water it swelled and sent out hairy tendrils until it looked like a shrunken head. Drinking the hot liquid was soothing, but if the infusion from the hairy ball had any effect, it was very subtle. Chinese medicines are mild, Julie told us, but they don't have the side effects of Western medicines.

The beginning of October is usually the best time of year in central China. We tried to appreciate the beautiful weather but we were already frazzled, tired, overworked. Our comfortable pattern of doing chores with automated machinery had been replaced by chaos and drudgery. At first it was a novelty; we were roughing it, camping out. By October, heating water on the stove to wash dishes by hand had become a drag, and we were disenchanted with our non-automatic washing machine which required filling, draining, filling, draining, filling, draining and then wringing out the clothes by hand. The challenge of working on our Chinese bicycles—joking that we bought them in kit form—had become tedious. We were annoyed about refilling tires that lost air every few days, readjusting brakes and seats and spokes and handlebars, unable to tighten the soft metal fittings adequately without stripping the threads.

Everything seemed to take longer than we were used to. Visitors knocked at our door too often. We couldn't find time to read and daydream and talk with each other. Too much was going on. In traditional Chinese medical terminology, our bodily energy, our *qi*, was out of whack.

On National Day no loudspeaker broadcast woke us but we still didn't get to sleep in because Old Ma and little Greg came to visit. Announcing that it was little Greg's birthday, Old Ma eyed one of our dictionaries, a thick one with maps inside, and asked if Greg could have it when we went home. We agreed, but felt a little put upon.

The Waiban had arranged a vacation trip for all the foreigners, a cruise down the Yangtze River to the mountain resort of Lu Shan. When our visitors left we hurriedly loaded backpacks with clothing and film and a collection of Dashiell Hammett stories, and boarded the university van that would take us to the dock.

Only Nelson was smart enough to choose second class accommodations on the cruise ship. (There were no first class cabins on these ships—only special tourist boats had them.) The rest of us decided to sleep with "the people" in third class and spent a restless night on cotton pallets covered with soiled bedding, listening to the coughs and hawks of strangers, worried that someone from the bunks above us would spit carelessly during the night.

At dawn we disembarked at Nine Rivers and boarded a small bus to go up the mountainside to Lu Shan. The driver popped the clutch and took off up the narrow mountain road, bouncing over ruts, taking tight curves with the bus leaning over precipices, the outer wheels where guard rails should have been. The driver sounded the horn as he overtook trucks and other buses, passing them around blind corners on a road that wasn't always two lanes wide. Yellow-brown dust covered the windshield so thickly the driver had to use the wipers in order to see. We yelled for him to slow down and begged Xiao Han and Little Lin to convey our messages but they weren't bothered by the reckless driving. Perhaps because they had never driven, they didn't realize the danger. The dust adhered to our sweat, forming a layer of gritty slime and turning our complexions yellow-brown. When we arrived in Lu Shan we were frazzled and our *qi* was more unbalanced than ever.

We had made no reservations and this was a major holiday but after some trekking around we were lucky and found rooms in a joint-venture tourist hotel that had just opened. The lobby sparkled, the rooms were clean and luxuriously decorated in shades of lavender, the beds were comfortable, the hot water seemed plentiful, the cost low. By the time registration arrangements were completed we were all hungry. Except for Pierre and Jeanette who had the foresight to bring their own food—granola, bread, dried milk and soup, the rest of us marched into the hotel dining room expecting a meal that matched the quality of the rooms.

"Oh, we cannot serve you," the manager announced.

"Why not?" we asked. They were serving a large group of Chinese and there were cooks in the kitchen and waitresses in the dining room doing nothing.

"We only serve tour groups," the manager said.

"Where else can we eat?" we asked him, forgetting that we also were a tour group.

He might have waved vaguely in any direction and saved himself some trouble because the town had several restaurants. Instead he said, "There is no other place."

"Well, then they must serve us," Helen insisted. We all agreed, forcing Xiao Han to act as our negotiator, trapping him between conflicting rudenesses. The manager grudgingly agreed to serve us.

"Okay, Okay, Okay," Xiao Han said to us, "Sit down. Sit down."

We sat down, eight of us at a stained tablecloth set with greasy dishes. The food was mediocre and outrageously expensive compared with our beloved Laurel Hill Restaurant. Before the meal was over, Janice received an urgent warning from her large intestine, heralding the dreaded *la duzi*. She slipped away to settle the emergency.

The next morning we went out to a mountain park, following the path through a bamboo forest at the top of a mountain. As we descended we heard haunting, beautiful music. Perched on a rock along the forest path was a man playing an *erhu*, a two-string bowed instrument. A sign in front of the musician said he and his family had hepatitis and needed money for treatment. We thought the state provided free medical care, but this didn't seem the time to ask Xiao Han about it. We foreigners gave him coins until Xiao

Han said, "Okay, Okay, that's Okay," monitoring our contributions lest they be excessive.

Pierre videotaped everything. Little Lin chided Nelson, worried he would get too close to the edge of cliffs. Xiao Han walked with Helen and worried about stragglers. Helen began to lag behind and Janice did too. Helen thought Janice was just being nice, keeping her company. And Janice, who thought ignoring illness would make it go away, didn't admit that even Helen was walking too fast for her.

When we got back to the hotel and tried to bathe, the hot water had turned brown and the cold water had run out completely. Janice's back, legs and arms hurt and she couldn't stop shivering. Her head ached, she was dehydrated and her skin looked yellowish and wrinkled. She hadn't eaten since breakfast and vomited up a small amount of dark green liquid.

Robin ran to Xiao Han to ask for a doctor. Within minutes the hotel's Beijing Jeep was waiting for us, and Janice, still shivering under all the sweaters and shirts we had brought, was half carried to the Jeep by Robin, Xiao Han and Little Lin. The Jeep seemed to have no springs or shock absorbers and the beams from its headlamps bounced across the faces of surprised Chinese tourists, past trees and animals as we shortcut over curbs and across parks to the local hospital.

The local hospital looked like a summer camp infirmary except for the spittoons on the floor. In less than a minute the head doctor, a pleasant looking woman in a white coat, her wavy hair drawn back, came out to treat the foreigner. Other doctors and their patients came in to watch her examine Janice. Even the Jeep driver was there.

The blackness of Janice's tongue prompted a conference with the three other doctors, pretty young women in white coats. The cause, Pepto Bismol, was unknown to them until Robin explained that it made the feces black. A thermometer appeared and Janice opened her mouth to receive it but the doctor indicated, as if to a child, that the thermometer belonged in the armpit. Heart and ab-

NUMBER TWO HOSPITAL 159

domen were stethoscoped and palpated, the doctor working discreetly under Janice's clothing as a crowd stood in the doorway watching. It was strangely comforting to have such a concerned audience.

Janice was given APC tablets, vitamin B6, six tiny glass vials of gentomycin to drink later, and then prepared for an antibiotic injection. In this infirmary, the furniture was old and rickety, the stone floor was grimy, but the syringe and needles came from a sparkling stainless steel autoclave tray wrapped in a cloth. Janice expected a painful injection, but in the Land of Acupuncture they knew how to stick needles into people.

As we were leaving the emergency room, nausea hit Janice again and she vomited into one of the hallway spittoons. The head physician put her arm around Janice and crooned in Chinese, "That's all right. You'll be all right. It'll be all right." Then everyone in the building, both medical staff and patients, escorted us to the door and waved good-bye.

Back at the hotel Janice took a bath to ease her muscle pains. The bath water was full of silt and rust, the color of strong tea. Robin felt sick and weak, partly from anxiety. The doctor from the hospital called to see if Janice was all right, cheering us with her concern. "Take the APC if there is a fever," the doctor said. Xiao Han offered to get up any time during the night, "I'm young and strong," he said.

Our worst fears had come true: we had gotten sick not only far from our US home, but also far from our Chinese home. All the warnings we had received about Chinese medical facilities had been true. The needle used for the injection had not been a disposable one and the hospital *was* dirty, at least the floors and the walls. But the care and concern and comforting was unlike anything we had ever experienced from medical professionals in the US. Imagine the heads of US hospitals holding patients in their arms to comfort them. Imagine the entire staff of a hospital, not to mention the rest of the patients, walking us to the door with wishes of good health.

Back at the dock in Nine Rivers, we discovered there was a four-hour wait for the ship. The two of us stayed in the waiting room to rest and mind the luggage while everyone else went for a walk.

Whenever a ship arrived, people filled the aisles leading to the gangway, carrying boxes and baskets on shoulder poles, pushing bicycles, stumbling over our bags, crowding us back against the benches. Peddlers wandered through the aisles of the waiting room, hawking hot meals in styrofoam boxes, peanuts, flat bread, sleeping mats, chickens cooked in soy sauce, sunglasses, new and used magazines. One man peered closely at Janice's notebook. She offered it for him to read, but he shook his head and backed away, as if he thought the English writing would hurt him.

Helen returned, chatting enthusiastically about Daumier faces and national minorities, delighted over a box of china she got for a "marvelous price." Pierre took pictures of the people who were staring at us, setting off the flash right in their faces. One laughed and wanted it to happen again. Another pushed through the crowd to run away.

A girl who looked like a kewpie doll sat down next to Nelson. She screwed a bright red-orange lipstick cylinder all the way out, examined it as if making a grave decision, and then applied it, exaggerating the bow in her lips.

Xiao Han was instantly suspicious. To him a Chinese wearing so much lipstick proclaimed moral degeneracy. He warned us to watch the luggage carefully.

Kewpie Doll talked eagerly to Nelson who couldn't understand her Chinese but seemed to enjoy the attention. She kept talking, changing the subject, trying to find some topic he would respond to. Robin explained to her that Nelson didn't understand Chinese but this didn't discourage her.

Finally our ship arrived and we boarded. Robin went with Xiao Han to the ticket booth to pay for second class tickets. People yelled at Xiao Han, accusing him of using the "back door," claiming they had been waiting for tickets longer than he had. Xiao Han

NUMBER TWO HOSPITAL 161

yelled back that there were other second class tickets, all they had to do is pay. The crowd quieted—they had been after third class tickets which were also in short supply. Xiao Han asked Robin to reimburse him for the difference between second and fifth class, not second and third. Robin didn't object, thinking the harassment at the ticket window made Xiao Han forget that the university had given him money for third class tickets.

Robin was weak, Janice was queasy, but our second class cabin had clean sheets, slippers, a thermos of boiled water, a pink enameled sink with hot running water, and only two beds. We managed to sleep through most of the night. In the morning, after the loudspeaker rousted us with martial music, Pierre and Jeanette brought us fruit-and-nut oatmeal. Helen and Little Lin arrived with Nelson, teasing him about snoring during the night.

Nick also came up to the second class deck. He was wearing sunglasses and a white sleeveless undershirt that showed his tanned well-developed muscles. A Chinese man called out at him: "Fake foreign devil," believing Nick was a Chinese pretending to be a foreigner by hanging out with us. To us he looked All-American, but Little Lin conceded that he looked Chinese.

Helen reported that during the night a man had walked up to Nick's bunk in third class, examined him carefully, then reached out and lifted up the covers until Nick awoke, scaring him away. We laughed over the story, wondering whether the man was interested in foreign currency or foreign anatomy. The fruit-and-nut oatmeal, the companionship and the little vials of medicine had pepped us up.

Being sick should have had its compensations. We should have been able to rest in bed and read and write. But as soon as we got back to Wuhan, students began to arrive to visit their sick teachers. They told us there was a hepatitis epidemic—twenty-five students in the neighboring university had come down with hepatitis. Pierre explained this was not unusual since sixty percent of the population tested positive for hepatitis antibodies. Wang Y, who had come to find out when we would return to class, said there was no hepatitis epidemic. He had not, you see, heard of one. Xiao Han told us the Waiban was arranging to have hepatitis vaccine flown in from Beijing to protect the foreigners.

By midweek the Guest House ran short of toilet paper because the foreigners were using it to blow their noses. Robin had a chest cold. Janice had a fever of 101° F. When we returned to the university clinic, Doctor Ming recognized us as the inadequate translators for Daniel, and said good naturedly, "You again?" She read the Lu Shan hospital records we brought her, took our pulses—short quick checks in different places—measured blood pressures, poked our livers, looked at our tongues, listened to our symptoms and prescribed for us.

Most tablets in the clinic pharmacy, regardless of composition, looked like small yellow M&Ms, indistinguishable from each other when removed from their labeled containers. We were given six packages of these tablets, various kinds of cough medicines and antibiotics, some to be take twice a day, some five times a day, some with meals, some at bedtime. We took all the medicine except the antibiotics, thinking they would be of no use for our colds. Janice was still anxious about not getting enough work done. By now her *qi* needed more than a tune-up; it needed a major overhaul.

Two days later Janice had a fever of 103° F. She had pains in her legs and shoulder and her resting heart rate was 118 times a minute, a big change from her normal 65. She began taking the tetracycline.

As word of our illnesses spread, our visitors increased. Golden Zhou came that morning to visit and checked whether Robin had a fever by touching his forehead to Robin's. He left and Li Meili arrived with eggs, spinach, fresh rice noodles and pork. She told us she had bought a chicken that she would kill tomorrow and cook for us. Our objections were ignored. Chickens were good for sick people, she argued. When Janice could not eat, Li Meili and Robin tried to convince her to see the doctor again. Janice admitted she was too weak to walk to the clinic. No matter, Li Meili said, in China doctors make house calls.

Intensive Care
Doctor Ming came to the Guest House, looked at Janice's splotchy white tongue, cried "Ai Ya!" and insisted that Janice have a blood test at the clinic. Li Meili offered to fetch what she called a "wheelbarrow," a two-wheeled stretcher cart. Unwilling to ride in a wheelbarrow, Janice made it to the clinic on her bicycle and then collapsed on a bench, her head on Robin's lap. Li Meili was delighted. It was almost as good as seeing us kiss.

When Doctor Ming saw the results of Janice's blood test she again cried, "Ai Ya!" The white count was 31,000. The clinic technician must have made a mistake, she said, because the white count was too high. She wanted the test to be done again but she couldn't ask the technician to repeat it or he would lose face. Janice must go to the Army Hospital for another blood test and an X-ray. Li Meili was ready to get the "wheelbarrow" to push Janice three kilometers to the hospital but Robin suggested calling the Waiban for a car. Li Meili hadn't even thought of this as a possibility. Ordinary Chinese didn't get car rides to hospitals.

Li Meili called the Waiban on Doctor Ming's bright orange telephone and told Golden Zhou about the blood test results, shouting into the receiver as if it were a string telephone. We could hear Zhou's voice from across the room. He would make the arrangements. Robin should bring the medical record, money, White Cards and Green Cards.

The Army Hospital, built by Russians in the nineteen-fifties, was very clean, the cleanest building we had seen in China, the lobby perfumed with phenol disinfectant. We were taken directly to the head doctor, no waiting. She examined Janice and asked about pain, especially in the liver. The blood test was repeated and the results were the same: a white count of 31,000. Janice was fluoroscoped and X-rayed and the hospital director came to tell her the diagnosis in careful English: "Pneu-mon-i-a." Doctors gathered around to teach us the Chinese for pneumonia, *fei yan*, smiling as we practiced until we got the tones right. So sorry, they said, but a foreigner couldn't stay at this hospital, which was only for military patients. We must go to Number Two University Research Hospital in Hankou, which was much better.

At Number Two Hospital, Robin was allowed (even expected) to stay with Janice in the special ward for high-level cadres and diplomats. It had large high-ceilinged rooms with only two beds per room and private Western-style bathrooms. The hospital officials had persuaded two high-level cadres to move in together to free a room for us.

A nurse came to give Janice a sensitivity test for penicillin and the driver came to take Li Meili back to the university. The doctors were unhappy Li Meili was leaving; they wanted us to have an interpreter. The doctors finally said we could use the interpreter who was staying with another foreigner down the hall. We were disappointed they thought we needed an interpreter but over the next few days we realized that we didn't know the words for fever, pill, allergy, cough, or even the polite term for bowel movement—a major concern in hospitals all over the world.

The nurse attached Janice to an IV drip, the first of many bottles of penicillin G and ampicillin that would be emptied into her veins. We looked up pneumonia in the *Merck Manual*, and learned that 31,000 was a very high white count; anything over 10,000 was too high. We deciphered "parenteral regimens" and "1 million u. IV q 4 to 6 h," and learned that intravenous rather than oral medication was for serious cases and Janice's IV drip would kill both gram-positive and gram-negative bacteria. The hospital was not taking any chances. We were reassured, our *qi*s were calmer, and so we slept.

Needles and Near-Sighted Nurses
The next morning we were awakened before six by the bustle of nurses, orderlies, and technicians. Some of the activities were different from those in US hospitals, but the hour of performance was

the same. Our thermoses of boiled water were replaced with fresh ones and the floors were mopped, leaving the scent of phenol rising from the wet tiles. Our wastebasket in the bathroom was emptied, using long handled tongs to remove each item piece by piece. This suggested there might be some truth to the rumor that we were not supposed to flush toilet paper into the sewer system. We hoped that we'd left enough toilet paper from blowing our noses to satisfy them.

Vitamin pills and cough medicine (an anise-flavored brown liquid that Robin identified from his childhood as "Stoke's") were brought in. A thermometer was placed in Janice's armpit and her pulses were taken. Breakfast arrived—four eggs boiled very long, two bowls of rice porridge, two covered bowls of milk. We westernized the meal by mixing the porridge and the milk, then adding the sugar and fruit that Pierre and Jeanette had stuffed into our suitcase.

As our *qi* improved, we noticed more of our surroundings. Our room was furnished with a dresser, a round table with a cracked glass top "repaired" with strips of surgical tape, a vase of brightly colored plastic flowers, assorted chairs of wicker and cane, vinyl covered folding chairs, and night tables.

The next in the series of IV bottles was brought by a different nurse, an older woman of about fifty. She tourniqueted Janice's arm with a rubber tube, but it popped off. She tried a longer one and this time it remained in place. Then she went through the now-familiar routine of connecting tubes to the bottle, expelling the air, unwrapping the needle, slapping Janice's hand to make the veins more prominent. She chose a vein and stuck in the needle but something went wrong and blood leaked from the vein and spread out under the skin.

The nurse made a sound of surprise, giggled nervously and tried another vein. This time the needle went into the vein and out the other side. More leaking blood.

She pulled the needle out again. If this intravenous business was so difficult, why didn't they just leave the needles in, Janice wondered, feeling somehow separate from everything that was going on. Her hand was now purple and blue, swollen and painful. The swelling prevented the nurse from locating any other veins. Robin hovered anxiously as the nurse looked around. What to do? Robin suggested she try the other hand. How to get at the hand that was on the side of the bed up against the wall? She began to turn Janice over. But then Janice would be face down for the entire three-hour IV drip. Robin suggested they move the bed out from the wall and put the IV bottle stand on the *other* side of the bed. This done, the nurse tourniqueted Janice's other wrist. Then she paused. What if she failed again? By this time we were tense, wondering what would happen. She giggled sheepishly, put her hand into a pocket and pulled out her special equipment—a pair of eyeglasses. She put them on and inserted the IV needle perfectly.

The Nurse-Who-Needed-Glasses was otherwise an exemplary caretaker. She took a special interest in Janice's health, especially in whether she was dressed warmly enough. The room was usually hot and Janice wore only a T shirt and jogging pants. The hospital personnel, who wore several layers of clothing under their lab coats—undershirts, blouses, corduroy jackets—were convinced that Janice must have been cold. The weather was like a pleasant summer for us, but to people who lived through tropical heat without air conditioning, it was a chilly fall. To be a good patient Janice kept a long sleeved blouse or a blanket handy to put on when anyone appeared. For The-Nurse-Who-Needed-Glasses this was not enough. She spotted a turtleneck sweater of Robin's in our suitcase and decided only that was warm enough. Whenever she saw Janice without it, she ran over to our suitcase and rummaged through until she found Robin's sweater, draped it over Janice's back and tied the arms carefully and stylishly around her neck.

She checked regularly to make sure Janice had taken her cough medicine and vitamin pills. She came in to sit with her at mealtimes when Robin was out, urging her with gestures and babytalk Chinese to eat more rice, expressing pride in her foreigner's ability to use chopsticks.

In addition to the hospital staff, the translator from down the hall became a frequent visitor. Little Zhang was a skinny, restless young man with blue jogging pants, designer frame eyeglasses, and a good opinion of himself. Little Zhang first came to see us soon after we arrived. He sat down on Janice's bed and introduced himself as a member of the Foreign Affairs Office of the Yangtze River Brewery. When Robin asked if the beer was good, he laughed and said that the quality of the beer depended on "his foreign expert," a consultant from a German brewery. His expert was Mr. Rad, an Australian from Sri Lanka who had been in the hospital nearly a month recovering from an operation for a blocked urethra.

We were about to ask him more about "his expert" when he suddenly jumped up and went to the foot of Janice's bed. "You know, this bed can be adjusted to make you more comfortable," he explained. Janice protested that she was comfortable the way it was, but Little Zhang took this as mere politeness. Saying he didn't mind doing the work, he turned the cranks through their full range of travel, describing each movement as the bed sat Janice up, laid her down, bent her knees and straightened them again. After he finished demonstrating the bed mechanism, Little Zhang told us that the former Mayor of Wuhan lived across the hall from us. Before we could ask him about the Mayor, he jumped up, excused himself and ran out of the room.

The Mayor, like Little Zhang, walked into and out of our room as if it were his own. He was curious about us and came over to talk as we ate breakfast. His voice was rumbly and he spoke the local dialect so we didn't understand much of what he said. He said disappointedly, *"Nimen bu dong"* (You don't understand). Guessing that he was asking about our Western food, we showed him the box of granola Pierre and Jeanette gave us. He seemed satisfied and went back to his room.

The next day Little Zhang appeared as we were trying to figure out whether to cancel our order for hospital meals. He suggested we order "steak and potatoes." We thought he was joking but he assured us his foreign expert had ordered it.

"Did he like it?"

"Yes, he liked it until his wife arrived and then he didn't like it anymore and his wife is thirty-six while he is fifty-three," Little Zhang told us, as if the age difference would explain Mr. Rad's change of taste. Again he left abruptly before we could question him about his incongruous answer.

When Janice's next IV drip bottle was empty and the needle removed, she was ready for an experimental walk in the hallway. At the end of our corridor was a large balcony with lots of plants—boxwoods, cacti, roses, citrus, and a lavastone terrarium. Our neighbor, the Mayor, watered and cared for these plants each morning.

On the balcony we met Little Zhang's expert, Mr. Rad, and his wife. She was a tall, handsome woman wearing gold bracelets and a bright green dress, a striking color against her creamed-coffee skin. Her dress was a unique style, a low narrow neckline, full around the waist and hips, narrow around her legs. She looked elegant and regal among the shorter Chinese hospital workers in their loose white garments.

Mr. Rad described his bladder operation. His surgeon was the best in central China, the operating theater very modern, the care excellent. Unfortunately he got double pneumonia and pleurisy while convalescing. He had been in terrible pain, couldn't breathe, required oxygen and four bottles of antibiotic IV drip each day. He lost fourteen kilograms before his wife arrived. She brought him Western food from Hong Kong and he got much better. If his next X-ray showed enough progress he would be allowed to leave the hospital. He said he was looking forward to a real shower when he got out.

Mrs. Rad, who had a pleasant lilt to her British speech, explained that Little Zhang had washed Mr. Rad's hair by dampening his head with a wet towel, rubbing in a cake of soap and then "rinsing" with a second damp towel. She pulled at her husband's hair to show the effect of the dried soap. She referred to Little Zhang as "Small Zhang," a translation of the diminutive *Xiao* that did not convey the affection of the original.

When we returned to our room we surprised a rat on the table near a bag of fruit. Remembering that other patients hung their bags of fruit from the IV stands, we hung ours too. The rat came back at night, lured by the smell from hanging string-bags of fruit whose number increased with every visitor—apples, pears, bananas, oranges, tangelos. The poor rat had to be satisfied with the fruit peels in the bathroom wastebasket and we slept through the sound of it foraging among our used tissues.

Many of our friends came to visit, cadging a car from the university if they could, otherwise riding public buses an hour and a half each way. Our first visitor was Little Lin, dressed in skin-tight jeans, a frilly pink blouse and a yellow sports jacket. It was Sunday, her day off, but Director Fang had ordered her to go to the hospital to take care of us. We could imagine her pouting at Director Fang's order the way she had when asked to give up her pretty postage stamps. We knew she would rather be home watching television on her day off so we thanked her for coming to see us. She replied, "Oh, there is no need to thank me. It is my duty to visit you."

Little Lin decided to fulfill her duty by translating the names of foods we might want to order. She began writing the Chinese characters for some foods she thought we might need, to save us the trouble of looking them up in the dictionary. She suggested ice cream, cake, cookies, chocolate. We doubted the hospital kitchen would supply these so we named some dishes we remembered from Laurel Hill Restaurant and added yogurt, milk, eggs, and fresh fruit to the list.

Little Lin then asked us to teach her some good things to say in English when foreigners teased her. She already knew "Bullshit," "You're putting me on," and "You're turning me off." We added, "Stop jerking my chain," to her repertoire and again cautioned her about "Bullshit." She bragged that she could say "Bullshit" to anyone in her office except Director Fang. Then she added, with a naughty smile, that she could even say "Bullshit" to her parents because they wouldn't know what it meant.

Margaret Xu, who was a friend of Li Meili and also one of our graduate students, was our next visitor. Margaret, a handsome woman with sparkling teeth and eyes, brought with her a bag of bananas and her parents. Her parents were both doctors in this hospital, her mother a radiologist, her father a neurosurgeon. Her father knew some English and enunciated "pneumonia" and "neurosurgeon" to show his daughter he could say difficult words in English. They asked if there was anything we wanted, and we realized Li Meili had sent Margaret's parents to be our *guanxi*.

The next morning Golden Zhou appeared, dressed like a high-level cadre, carrying a huge bag of apples. He had also come prepared to use his power and influence to help us. Janice felt so much better she wanted to leave right away but the doctors wanted to keep her in the hospital for at least two weeks. Zhou went out to talk with the doctors and convinced them to let Janice leave on Thursday if her blood test was normal and if she agreed to rest and return for X-rays. Zhou then asked the doctors whether they wanted the Waiban to send a translator to stay with us. We were delighted when they said it was not necessary.

By the end of the day the pain in Janice's side was almost gone and her temperature and heart rate were returning to normal. Pierre and Jeanette arrived, bearing an electric cooker, coffee, and lots of other food. The hospital lunch, which we had tried to cancel, arrived cold. Jeanette heated it in the cooker and fed it to Janice as the IV dripped. Pierre got excited about our *Merck Manual*, part of his fascination with knowledge that we liked so much about him. Then Janice showed off her X-rays, teaching them that the ominous black spot was only a gas bubble in the stomach, the white shadow over the left lung was the heart, and only the innocent-looking hazy section on the outer part of the left lung was the pneumonia.

The next morning Daniel and Julie arrived with bags of giant pears and oranges. Like Pierre and Jeanette they had taken public

NUMBER TWO HOSPITAL   171

buses to get to the hospital. On the bus they met a third martial arts teacher who invited Daniel to study with him.

Even the unappreciated Wang Y came to visit, along with two other teachers and more bags of fruit. They had taken a university car because it was an official visit. One of the teachers had come to see his father who had stomach cancer and was in a ward on a lower floor. They told us how much better our room was than his, leaving us to wonder whether we should express gratitude for our special treatment or apologize for the injustice. For lunch we had yogurt and fruit salad, two huge helpings, and went out to sit on the balcony.

That night we canceled our order for the hospital meal and feasted on Li Meili's "Glorious Chicken Stew with Ginger and Eggs." The night air was fresh and cotton-puff clouds were highlighted by the moon and a few bright stars. As we ate, we saw what looked like fireworks outside our window, streams of bright orange sparks shooting into the air high above the fifth floor of the next wing of the hospital. We went to the window and realized we were seeing a fire. Robin ran to the nurses' station to tell them. They ran to the phone and a few minutes later we heard sirens. Since our room had the best view, the Rads, Little Zhang, the Mayor of Wuhan and others came in to watch from our window. Little Zhang skittered back and forth, trying to see more of the action and finally asked the Rads' permission to run outside and look. When he returned, he reported eagerly that the fire was in temporary workers' housing next to the construction site and had been started by a discarded cigarette. He added, only when we asked, that no one had been hurt.

The next morning we went out on the balcony to stretch. The Mayor was there in bright blue pajamas and a striped terrycloth bathrobe tending his plants. Down below on the lawn a group of stocky older people in dark jackets and trousers were doing morning calisthenics. We imitated them, worried that the Nurse-Who-Needed-Glasses would see Janice wearing only a T-shirt and jogging pants.

Mrs. Rad came out to show us the track suit she had just bought. It was just like Janice's. All the time we had admired her wardrobe she had been interested in ours. Mrs. Rad told us that a rat had been in their room too, referring to the rat as "that small fellow," the same expression she used to identify their translator.

On Thursday Janice's white count report was good—only 8400, low enough to go home. After several attempts to phone the Waiban, we finally got through, made arrangements for a ride back to the university and went out onto the balcony to watch for the car. An hour later a gray Toyota pulled up to the curb, Little Lin's pink-bloused arm sticking out the window. We called and waved until she looked up. She yelled back impatiently, "Come on down! Hurry up!" We hadn't begun to pack, and had acquired more from our visitors than we could carry. The Nurse-Who-Needed-Glasses commandeered a hospital cart and helped us load it. She also slipped us extra packages of vitamin pills.

Little Lin came up just as we finished loading the cart. She told us we were supposed to pay our own food bill; the university would cover all the other hospital costs. A woman from the kitchen accountant's office came to the fourth floor to lead us downstairs, through a long hallway, across a sunny courtyard, into another doorway and through a strange unlit corridor whose walls and ceiling were painted black. We continued through the main kitchens, and into an office crowded with cabinets and desks. Rapid discussions took place between the workers and Little Lin, always sounding angry. People left the room and returned. They looked up bills and charges, asked us if we were German, and finally said that the bill was thirty yuan. Fifty minutes had gone by. Janice felt weak and sat down.

Did we want a receipt, they asked.

We said yes.

But the receipt person was not here right now, they said.

Little Lin said maybe we did not need a receipt.

We offered to wait.

Little Lin said maybe we could leave without a receipt and get it when we returned for the X-rays next week.

We said, fine, we'd pay next week when we returned for the X-rays.

No no, Little Lin said.

Okay, then we would wait for the receipt person. We waited. Robin proposed that he and Little Lin load the car with our luggage while Janice remained seated in the office, waiting for the Responsible Receipt Person and taking notes on all this.

Janice waited, wrote in our journal, looked around. She asked the reason for the black corridor and was told it prevented flies from going into the kitchen. Discussions among the workers took place in another room, sounding harsh and angry, accompanied by anomalous laughter. The angry sounds had to be the Hubei dialect. "In heaven there is the nine-headed bird, on earth, the Hubeinese." When the Responsible Receipt Person arrived there was more discussion. She picked up the money from the table but didn't write anything.

One of the workers said, "What Is Your Na Ma?"

Janice wrote her Chinese name for them.

They wanted her husband's name, they said.

So she wrote Robin's Chinese name too.

The Responsible Receipt Woman hesitated, then left the room with the money. Five minutes later she returned with a ragged little pink slip that was our receipt. Surely they had never done this before.

Why had we insisted on a receipt, despite Little Lin's strong hints we should not? We were tired and annoyed with the delay and spoiled by the good care we had received during the past week. If they could make us wait fifty minutes to let us know how much we should pay, producing what was clearly an ad hoc bill, then we were going to be as willful and stubborn about getting a receipt. We'd show them. Our hospital stay had made us forget the world of daily life and bureaucratic frustration. We liked it better inside.

10

SCANDALS

Sex, Spies, and Kodachrome.

Like the Chinese, we foreigners learned how to tap into the bamboo telegraph and indulge in the pleasures of gossip, retelling the "secrets" everybody knew. The gatherings at Nelson's apartment, Saturday van rides and parties became opportunities to find out the latest. One subject that always came up was the constantly changing romances among the young foreign teachers at nearby universities.

Fiona, who taught at the Cartography University, described their behavior as "musical beds" and said it was a reaction to loneliness, to being away from friends and family, a desperate need to feel close to someone. Loneliness was part of it, but there was something else going on—just being in China magnified the intensity of our emotions. Perhaps it was a romantic reaction to exotic surroundings, things we'd never experienced, like the haunting sound of *erhu* music or the mist on terraced fields of sorghum. We felt warmth and love well up at unexpected moments: when Li Meili got excited about a computer game, when we saw our students racing on the athletic field, when we helped Little Greg master his lesson.

The foreign teachers tried to keep their romantic affairs secret because they thought the Chinese would be shocked, but Chinese authorities didn't care about intimacies among the foreigners. Chinese vigilance focused on protecting the natives from Western "Spiritual Pollution," a state of ungrace requiring periodic moral clean-up campaigns.

During one of these campaigns, large posters appeared on the campus bulletin board describing the various moral offenses of five students: having affairs with foreigners, having multiple sexual relations, having a sweetheart earlier than the permitted time. The posters named the offenders and described what each had done, with enough detail to attract huge crowds. Official pornography for the masses. Romance and sex might have been forbidden, but reading about them was not. Everybody on campus and many visitors came to read the posters, which were so popular they stayed up longer than photography exhibits and other displays. They were taken down only when the crowds dwindled, more than a month later.

One of the notorious offenders was the Girl Who Had Two Boyfriends. In addition to her offense of romancing Ethan, she had been arrested trying to register at a hotel with a Taiwanese man. Daniel told us she and the Taiwanese had taken separate rooms, but this detail was omitted from the poster. Although her "crimes" were over a year old they were described in detail. Her punishment was that she had to attend classes for an extra year and be subject to "close supervision." Requiring her to stay at the university was a way of keeping track of her, of restricting her freedom. The more serious punishment was that her crimes would be entered on her record and would count against her for the rest of her life.

We wondered why the poster appeared so long after her deeds until we heard that the American boyfriend, Ethan, was planning to return to China and would be granted a visa on condition that he stay away from Wuhan. Close supervision, like criminal parole, meant that the girl would not be able to visit him in another city.

Except for the final red check mark, the moral-transgression posters were similar to the public notices describing the crimes and punishments of murderers, rapists and thieves of government property. For sexual behavior, something we regarded as a private act, the public condemnation and humiliation seemed inappropriately severe.

We talked about the posters with our tutor, Julie, who told us about her own experience. When she and her boyfriend were students, they studied together more than anyone else until they were at the very top of their class. Although they had never thought of each other as romantic partners, Julie's political adviser told her they must not continue to study together because she would get pregnant. It seemed to us the political adviser had started the romance she was trying to prevent, giving Julie and her boyfriend ideas about each other they didn't have before. Julie believed that only their good grades kept their names off one of those humiliation posters since the authorities tended not to punish the best students. They did, however, reassign the boyfriend to teach at another university, justifying the separation on the grounds that "they would have more to talk about" if they worked in different places.

Unlike Julie, Li Meili and older Chinese found nothing wrong with the posters. "It is different in China," Li Meili said, "It is all right for you Americans to do such things, but not for Chinese." Li Meili and Golden Zhou tried to explain the Chinese values—that premarital sex was moral chaos; that undergraduates were not considered adults; that students had to devote all their time and energy to their studies and not distract themselves with romance. And romance had a trickle-down effect—Zhou gave us a copy of a *China Daily* article: The "problem of puppy love" in middle schools had made the front page.

Golden Zhou and Li Meili were both older, married, and in authority roles, so we were not surprised by their views, but we expected the students themselves to be more sympathetic. They were not, at least not openly. The five described in the posters "deserved to be punished," most of the undergraduates said during a class discussion. They asked us how we handled the "problem" of premarital sex in our country.

"In our country," we told them, "many people do not consider such behavior wrong if it does not hurt anybody."

"Oh, but here in China it hurts the families and the university."

"But don't the posters themselves hurt people?" we asked, thinking that this was the real source of harm.

"Only bad people," they responded.

Jeannie, the Communist Party applicant, volunteered a different opinion: The trouble with the posters was that they probably would not help the notorious five to reform. "Because of the posters, they will be like outlaws and perhaps go on to do even worse things." Ah, Jeannie, we thought, good for you. You are going to make an excellent Party leader.

Our counsel in matters of spiritual pollution was sought almost as much as Daniel's. A young teacher told us that when she was fifteen she read a book that described a man resting his head on a woman's chest. She feared the book had affected her thinking in a bad way.

Other stories were more juicy. Some confirmed Pierre's assertion that in China a marriage license was a license to philander. Marilyn Zhang from Fiona's Waiban confessed that she was having lots of affairs, many with foreigners. They gave her presents and wanted her to leave China with them. Once her supervisor caught her necking with a visiting scholar from France, but since the work-unit "family" protected its own, she did not get into serious trouble and continued to carry on her affairs. Perhaps she was immune from punishment because she was already married and everyone knew she was only interested in foreign men for One Thing. If her affairs did not threaten the moral order of the country, they did upset her husband. When he found out about her infidelities he thought that he too should have affairs. She thought this would break up their marriage. "Should I get divorced?" she asked us.

Golden Zhou told us about "a friend" of his who was married but had an affair with an unmarried girl. They were discovered the day before the girl herself was to be married. The friend didn't know what to do, didn't want to hurt his wife. He finally confessed to her before someone else told her about it. It was a big strain on their marriage, a permanent scar, but the friend had learned a lesson.

While young people wanted to confide in Westerners about sex and love, older people wanted to talk about politics. Many who had suffered during the Cultural Revolution still felt in danger. They would not come to the Foreign Experts' Guest House where a record might be kept of their visits to foreigners, fearing contact with us might someday be used against them. We met them elsewhere.

Even if there had been no Cultural Revolution, there were still professional jealousies. Our linguist friend Wang Wei, for one, did not want people to think he was trying to get special favors from foreigners, so he only came to see us at the Guest House on official business. Once he took us on a tour of the countryside, showing us where he had been sent to learn manual labor during the Cultural Revolution, driving water buffalo and building dikes and causeways in South Lake. Everyone was miserable, he told us, but we detected a certain pride that he had built those dikes and knew how to handle a water buffalo.

We walked our bikes over a rough section of field past a peasant plowing with a water buffalo. The animal's placid movements contrasted with its fierce snorting exhalation. Wang Wei asked if we would like to drive the plow, taking for granted that the peasant would allow us to take a turn. We looked at the animal's huge horns and declined.

A physicist we met through Pierre never came to our Guest House. We would meet him at the computer center or on the athletic field. We learned most of his life story. At the beginning of the 1949 revolution, part of his family fled to Taiwan where his older sister lived now. During the Cultural Revolution many of his relatives who remained in China were falsely accused of being secret agents for the Taiwanese and were beaten to death. He was so frightened that he changed his surname and assumed a new identity, something that was possible in the chaos of those years. Recently, he tried to contact his sister by having a student who went to the US place an ad in a Taiwanese newspaper. The sister finally wrote but the letter was very formal, containing nothing about herself or the family, and our friend was very disappointed.

The physicist told us other interesting things:

> During the Cultural Revolution, the Red Guard at Central China University decided that one professor was a traitor. The evidence against him was mainly that he was fat. They beat him with bamboo sticks until he died and then they took turns jumping on his belly.

We heard versions of this story from other people, so we believe it really happened.

> One foreign teacher, upon returning to the US, wrote an article critical of the food and accommodations at the university. A Chinese student in the US translated the article and sent it back to the university authorities causing a furor that resulted in the firing of a vice president and the banning of this foreign teacher from ever returning.

We did hear from other sources that such a critique was written but we couldn't find any confirmation that the author had been banned.

> Praise from foreigners could be dangerous. We should be careful not to praise Chinese friends to other Chinese. Jealousy and suspicion could hurt them.

Unlike the physics teacher, most students were too young to have emotional scars from the Cultural Revolution. They were still willing to risk official wrath in order to express how they wanted their country to change. Every year there were student demonstrations of some kind. During our stay, the first protest march in Wuhan was scheduled for October 9th, coordinated with demonstrations in Anhui and Guangdong. Despite the local reputation for bellicosity, the student marches in Wuhan were peaceful. Students from the major universities, including ours, paraded on the main street, demanding more "democracy." Public Security handled it very well, deploying officers only to minimize traffic disruptions. Although detectives tried to get names and photographs of the marchers, we heard of no arrests.

We asked our students what they meant by "democracy," which they pronounced so strangely in English they didn't recognize when we said the word until we used the Chinese *min zhu*. Some said it meant more choice in selecting their courses. Some wanted to be able to cut classes without being penalized. Some wanted to be rid of their political advisers—girls mostly, who claimed they were hassled about their personal lives and cut off from romance. Some wanted the freedom to choose their own jobs after graduation. Some had much bolder aims—to improve China and help the economy and replace the nation's old leaders with younger, more progressive ones to speed up improvements.

Free speech was a popular demand but other students said, "No, we already have free speech."

Then someone called out, "Don't say anything more. It will all be reported back." No one laughed.

After class, some of the students came to talk with us privately. Jim (of the "Dating Rats" and cheating girlfriend) said the vagueness of their demands didn't mean that the demonstrations were about nothing.

He was right of course. Like having an illness, people can be discontent without understanding the cause. And we knew some of what was bothering them. Students were assigned a field of study before they entered the university and studied almost nothing else during their four years; then they were assigned a lifetime job at a university or middle-school for lower wages than paid to many factory workers. With economic conditions improving, the economic security of a lifetime job no longer seemed valuable. Students were dissatisfied with their too-predictable futures and wanted to make more of their own choices about courses and future employment; they wanted to be treated with more dignity. Beyond their immediate concerns, some students also wanted faster economic reforms; they didn't want Party officials vetoing decisions made by factory managers; they didn't want the "back door" used for political favors and privilege; and they wanted the "Open Door" to the West to remain open. One student conceded that leaders needed to be somewhat conservative, but he was passionate in proclaiming that it was the mission of the new generation to compensate for the stagnancy of the old.

University authorities tried to discourage students from participating in further demonstrations. Student leaders were interrogated to find out the names of those who had marched. Authorities especially wanted to know who helped coordinate the demonstrations with those in other cities. Unlike their apparent willingness to turn in schoolmates for sexual activity, the students stuck together on political issues. Nearly all were sympathetic to the demonstrations and many were disappointed that nothing changed as a result of their protests, regretting their demands had not been more clearly expressed.

When students asked us what we thought, we told them we believed public demonstrations were expressions of opinion, a way to inform fellow citizens and public officials about our views. We told them proudly about our participation in protests against the Vietnam war. In our country, we said, there are so many demonstrations that large cities have a special office to issue permits, and some streets in New York City are closed to traffic nearly every Sunday for one kind of parade or other.

We assumed someone reported our class discussions to university authorities, but there was never an objection to anything we said. Foreign teachers in other schools were asked to change essay topics and to withdraw exam questions that were politically sensitive. We never were.

Xiao Han told us that a Public Security officer came to the Waiban to investigate us. The Waiban told the officer that no one was going to interfere with *their* foreigners and if the officer from the Public Security Bureau did not have anything more important to talk about he could leave! The anecdote told more about how the Waiban viewed us than about our rights. They were annoyed because Public Security tried to encroach on their turf, not because our freedom was threatened. We were *their* foreigners and interference with our behavior was the Waiban's prerogative.

The bamboo telegraph carried the stories of two foreigners who were at the October demonstration. One story was about our own Bud. He was riding his bicycle and saw a huge crowd. He wanted to know what was happening, so he stood on his bicycle luggage rack to get a better look. The next day students told us Bud had made a speech at the demonstration. Standing on a bicycle in China was a signal of speech-making, like standing on a soapbox in the US. Everyone who saw Bud standing on his bicycle thought he had made a speech, but no one knew what he said. We weren't surprised, given that he spoke no Chinese and mumbled his colloquial English. We teased Bud by imitating what he might have said:

"Hey mon, whuzz happ'nin mon?"

The other story was about Nick, the tanned foreigner who with sunglasses looked Chinese. He had been trying to decipher one of the student posters when Public Security officers told him to go home and stay away from the demonstration. He told them that this was a public street and refused to leave. The officers ripped up the poster but did not arrest him, so Nick took a piece of the torn poster home to translate. He left it in his apartment and went out for dinner but when he returned, his rooms had been searched and the poster was gone.

In Shanghai we heard that an American rock group giving a concert had invited student leaders to come up onto the stage. The vice-president of the student body was stopped by security guards, dragged away and roughed up. They could have gotten away with this treatment if their victim had been a worker, but it was considered an outrage to treat a student that way. The student leader reportedly said to them: "*You* have made a big mistake." The next day foreign business executives boycotted a Trade Ministry banquet to protest the assault on the student leader and students vowed more demonstrations to show the authorities they couldn't mistreat students. Bud, Fiona and Nick went off to Shanghai for the weekend hoping to see a demonstration, but they arrived too late.

On January first, a rainy New Year's Day, the Guest House was alive with festivity. We started a brunch in Nelson's apartment with real brewed coffee then moved to Pierre and Jeanette's apartment for Belgian waffles. Foreigners from other schools drifted in and out. When a Chinese graduate student told us about a demonstration planned for that afternoon, we donned our rain parkas, mounted our bicycles and rode out the university gate to look for the action, hoping for An Event to pep up this slow, wet, overfed day. Even Helen was ready to wade through the mud to see the parade. Pierre and Jeanette were eager; Nick, Bud and Fiona were excited. We two were less enthusiastic because we had heard too many false rumors about demonstrations and besides we wanted to go to the big dance that evening.

After waiting in the rain and posing with water dripping off our hoods so Fiona could take pictures, we decided not to hang around for a demonstration that might never take place. After the dance we learned there had been a demonstration, a small wet one, and that Fiona had taken photographs and then was followed by a white car. We heard that Director Fang too was out in the rain watching the demonstrators march by. Helen said to him archly, "Are you here to support the students?"

Fang replied, just as archly, "Maybe."

It is possible that Director Fang's "Maybe" was a response to an entirely different question he imagined Helen had asked, but we began to appreciate him more for all that, especially because of what happened afterward.

The next day Fiona came to see us, nervous, frightened. The previous evening, after the demonstration, she went to a New Year's party at her university. Parked outside was the white car that had followed her that afternoon. At the party Marilyn Zhang tried to interrogate Fiona about the demonstration. Marilyn pretended it was casual conversation but the intensity of her questions made Fiona uncomfortable. Marilyn went into another room to confer with her boss and reappeared a few minutes later with another set of questions: "Why did you go out in the rain? Did you see anything? Did you see the leaders of the demonstration? Who was with you?"

Again Marilyn left to confer with the boss and returned to press Fiona for more information, "Did you see anyone taking pictures? Did you take any pictures?"

And again: "Do you have a camera? May I see it? Did you take any pictures? What sort of pictures?"

Into the other room and back again. "If you have pictures of the demonstrators I would like to see them. Would you give me the film?"

Upset by the questioning, Fiona lied and said she no longer had the camera. Then she rode over to Nick's university and gave the camera to him without saying what was on the film. The next day she found the lock to her apartment door broken but since her apartment usually looked ransacked, she couldn't tell if it had been searched.

What should she do, she asked us. Should she give up film that might have a clear picture of the student demonstrators? Should she admit she lied? She wanted to do the right thing but she didn't want to be a wimp.

Pierre, eager to be part of the adventure, got a new canister of film and set fire to it. He proposed that she place the charred canister in her wastebasket so the authorities would think she had destroyed the film. This didn't seem to be terribly clever spycraft, but we weren't taking it very seriously.

Five days later Fiona visited again, her voice quavering, hands trembling. Public Security had taken her and her Waiban's Marilyn Zhang to their headquarters and grilled them, threatening arrest, heavy fines, deportation, prison. They asked her repeatedly: Who are your friends? What are their names? Who told you about the demonstration? Fiona refused to answer. Marilyn Zhang, who was planning a trip to Germany, feared she would lose her passport.

After several hours of questioning, the two women were released and told to return the next day with the film. Fiona was frightened and also ashamed of her fear.

Robin realized the seriousness of the story and warned Janice: "Don't commit us to anything before we talk it over." But Fiona no sooner said, "If only someone could come with me," than Janice blurted, "Of course we'll come with you." Helen kept her mouth shut. Nelson, who was preparing the meal, didn't volunteer either.

Fiona said she was afraid to sleep at her own place because the lock on her door was broken. Helen offered the extra bed in her apartment. Fiona could not decide where to sleep; first she said she'd go home, then she said she should get her camera back from Nick so he wouldn't be caught with incriminating evidence. She put on lipstick before going to get the camera. Helen began to worry when Fiona didn't return, but we assured her that Fiona was probably in very capable hands. Ohh, said Helen.

The next morning Fiona telephoned: Public Security wanted her to come right away. We tried to contact Golden Zhou but he was out on business. Fiona called the American Embassy legal officer who told her she was on her own, that Chinese authorities could claim nearly anything was against the law. Crimes Against the State, "Disturbing the public harmony." The Embassy legal officer said something noncommittal like, "Keep in touch." Following our advice, Fiona told her Waiban that the Embassy wanted to hear from her regularly.

Off we went, Janice regretting her impetuous offer, Robin in his Mao jacket with his work-unit badge and two gold pens in the pocket, imitating a conservative high-level cadre. Fiona also dressed up for the occasion, in a short leather skirt and high heels. As she applied dark red lipstick, Robin quietly suggested she soften it a bit for Public Security. "Oh," Fiona said, and blotted her mouth on a tissue.

As we rode to Public Security headquarters, Fiona and Marilyn Zhang discussed how to explain our presence. They began to invent stories. We who hadn't yet been intimidated, insisted on the truth. "We'll tell them Fiona came to see us because she was frightened. We are here to help you and because they wanted to know who you visited on the day of the demonstration. You visited us, so we're volunteering to answer any questions they might have."

One thing we agreed on without mentioning it: we would not remember how we first learned about the demonstration. Although the information came as one more piece of gossip, the authorities were so paranoid about "outside agitators" and "Western bourgeois influence" they would crucify anybody suspected of trying to involve foreigners in the demonstrations.

We expected one of the interrogators to be the Public Security detective whom we had met back in October when he visited us, claiming he only wanted a chance to practice his English. We described him to Fiona who said he had been at her previous interrogation, wearing a leather jacket and carrying a satchel, which she thought contained a tape recorder. We reassured her that we knew this man, that we were on friendly terms. We had *guanxi* with him. Not much, but certainly enough to expect to be treated politely.

But our friend was not there. A different detective came into the interrogation room and placed an unzipped leather satchel on the floor. A young woman and two high-ranking uniformed officers also came in, one about sixty and the other in his forties. The younger man leaned back, crossed his arms, narrowed his eyes and looked at us from under the edge of his cap visor. He must have watched a lot of old movies about the Gestapo.

"Who are they?" he wanted to know about us. When Marilyn Zhang introduced us using the title *jiaoshou boshi* (Professor-Doctor), they quickly led her to another room to confer. When she returned she said Golden Zhou had just telephoned to inform Public Security that we two were "very important people in the United States and also very polite."

Perhaps as a result of Zhou's call, they served us tea and turned on the room heater, allowing Robin to open his down coat so that his Mao jacket showed. The detective reached into the open satchel and they began.

The woman officer had translated yesterday but had not done a good job. The Chinese expression that meant, "It is not clear why you said . . ." had been translated as "You are not being rational about . . .," not the sort of paraphrase to calm a frightened witness.

This morning the Gestapo-interrogator type spoke rapidly for five minutes and then turned to Marilyn Zhang for a translation. She began nervously, sure she would not remember everything. Despite his dialect we caught enough to understand that he addressed us as "you two honorable people."

As this officer talked, the detective watched us intently, occasionally reaching into the satchel. The woman officer frowned as she tried to follow Marilyn Zhang's translation: They hadn't intended to frighten Fiona yesterday but we two honorable people should know that if we participated in a Political Movement we would be breaking the law. The government had ruled that the demonstrations were illegal because the demonstrators had not gotten a permit from Public Security. We two honorable people had been invited to China to teach and we had no business getting involved in Political Movements. We should stick to our teaching and not interfere with Chinese internal politics.

Very interesting, we thought, that they were honoring the demonstrations with the title of "Political Movement."

Janice, thankful for years of practice with hostile questions at philosophy colloquia, responded: We went to see the demonstration just as we would go to see a parade, because it was an interesting event. Fiona took a picture of the demonstration just as she took pictures of the Yellow Crane Pagoda, because it was interesting. We are teachers and we are only concerned with our teaching. We value the friendship between our two countries and would not do anything to hurt China. We appreciate the freedom we are allowed in this country. However, we no longer know where we are allowed to go and what we are allowed to look at.

This was all duly noted, but it was only preliminary. The real challenge was yet to come. Our interrogator said, "Perhaps you can tell us what you know about the demonstrations." He leaned back, eyes narrowed under his visor, smug, as if he had caught us off guard. He continued, "Perhaps you can tell us about the foreigner at your university who gave a speech at the demonstration." He suddenly leaned forward.

The three of us laughed, not the nervous laughter of people who have something to hide, but the laughter that greets an unexpected joke. He meant Bud! Our Bud, Bud-the-Mumbler, The-Foreigner-Who-Wore-Underwear-On-the-Outside. That's what this had all been about! We straightened our faces and explained that the foreign teacher who stood on his bicycle could barely say hello in Chinese, let alone give a speech. The detective began laughing and the others joined in. None of our explanations, none of our professions of respect for China and claims to be neutral toward its politics could have done as much as that spontaneous laughter.

Now we understood why Fiona had been harassed. She and Bud and Nick had gone to Shanghai together to see the demonstrations. The Watchers, if they were watching that closely, might have thought that Bud, Nick and Fiona were conspiring to "disturb the public harmony," one giving speeches on his bicycle, one translating student propaganda, and Fiona amassing photographic records of political unrest.

They wanted to know the name of the foreigner-on-the-bicycle. We politely declined to give Bud's name but we offered to ask him to contact Public Security. They accepted this compromise. Then they seemed to have nothing more to say. The meeting should have been over at this point, but the Public Security Bureau had scheduled the entire morning for the interrogation. That all their questions had been answered did not call for a change in plans. There were long pauses. They repeated some of the earlier questions. They assured us that they wanted to be our friends, that we should not be afraid, that they wanted to promote friendship between our countries (our line earlier). We in turn assured them that we valued China and respected China's laws.

Although we didn't use adjectives like "illustrious" and "humble," the exchange was everything we imagined a formal dialogue in China should have been, full of polite superlatives and self-deprecating disclaimers. The detective spoke now for the first time, suddenly taking charge. He assured us that we were free to visit anywhere, to watch anything we found interesting, that we should not feel our actions were restricted in any way. However, if we wanted to take pictures of a "Political Movement," Chinese law required us to apply for a press permit.

Only then did they ask for the film. The camera had been in Fiona's lap all morning. Now that our differences had been resolved, at least officially, Fiona could give them the film in a spirit of cooperation, not under duress. She would not lose face. She opened the back of the camera and began unwinding the film from the take-up spool, pushing it back into the cassette. They accepted it very graciously, saying that after they developed the film they would return any personal pictures to her. Robin said that perhaps the film was spoiled. The detective said yes, but seemed happy to receive it nonetheless.

At noon the meeting ended. The Public Security officers shook our hands and accompanied us to the university car, waving good-bye as if they had just given a party. We were relieved, euphoric at our own ability to handle a difficult situation, feeling safer than ever in China because now we knew the leaders of the Public Security Bureau. Marilyn Zhang would keep her passport, Fiona had been saved from deportation and we had helped.

Fiona's emotions were more complex than ours. She had been frightened and humiliated by Public Security and all their politeness could not make up for that. Her friend Marilyn Zhang had been used against her and she would never be able to trust Marilyn again. And despite the relief, Fiona was disappointed because the adventure was over.

When we got back to the Guest House, we told everyone that Public Security was interested in "the foreigner who made a speech at the demonstration." We pressured Bud to call Public Security. Even Daniel urged him to call and clear things up. Bud resisted, got upset, delivered a diatribe against authority, called Daniel names and stormed out. A few minutes later Bud came to our door, remorseful about fighting with Daniel. He felt bad, he was wrong, but he didn't want to have anything to do with those muh-fuhin Security shitheads, he didn't trust them, he couldn't stand their asses.

"Right. Okay. We understand. But Daniel was just trying to help you by getting them off your back once and for all."

Bud paced the floor. He felt so bad for yelling at Daniel. How could he fight with Daniel? It's those Fascist Security creeps' fault. He'd do anything to make up. Where's the phone? What's the number? He'd call them, he'd do anything. He was ready to call Public Security and answer any questions as penance for saying harsh things to Daniel. We reminded him he would need a translator.

Just then Golden Zhou arrived and we told him the story. He was angry at Public Security, and said "I know this story and I know Bud would never do this speech. Public Security has no business with you. They must contact the Waiban and talk with us first. If they had done that I would have told them the whole story was wrong." Golden Zhou told Bud not to make the call.

There was a sequel to the story. The President of the Provincial Ministry of Education paid Fiona a visit to apologize for the treatment she had received from Public Security. He and her Waiban gave a banquet to honor her. It would have been a very nice occasion, she reported, but the director of her Waiban got drunk and rubbed her face with his hands, saying over and over, "Poor Little Fiona, Poor Little Fiona." She would rather be known as "Tough Competent Fiona, Sharp Savvy Fiona," and she certainly didn't like her face rubbed as if she were a child.

But what was the effect of the demonstrations on the university? Students were ordered to stop demonstrating and return to their studies for the good of the country. Some told us they thought they had been involved in a worthwhile cause but now they knew they were mistaken. Others said, "Next time, it will be better. Next time we will be more organized."

The demonstrations served the government as an excuse to shuffle power at the upper levels but the changes in leadership did not seem to affect daily life at the universities, except for one thing: A politically correct attitude became a formal requirement for university admission.

11
GOOD TIMES

Guest House Follies

We used to think pranks and raucous parties were only for adolescents until we discovered they were inevitable for people, whatever their age, who lived on a university campus. Although we had separate apartments and were all past our teenage years, something turned the Guest House into a dormitory, with childish jokes, changing alliances, and morning wastebaskets full of empty beer cans.

There were certain aspects unique to our setting. "Oh! I feel evil spirits near the building," Robin would say and jump up from his Chinese vocabulary exercises, run to the balcony with a string of firecrackers and a stick of burning incense. Nelson and Daniel would go out on their balconies to cheer as the evil spirits were driven away by the fusillade of explosions. Bud would scream in mock outrage, "Whuh the Fuh! I was trying to sleep, you bat breaths," but he had to turn down his reggae music so we could understand him. Helen heard the commotion from her balcony at the other end of the building and joined in the shouting, delighted that the soft-spoken Robin had this unexpected love of pyrotechnics.

During the rainy season, most of the horseplay took place inside the building, like the time we challenged Nelson to a game of corridor soccer. Enthusiastically Nelson tried to score a goal, missed the ball entirely and sent an empty thermos bottle skittering down the hallway. The crump of the imploding vacuum bottle and the sound of glass fragments spinning inside the metal case put an end to the game. Nelson laughed. "It's worth a few yuan to smash one of those fuckers."

Nelson, intent on denying his professorial dignity, was often the instigator of mischief. After hearing that Daniel's sweater and jeans were stolen from his first floor balcony clothesline, Nelson used a long bamboo pole to snatch a pair of pants from his neighbor's second floor balcony. When the new theft was discussed he acted indignant:

"They stole your pants too? The nerve! How did they get to the second floor balcony?" And then, completely unsuspected, he produced the purloined pants.

On April first, with the help of Little Lin and others from the Waiban, he composed a letter to Robin on university stationery, forging Director Fang's name.

> It has been called to the attentions of the authorities that I am serious to tell you that it is against law for you to have fire-works in your partment. I am sorry to tell you that you must give all fireworks to Office of International Exchange tomorrow in the morning. So that we can give fireworks to the Security Bureau. They told our office that they will have formal talks with you. They said it is a new law. We have just receive it. You have no choice because we just knew it is a new law.
>
> I am sorry to say that workers by your building told Public Security Office during spring festival that you burn grass by the guest house. Also they can not sleep or do work on the new building late at night. In order to keep safety we advise that you not have fireworks any more or you will get problems.
>
> Bring them our office tomorrow mornings. I am sorry to have to do this, but I have no choice. Please understand me.
> Truly,
> Shoubai Fang
> Director, Exchange Office of International Educational.

The style and wording and bits of Chinese syntax fit what we expected of Fang. Even reversing his name to Western order was something only Fang would do. The phrase "it is a new law" would convince anyone with experience of China that it was genuine. We were furious at the false charges but never skeptical about the source of the letter. Nelson aided the deception by listening to our outrage and sharing our feelings. "Those bastards! Those bastards!" he said over and over. So effective was the hoax that we didn't realize that a law banning firecrackers in China was as plausible as a law banning milk in Wisconsin.

Our anger turned to rebellion. "They're not getting *our* firecrackers." We invited everyone to help us set them off and led a big procession to the open field near our building. Nobody let on that this was a hoax until just before Robin ignited his precious "Big Fountain," Nelson said innocently: "What day is today?" We set off the Big Fountain as a toast to those who took us in so completely.

Grousing and other Hobbies.
Days and days of heavy rain. Dew coated the furniture in the morning. Our laundry took forever to dry; the only way to speed it up was to pin our socks to the grill of the electric fan and hang our jeans over the warm air rising from the refrigerator condenser. We wore our Chinese galoshes and Chinese bicycle ponchos to class, looking like the parents of ET. Our pants became splattered up to the waist with wet clay. We began to wear *xiu tao* (sleeve covers) on our legs instead of our arms.

Nelson's poetry production soared, lyrical and witty. Inspired by a ruined temple, the taste of chloroquine, the bark of a Chinese dog at three in the morning, the shaved and saffron-robed monks walking down the median strip of a Bangkok highway, Nelson evoked lost emotions and wry memories on his word-processor. He would write from early morning until late afternoon when he tuned in the BBC, poured his Jack Daniels and played host to the early evening gathering.

His apartment had become the local hangout. He shared the bottles of Jack Daniels and Beefeater that he bought at a large premium and even shared the packages of chocolate-covered peanuts he got from home. On Saturday afternoons he cooked vats of Texas chili for everyone.

Bud adopted Nelson as a father confessor and Nelson never threw him out when he came late at night to get drunk and tell his troubles. Daniel stopped in occasionally, usually after his Chinese friends had left for the night. "Where does Daniel get all those beautiful women," Nelson soliloquized, "And what does he do with them?"

Daniel opened his *Jianlibao*, a carbonated version of Gatorade, and smiled. "I'm not going to tell you," he said, trying to look arch.

The relentless rain gave the cocktail hour new importance. Nelson would pour Beefeater gin into our glasses and use a tiny spoon to add Martini & Rossi vermouth. He poured himself a glass of Jack Daniels as we tuned in the BBC. Nelson's refrigerator was stocked with *Jianlibao* for Daniel and *Ding Hu* beer for Bud. Helen and Nelson were not on good terms, so she rarely came.

The deep-voiced BBC announcer would describe the latest stupidity in the Middle East, perhaps a plane crash, a tourist bus diving into a lake, an uncontrollable fire burning up the forests of Heilongjiang Province, the current embarrassments of US foreign policy. The gloomy news combined with the rain to set the tone for the evening. We complained about the dirt and the disorganization of our surroundings, cataloging what was not going well.

We stopped getting hot water as soon as the outside temperature reached fifty degrees. The *fuwuyuan* told us that the university had run out of coal, as if that were a good explanation in a country with the world's largest coal reserves. They shrugged when we mentioned the huge pile of coal near our building.

After the Golden Smoothie went to see "the new Vice President in charge of this matter," telling him about the supply of coal we had "discovered," the hot water returned. We should have been happy about our success but we were depressed that we had to intervene yet again.

When the weather became rotten, the hot water unreliable, and the world news gloomy, it was hard not to grouch. As our martinis disappeared and Nelson poured himself a third shot of JD, we reminded ourselves that we had similar complaints about our own country—the insurance industry, Detroit auto makers, American high schools, the IRS (who had just misfiled another of our tax returns and was sending us nasty letters), our academic colleagues.

Bud complained about the two night guards at the front desk. He called them "Goebbels" and "Himmler." To us they were just two old men who controlled our hot water and were pretty casual about supplying for us what they never had for themselves, but Bud's nicknames soothed our resentment. We felt better when we heard other people get angry. It helped to criticize the things we couldn't change. Grouching and grumping had become part of our leisure activities.

We did have more respectable forms of entertainment. We went to concerts and performances and art exhibits. We traveled around China and to Hong Kong, Macao, Thailand. We had visitors, most of them welcome, some from as far as the US. And we had hobbies.

Bud played basketball and lifted weights with Nick and some of their students. Daniel took lessons in *Wu Shu* (martial arts), practicing a combat style of *Tai Qi* and sword play. These lessons were beautiful to watch, a combination of ballet and movie fight scenes, carefully choreographed by Daniel's teacher, a *Wu Shu* master who had refused to take any new students until he saw

Daniel's foreign face. He agreed to teach Daniel and refused any payment for the lessons.

Helen's hobby was ethnic minorities. She gave lectures at the Institute for National Minorities, interviewed their scholars, returned with cork sculptures and tapestry samples. Through a friend in Washington she arranged an exhibit of these fabrics at the Smithsonian.

Nelson's hobby was art. One of his graduate students had become his Chinese tutor and friend, a woman who wanted to be an art historian but instead was assigned to study English. She knew the local art scene and took him to exhibits and museums. With her interest in art, her grace and conversation, Judy Liang replaced Little Lin's child flirtation as the object of Nelson's romantic fantasy. Judy's perfect figure (she took special "beautiful body" training classes), delicate good looks and pale perfect skin made it easy for Nelson to abandon Little Lin.

Judy Liang believed she was too old to marry. Nelson called her "Old Girl" and she called him "Old Boy." He worried that his caring for her might cause her trouble, that someone angry at him would try to hurt her. We knew by this time how a person's behavior could affect their friends and relatives. In the US, one's own reputation might escape harm if friends and associates did wrong, but in China, where reputation was more fragile and relationships more salient, the negative effects were certain. Nelson was therefore very careful not to put Judy Liang in jeopardy.

And so were we. One Saturday Nelson left the shopping outing to meet Judy Liang and walk with her to her parents' home. We saw them go off, sharing an umbrella in the rain. When Little Lin returned to the van and demanded to know where Nelson had gone and with whom, we tried to protect Judy Liang from gossip by changing the subject, distracting Little Lin with jokes and teasing.

Except for keeping our journal and studying Chinese, we didn't have a special activity at first. We played soccer with the students in the English Department and practiced kicking the ball in the Guest House yard with some of the other foreigners. We played a little volleyball with Julie. We attended the English Department's sports festival where Janice won second prize in the women's division of "grenade throwing." A softball replaced the original missile but distance and accuracy were still the goals. We rode our bikes around East Lake, past flowering orchards and public parks and fishermen reading books. We went to art shows with Nelson and his tutor, attended movies at the university's open air theater, watched language lessons and sports on television.

And then we became fans of what everyone called "traditional Chinese dancing." When we first heard the term we thought it referred to the stamping, arm-waving routine popular during the Cultural Revolution for singing praises to Chairman Mao, but "traditional Chinese dancing" turned out to be old-fashioned ballroom dancing—tangos and waltzes and rumbas and two-steps with lots of crossover routines. Janice had not done this kind of dancing since she'd been a teenager. Robin had not done it ever.

Charleston Fever
Our dancing hobby began one wintry Saturday night when Old Dong came to our door and said, *"Dian hua! Dian hua!"* (telephone). Janice followed him downstairs to the telephone at the front desk. It was Golden Zhou on the line inviting us to go with him to a student dance. Janice was delighted with Zhou's proposal because we had not seen him for weeks. She wanted to go, but Zhou had to persuade Robin, she told him, because Robin didn't know how to dance. She ran back upstairs. "It's Zhou on the phone and he has an offer you can't refuse." Meanwhile Zhou had worked up the perfect sales pitch. He told Robin how this would be a valuable opportunity for him; he could study Chinese student life, social customs and folk dancing, was that right? Zhou had tickets

for the three of us but he would go only if we joined him. He very much wanted to go, but it was up to us.

We rushed through dinner, dressed hastily and rode our bicycles in the dark through mud and ruts and crowds of people, our bells ringing and the beam of our tiny flashlight bouncing ahead of us. Golden Zhou was waiting near the entrance, dressed in Ultimate Western Cool—a sports jacket over sweater and open collar shirt, jeans and boots below, cigarette held just right.

Inside the hall where we had seen performances of acrobatics and Hubei opera, most of the pew-style seats had been moved to one end. Mercury vapor lamps in the ceiling turned the center of the huge room into a harsh arena until someone switched them off, allowing the red and green lamps on the side walls to glow like the pillars of an old juke box.

The band arrived—drums, electric guitars, trombone, trumpet, electronic keyboard, male and female vocalists. People crowded the edges of the huge room, leaving the dance floor an empty field. The first number was a tango with an elaborate melody and an overly embellished rhythm. Brass cadenzas, drums, electronic marimbas competed with the female vocalist who concentrated her acoustic energy in the narrow band of frequencies traditional for Chinese opera. The audience was intimidated by the complexity of the music and for several minutes, nobody went out onto the dance floor. A few people tried to match their steps to the music, heads bent, watching their feet. Then one couple moved out onto the floor, dancing conservatively but well, their movements synchronized with the stronger beats of the rhythm. Soon many couples were dancing.

We had never done this kind of dancing together. But one winter, living in a huge loft with a quarter acre of floor space, we did aerobic dancing for exercise whenever our soccer field was covered with snow. Our favorite routine was the Charleston. If the music was fast enough and had the right beat, we thought we could try a Charleston. It was unlikely that anyone had seen a Charleston to know if we were doing it wrong. What did we have to lose?

The tango rhythm was not right and the next piece was much too slow. Golden Zhou went off to mingle, nearly resigned to us not dancing. But the third number was faster and we decided to try. Other Chinese stopped dancing to watch the foreigners and more gathered until there was a crowd cheering our hops and turns. A Boop-Boop-Be-Doo hand wave wowed them. Heel slapping knocked them dead. Golden Zhou beamed with pride. At the end, we were breathing so hard we barely heard the applause from the crowd. They gathered closer, begging us to teach them what they thought was the latest American dance. We apologized, explaining that it was really a very old dance and protesting that we did not do it well. In a country where modest denial is the response to all praise, the truth of our claim was not accepted. We showed the steps in slow motion to an eager audience.

Zhou then danced with Janice, touching her for the first time since she had grabbed his arm to cross a Beijing street. He began a routine of intricate steps for the rumba, and after a few bumped knees and toes, Janice learned to follow and they twirled together around the floor, Zhou masterfully weaving through other dancers.

It might have been because Zhou, unlike Xiao Han and Little Lin, had never touched Janice before, it might be because dancing again after all these years was so enjoyable, and it might have been because Golden Zhou was so good looking, but Janice felt flustered, as if dancing were an inappropriate intimacy. If it was for her, it was not for him. From then on touching between them was permitted—he grabbed her arm, her shoulder, her hand to make a point, as one would touch a sister, an old friend. Perhaps *not* touching had been the intimacy.

In China there was nothing unusual about two men dancing together, so Zhou then danced with Robin, giving Robin his first lessons in ballroom dancing. We then danced with our students, sometimes male with male, sometimes female with female, sometimes mixed. When we returned to the Guest House, we compared notes on the partners we shared.

A few days after the student dance, there was a "dance for young teachers," and a few days after that a "dance for old teachers." The music was the same except for fewer Latin rhythms at the old teachers' dance. Helen came with her students who danced with her, honored to be so employed, comically dwarfed by her size. Bud came with his basketball buddies and hung out with them at the edge of the dance floor. Julie tried to get her boyfriend to accompany her to a dance but he refused because he didn't know how and didn't like to try things he was not sure he could do well. Finally, she came with us.

Robin did learn to dance, finding eager teachers and partners everywhere. The graduate students came to our apartment to give us lessons. Little Lin came one Friday afternoon, escaping from the mandatory "Political Study" meeting on an imaginary errand so the three of us could practice dancing. She claimed she didn't really like dancing and only went to the dances because it was her duty to learn anything that would help her do her job. She said mischievously, "If Mister Zhou heard what we did today he would be angry." Surprised, we asked her why. Because he too wanted to get out of Political Study, she said. If he had known we were going to dance he would have wanted to come.

As Robin learned to dance, we told Zhou he should teach his wife also. If Robin could learn from him, she could too, because Zhou was such a good teacher. "I know," he said laughing, and brought her to the next dance. The time after that neither came. "She wanted to go to a movie instead," he explained the next day.

Guest House Parties
The Halloween party where Bud distinguished himself was the first, but the party season began in earnest with Thanksgiving. By that

time we American expatriates were ready to express our culinary chauvinism. We pooled our furniture and tableware for a banquet in Nelson's apartment and then sat down to plan the menu.

Unfortunately, the only turkeys in Wuhan were honored residents of the municipal zoo. The Chinese considered turkey an exotic animal; eating one for them would be like our eating a zebra. Little Lin believed *huo ji* (fire chickens) were not even edible. Deprived of our traditional fare, we settled for canned ham with orange sauce, candied sweet potatoes, mashed white potatoes, crepes, mushroom gravy, cauliflower, and apple pie for dessert. This was the first of many feasts where Western food was the reason as well as the means for celebration. After several months of a Chinese diet, Western food was so alien to our digestive systems that half the guests got diarrhea afterwards.

The party with the most elaborate preparation, the largest attendance and the longest duration was the Christmas party. Helen was in charge, euphoric with her new apartment, enthusiastic about assigning people to committees, leading, exhorting, coordinating. One of our jobs was to type lyrics so people could sing Christmas carols. We prepared our favorites for duplication and even made up some lyrics of our own:

> On the twelfth day in China, the Waiban gave to me:
> Twelve hours a-teaching, eleven days a-waiting,
> Ten bikes a-breaking, nine toilets leaking,
> Eight chickens squawking, seven children staring,
> Six students cheating, FIVE STO-MACH CRAMPS,
> Four hungry rats, three hard-seat tickets, two Wuchang
> fish, And a taxi tour of Beijing.

When Bud announced that he wouldn't attend the Christmas party, Helen's motherly instincts were aroused; she imagined him sad and alone in his room while the rest of us were making merry. Recalling his drag queen costume on Halloween, we realized how to appeal to him. Janice ran downstairs, Helen trying to catch up. "Bud, we have a problem and we need you to help us."

When Helen explained that we needed him to be Santa Claus he yielded. Helen collected cotton from medicine bottles to stick on Bud's red T-shirt and a pillow to go under it. Janice looped a white plastic bag over his ears so it would hang under his chin like a beard. The transformation was complete when Helen applied lipstick to make his cheeks oh so rosy and his nose like a cherry.

We had invited forty guests but well over a hundred people showed up, fulfilling the Chinese expression for an ideal social occasion, "heat-heat noise-noise." The celebration spread out over the lobbies of the second and third floors as the guests danced to rock music tapes, sang carols from mimeographed lyrics, drank orange soda, soy milk or beer. Suddenly, above all the other sounds, we heard a distant cry, a scream, and then a crescendo of high-pitched voices. Dozens of children came running up the stairs waving toys and fists full of candy, followed by Santa Bud shouting "Ho! Ho! Ho!" The kids were ecstatic that the "Children's God of the West" had come to life in their presence. One little boy, who had been drinking beer instead of orange soda or soy milk, demanded extra toys from Santa. His father apologized, "He is very bourgeois."

Nearly any holiday or event became the excuse for a party—Halloween, Thanksgiving, Christmas, Hanukkah, New Year's Eve, Chinese Spring Festival, birthdays, going-away parties and coming-back parties; American food parties, Chinese food parties; cheese cake parties based on a no-bake cheese cake mix we brought back from Hong Kong; ice cream sundae parties with homemade ice cream, bananas, fruit preserves and melted Shanghai chocolate; pasta parties to celebrate the arrival of the oregano, basil and Parmesan cheese we ordered from Hong Kong; local wine and foreign cheese parties.

When Chinese friends were invited to our "cheese" party they were wary, for cheese was almost universally disliked. Brave Xiao Han, believing that all cheese smelled terrible, brought bricks of "stinky" tofu to challenge the Western contributions. He tasted each of the cheeses and looked on triumphantly as most of the foreigners declined to taste his offering.

A UN expert studying giant salamanders that lived only in our province stayed in our Guest House for a month. When we had a welcoming party for "Salamander Dave" he brought one of his charges back to the Guest House. The specimen, shorter than the two-meters many of these salamanders reached, lived in his bathtub, keeping cool in shallow water. The salamanders were called "*Wawa yu*" (baby-fish) because they made sounds like human babies crying in distress. Little Lin wanted to make it cry, but was afraid to touch it herself so she tried to convince other people to poke it. Salamander Dave distracted her by suggesting that we all help him name the animal. "Nelson," suggested Little Lin gleefully, for he was away that weekend and couldn't defend himself. When Salamander Dave and his slippery friend left, we threw a going-away party.

Another party centered around a treasure hunt with doggerel verse "clues" hidden all over the Guest House:

> Buddy's was the worst of all,
> A thousand flaws you will recall.
> But now beneath its dainty seat
> You will find a useful treat.

This clue directed clever players to the bottom of Bud's bicycle seat. The verses also contained bilingual English-Chinese puns to encourage international cooperation, but most of the Chinese laughed too hard at the antics of the foreigners to hunt seriously. Li Meili wanted to search, but her teammate Fiona gave up early.

They won the booby prize so Li Meili wasn't too disappointed. The treasure hunters ran through the building collecting clues from Bud's bicycle, from Old Dong's newspaper (to his amazement), from the "Comment Book" the *fuwuyuan* had installed in the Guest House for us to make suggestions (although none of them could read anything most of us could write), from the cuspidor at the end of the hall corridor, from the ladder to the roof.

Jeanette and Pierre had a party to celebrate their last hundred days in China and nearly a hundred days later we had a going-away party for them. They planned to give away everything they were not shipping home. Helen was willing to accept everything for free but because they had always been so generous, we insisted they have an auction and not just give away their appliances, cookware, foodstuffs and clothing. Also we were angry at Helen for selling FEC to Bud at black market rates.

Pierre and Jeanette agreed to the auction but were reluctant to take money from their friends. Whenever they faltered, we suggested an opening price to start the bidding and whenever Helen seemed about to get something too cheaply the rest of us bid up the price.

Helen's move to the end of the corridor had changed the dormitory dynamics. She and Nelson no longer ate together. Nelson complained about her "presumptuous mothering" and her meanness—borrowing a bottle of scotch and returning a glass of gin, saying, "Now we're even." Helen complained about Nelson's latest outburst of anger—losing his temper at Old Crabby the driver and slamming the van door. When the driver and Little Lin then scolded Nelson for mistreating the vehicle, Helen joined them, treating Nelson like a naughty child. Hostility, Nelson could forgive, but being patronized was too insulting.

She came to fewer parties and talked to us only in the hallway, often to request a favor, "Would you take this to . . . .?" "Would some man help me lift . . . .?" These requests produced mixed emotions: we were ashamed of our resentment but smugly amused that once again she had confirmed her character as a user.

When we were much younger we believed all our likes and dislikes had a moral basis. Now we knew better. We found ourselves siding with Nelson, not because he was morally superior but because he was wittier in his criticism. We joined him in imitating Helen's mannerisms and dubbed her "The Empress."

When two of Helen's friends from Washington arrived she decided to throw a party. Nelson said he was not going. Instead of preparing the food herself, Helen assigned the task to Little Lin and our Chinese tutors. She told Little Lin the party was on Friday but when they arrived on Friday, Helen changed the time to Saturday at five o'clock.

On Saturday at seven the campus open air theater was showing a foreign movie, supposedly a John Wayne western, which the Chinese all wanted to see. They thought they could prepare and serve the food in time. Helen's cooks arrived at the Guest House at five and sat in the lobby until Helen and her friends returned from their day of shopping at five thirty. "We want to take baths," she told her Chinese help, "Come upstairs about six."

We had some leftover jiaozi in our refrigerator so Little Lin, Li Meili and the others came to our apartment for dinner. At six Janice checked with Helen: the three women had just finished bathing. No preparations for the meal had been made so Janice set a basin of flour and water in front of Helen for her to knead, and encouraged the friends to begin chopping vegetables and cutting meat. Only then did Janice fetch the others.

As the Chinese entered, Helen jumped up from her kneading and said coyly to Li Meili, "Would you like a turn?" Helen never again made any attempt to help with the food preparation. We worked like mad to prepare and serve the meal for Helen's visitors before excusing ourselves to run to the outdoor theater, leaving the three women to enjoy the food.

The movie turned out to be a Romanian swashbuckler about Gypsies and revolution, not the John Wayne western we had anticipated. An hour into the movie the air got misty and rain threatened. When a few drops fell most of the audience left. Chinese were soft after all, we thought as we continued watching. A few minutes later the audience returned with umbrellas and when the skies opened up it was we who ran away while the rest of the audience stayed hunkered under their umbrellas watching the movie to the end.

It was dark when we returned to the Guest House and saw lights on at Helen's. We went down the hall to see if the party was still going on, and to relieve a bit of guilt for leaving so abruptly. Nelson was the only guest there, chatting amiably with Helen and her friends. Afterward we accused him of having a soft heart, of being less willing to abandon Helen than we were. Embarrassed, he claimed he only went to drink up her liquor.

Western Faces for TV Ads

Despite official government warnings against creeping Western influence, many new entrepreneurs believed that "West is best" for boosting sales. An executive of the local "Discar" company decided to make a television commercial to introduce his new toy, so he called a friend in our Waiban and asked to borrow some tame foreigners. Xiao Han came to enlist us for that afternoon. To be models in a Chinese TV ad! Our fantasies blossomed: Our faces would become familiar to the half of China's billion people who watched television, rivaling Mickey Mouse in popularity, perhaps even helping us get train and boat tickets. . . .

A Toyota van with DISCAR decals on the windscreen and door arrived at the Guest House. We were driven to the center of Wuchang where we left the main street and snaked through alleys and driveways into a courtyard in front of the company building. Large signs in English flanked the doorway: TIME IS MONEY,

EFFICIENCY IS EVERYTHING. Was China changing faster than we realized or were the signs posted just for their trendy English?

Inside we were led through a series of moongate doorways past several empty rooms into a hall the size of a gymnasium where children and adults were riding the "Discars," weaving, gliding, dodging.

Discars came in several sizes, shapes and colors. All had a small platform about the size of a garbage can lid. The rear wheels were relatively close together, the front ones wide apart and steerable by ski-pole handles that stuck up through the platform. Pushing the right handle forward and the left one back caused the wheels to turn to the left. With the encouragement of company officials we mounted the platforms and discovered a sideways version of pumping on a swing that would propel the Discar. The weight shift had to come at the right time or the car wouldn't accelerate. The motion of the upper body resembled skating except that the feet were planted, hips moving like an exotic dancer's. By steering a zigzag course and shifting weight from side to side, we could pump the Discars to over twenty kilometers per hour.

A giant boom box played classic Chinese rock-and-roll songs: "I Am the Batman of Love," "You're Too Late," and "Ali Baba." The concrete floors of the room and the roar of the wheels made it sound like a rock concert in a subway station.

Young women wearing short tunics, tights, high-heeled leather boots and much more make-up than Chinese women ordinarily wore, were skilled and very graceful on the Discars. They were dancer-acrobat-martial artists from the Hubei Chinese Opera Company. Just a week before, we had seen them perform. Singing, dancing, swordplay, tumbling, juggling—no Western performance combined so many talents.

One of the Hubei Opera dancers hopped on behind Janice, hugging her around the waist and molding herself intimately to the curve of Janice's back. The dancer matched her rhythm perfectly. The company photographer took pictures of the couple.

When they dismounted, the dancer took Janice by the hand and led her over to the boom box where the Chinese rock music had turned sinuous and less frenetic than the American style. The dancer taught Janice the steps by holding their bodies together, back to front. Janice's "girlfriend" now wanted Janice to teach her an American dance. When a fast song came up and Janice stepped into the Charleston, all the dancers gathered around her, imitating her movements closely—the roaring twenties had met the roaring dragon. They caught on quickly, much faster than students and teachers at the university dance party. Robin joined in and tutored another dancer. Together Robin and Janice introduced the flourishes, the high knee slap and the thumb-to-heel variant. The dancers applauded and copied the steps perfectly. The Charleston would have been in danger of upstaging the Discar were it not for the children, who now had the vehicles to themselves and went roaring through the moongates at speeds we had been too cowardly to try.

At the company banquet afterwards, Janice's girlfriend sat next to her. "I like you. I like Americans," she said over and over. After the meal the company president announced that today had only been a rehearsal. Later they would videotape the real commercial on the university campus. They would let us know which day.

Although the company's sign proclaimed that time was money, advance notice wasn't yet part of their capital. The following week they called us from the university Waiban office announcing they were ready to videotape and we must come to the Waiban's courtyard right away, hurry up. It was a beautiful day and every foreigner came out to ride the Discars, even Helen who wouldn't ride a bicycle. Director Fang came walking up the path and we encouraged him to try a Discar. Like a good sport he tried to ride but soon fell off. Golden Zhou, Xiao Han and Little Lin all took turns.

The Discar company had worked out a skit. A feeble old person notices a young woman zipping by on a Discar. Cut to new scene: The old person decides to try the Discar, mounts, succeeds and is rejuvenated by the experience! The script reminded us that Chinese advertisers often touted the curative benefits of their product, whatever it might be.

Nelson was enlisted to play the old person. He walked slowly, exaggeratedly decrepit. Janice's girlfriend from the Hubei Opera Company zoomed by on her Discar. Nelson stopped hobbling, his mouth dropping open in amazement as he turned his head to follow the Discar, his hands spread in wonder. The crowd cheered and applauded. He mounted a Discar, suddenly losing his infirmities and looking ecstatic as he spun past the cameras. More applause. There was another banquet, and this time Janice's girlfriend sat next to Nelson, saying over and over to him, "I like you. I like Americans."

12

SECRETS

The Saga of Driver Li

Janice learned of the accident when she went to the photocopy machine during a class break. The office was closed and as Janice left, she was beckoned by Wang X. There is some very sad news, he said, six people from the English Department had gone on a trip to a remote county and the university van was hit broadside by a lorry; two were dead and the others were seriously injured; four university leaders, including Wang Y and Wang Z, had been rushed to the scene but it was being kept secret until the families were notified. The eagerness in the telling vied with the sadness of the tragedy.

Nelson was told the same story by Wang Y, who asked him to keep it a secret. We were told again, always in confidence, by several other people, teachers and students, each of whom swore us to secrecy. We foreigners were the only ones who didn't pass on the story because we didn't appreciate the resale value of information, didn't realize the label "secret" was not an injunction against telling other people, but a phatic enhancement of the value of the news. Soon everyone knew what had happened.

The accident had occurred in the countryside. Both vehicles were traveling downhill toward each other on a narrow unpaved road made slippery by rain. The university van skidded sideways and the truck hit the middle of its right side. Two of the survivors were probably paralyzed.

The university was responsible for arranging hospital care, memorial services and much more. The rural medical clinic did not have modern equipment and could not provide the best care but the rural roads were too bumpy to bring the injured back to the city in a car or van. University officials could have paid for a helicopter to fly the injured back to Wuhan, but decided not to. Perhaps if the injured had been more important, Wang Y confided to Nelson, the helicopter would have been hired.

The university also had to decide whether to transport the dead or arrange a cremation in the remote county. The bodies remained in the countryside while their fate was negotiated.

University officials had to negotiate the sorts of things that police, courts and insurance adjusters would decide in the US. No outside agencies assigned blame and dispensed compensation; even the police played a minor role. It was the university against the trucking company, not one driver against the other. The negotiating teams represented the interests of the work units, not the individuals who were involved.

Since the dead and injured were from the English Department, Wang Y was one of the university representatives. He passed on each bit of "secret" news to Nelson, advanced payment for Nelson's recommending him to teach at the University of Tennessee. He must have thought the information itself very valuable because the stories themselves did not present him in a good light.

The typing pool had lost two workers. One was dead and the other, Little Shu, had a broken pelvis. A month after the accident Little Shu got out of the hospital to convalesce at home. We told the remaining typist that we would like to visit her injured colleague. She said immediately, "Oh I will take you," closed up the office for the afternoon and led us to Little Shu's apartment.

Little Shu's husband answered the door, surprised and happy to see us. Little Shu was lying in bed. Tears came to her eyes as she took our hands. She said she had to stay in bed for five more months and pulled down the blanket to show us her bandage, a canvas wrapping with buckled straps pulled tight around her tiny hips. She said everyone told her she was lucky to be alive, that she should be happy but all she could think about was her dead friend, Little Hu. She missed her so much she did not feel lucky. Her husband offered us peeled oranges, and we were suddenly very glad we had come because it seemed important to Little Shu and her family that the foreign professors cared enough about her to visit.

The driver of the wrecked van was friendly Driver Li who took us to Hankou on Saturdays. New gossip said Driver Li had been recklessly trying to pass another vehicle when he collided with the truck. Wang Y and his cohorts suggested that Driver Li deliberately swerved to the left to avoid getting hit, sacrificing the others to save himself. Driver Li had the misfortune to have escaped serious injury. If he had died or been paralyzed, perhaps his reputation would have been spared. The university representatives, along with those from the trucking company, decided Driver Li was sixty percent at fault for the accident and that the university had to pay sixty percent of the damages.

In the US a driver could be responsible for a road accident without receiving moral recriminations. Carelessness, lack of skill, even stupidity are alternatives to moral reprehensibility. In China few people drove, so few appreciated how easy it was to make a mistake. Driver Li might have been assigned only sixty percent of the responsibility, but he got all the blame. The conjecture that Driver Li deliberately swerved to save his own life spread across campus with the speed of other secrets.

The university investigating committee had to compensate the families of the people who were killed. One of the dead, the typist Little Hu, had been married for only three months and had been pregnant. Her parents asked the university to give their dead daughter's job to her elder sister who could then live with them and take care of them in their old age.

However, the widower wanted to be hired by the university himself. He said *he* would take care of his parents-in-law. His own parents supported his claim, arguing that according to Chinese tradition, when a woman married she left her father's family and became part of her husband's. Therefore *they* should be the beneficiaries of any compensation.

The widower's family had authority over the dead secretary's body. By law, the husband had to sign the cremation order. The bodies were transferred to a local mortuary after the university paid to move them from the remote county. The widower and his parents used their authority over the body as a bargaining chip by announcing that they wouldn't give permission for cremation until he was hired. People feared that the dead woman's ghost would be unhappy.

Public opinion was against the widower. People thought he would remarry and then he would no longer be able to support his first wife's parents. With that argument, the university decided to hire the dead secretary's sister, not the widower. But before this could be done, public pressure had to persuade his family to allow the body to be cremated. There were no editorials or letters in the university newspaper, no legal proceedings or public pronouncements. Instead visitors to the widower's family expressed their views, one by one, until minds had been changed. Such persuasion took time. The uncremated body waited, the ghost unlaid.

By the time the secretary's body was cremated and her sister was hired in her place, the story was no longer news. The new typist didn't know English and had never typed before, a shortcoming irrelevant to her getting the job. She had to place one finger on the handwritten manuscript she was supposed to type while another hovered over the keyboard looking for a matching letter. It took her nearly a minute to find each key.

The story wasn't quite over. Little Lin complained to us that she had trouble getting a car. Since the accident the university drivers had been too busy; the families of the dead and injured were requesting rides and the university dared not refuse them.

Next we heard the families of the dead had demanded better housing as compensation for their losses, but at this request, the university authorities played a trump card: The ill-fated group hadn't gotten official permission for their trip. And since it was not an official trip, compensation in the form of better housing was not required. Moreover, the very purpose of the outing had been illegal!

The group had gone to sell lithographed copies of old college entrance examinations, an entrepreneurial sideline. The central government had just outlawed these "study guides." Old Yao, the man who led the group, would be "criticized" for arranging the trip, when he recovered. This threat tempered the demands of the survivors.

Driver Li lost his license. For a whole year some people told us. For a very long time, others said. He would never drive again, we were told by someone else. Little Lin told us that the other university drivers said Driver Li was never really qualified, that they had been covering for him, that this was Driver Li's second fatal accident. Were the other drivers whistleblowers or rats abandoning a sinking friend?

What would become of Driver Li, we asked. Would he be fired?

Oh no, he would be assigned to another job in the university.

Office work? Latrine duty? we asked. No one knew.

There were other automotive accidents. Helen was riding in a university car when it was struck by another car. She was not hurt but the bumper was crushed. She reported that the driver was terribly upset at the damage to "his" car. At the front gate of our campus a bus overturned trying to avoid a cyclist. One person was killed and others were injured. Across the street, a Beijing Jeep ran out of control and crashed through the *shao bing* cook's steel-drum oven into a little shed, injuring an old man when the roof collapsed. The *shao bing* cook didn't appear at his usual place and we missed him and his salty roasted bread.

An article in *China Daily* announced that 42,000 motor vehicle fatalities had occurred in China the previous year. This was nearly the same as the number of auto deaths in the US, a country with more than twenty times the number of motor vehicles as China. We wondered why this was not a secret.

Nelson's Tale

Nelson had a graduate student, an attractive woman named Eleanor Fu, who worked with him translating the works of a Song Dynasty Chinese poet. Although they worked together on their project nearly every afternoon, Nelson, honoring local custom, kept their collaboration a secret.

Nelson, always generous with his time, had also agreed to work on a translation project with Vice Chairman Wang Y. But the Vice Chairman was so stilted in his view of literature and so afraid of offending Nelson that very little had been accomplished except to exasperate Nelson. Eleanor Fu on the other hand, was smart and willing to tell Nelson, "No, that's not the right word. It's more like this." Teacher and student worked well together, using explanations and annotations of the work prepared by a former professor of Eleanor's. Soon they had almost completed the book they would submit for publication.

Nelson and Eleanor Fu made plans to visit the university where Eleanor had taught before she went to graduate school. There Nelson was to meet her professor and discuss the manuscript. Eleanor went to the Waiban to ask for a university car to make the trip but she soon came running back to Nelson's apartment, in tears.

She reported that Xiao Song, who was temporarily in charge while Golden Zhou and Director Fang were away, had challenged her. "What do you want to go there for? What are you going to do there with Nelson? Who do you think you are, a mere student, that you think you can write a book? What is your relationship to Nelson? Do you have sex with him?"

Eleanor Fu was not the kind of person to get upset easily. She was confident, almost arrogant in her intelligence. But she had come back from the Waiban office weeping and distraught. Nelson was furious over the affront to his student and the implication that he was having a sexual relationship with her. He began writing a letter to the university president denouncing Xiao Song.

We had always liked Xiao Song. She was pleasant, quiet, hardworking, plain. She didn't have the fire of Golden Zhou, the good looks and pertness of Little Lin, or the warmth of Xiao Han. What she had done seemed out of character. We told Li Meili what happened as the three of us were sitting outside enjoying the cool night air. Li Meili said, "How do you know it is true?"

"What?"

"How do you know it is true? I have known Xiao Song for many years and she wouldn't do this. She just wouldn't say that sort of thing."

It had never occurred to us to doubt Eleanor Fu's story. We knew Xiao Song and we trusted her. We trusted Nelson too. But we didn't know Eleanor Fu very well. Perhaps she had misinterpreted, distorted, imagined.

The next night Li Meili came to us, contrite because she had told Xiao Song what we said. She apologized over and over for not keeping the secret. But what did Xiao Song say, we wanted to know.

Li Meili told us Xiao Song's version: Eleanor Fu walked into the Waiban office as if she owned the world. She ordered a car as if talking to servants. Xiao Song didn't like her attitude and didn't smile at her. She was brusque, perhaps even unfriendly to Eleanor. Eleanor asked for a car to go to the town across the river from her former university, to the home of her old professor. But that town was in a restricted zone and Nelson would have had to get a special travel permit. These permits were available and we got them for other trips, but doing so involved a tiresome visit to Public Security headquarters and a lot of paperwork.

Xiao Song said she had asked Eleanor Fu only why she wanted to go the small town instead of to the university city. Xiao Song admitted she didn't ask this in a friendly manner, but Eleanor's arrogance didn't encourage friendliness. Xiao Song insisted that she never said anything about sex or even hinted at anything immoral between Nelson and Eleanor. She was upset that Nelson was telling people such a story.

This gave us a little insight about how stories got out of hand. Perhaps Eleanor took Xiao Song's question about why they wanted to go to the city across the river as an accusation. Perhaps Eleanor had her own romantic thoughts about Nelson. Perhaps Xiao Song did ask if they were staying overnight. Eleanor may have thought Xiao Song was asking if they were staying overnight *together*. In a society where talking directly about sex was taboo, people had to learn to read between the lines. But in this land of subtle metaphor that empty space left a lot of room for misunderstanding.

The Wang and Li Dilemma
Wang Y, a font of information for the auto accident story, himself became the subject of gossip. Our linguist friend Wang Wei came to us on behalf of a colleague, Teacher Li, who was distraught and asked his help. Teacher Li believed that Wang Y had been trying to prevent him from going abroad on the University of Tennessee exchange program. Nelson had already interviewed Teacher Li and agreed to recommend him for the exchange program. But Teacher Li believed (correctly) that Wang Y also wanted to go the US, that he was trying to take Teacher Li's place. Teacher Li said that Wang Y had him "caught by the throat" but that he intended to fight back by complaining to the Vice President that Wang Y was trying to steal his trip abroad. Wang Wei had come to find out the truth for his friend, Teacher Li.

We checked with Nelson. As far as he knew both Wang and Li could go to the University of Tennessee next year since there were two positions. This news did not reassure either Teacher Li or Wang Y. Teacher Li heard that Wang Y was telling people that Teacher Li was not qualified. Teacher Li told his ally, Director Fang, about Wang Y's calumny. Director Fang, in retaliation, told Nelson that he didn't think Wang Y was very smart. Nelson stirred things up even more by telling Wang Y what Director Fang had said about him.

Finally Director Fang and the Vice President visited Nelson to inform him that Wang Y would be unable to go to the US next year because he had not finished his three-year term of office as Vice Chairman. This must have been one of those "new rules" because

Wang Y hadn't known about it. Desperate, Wang Y asked Wang Wei to become Vice Chairman in his place, but was refused. Wang Y visited Nelson every night, trying to consolidate his position, sure Nelson would forget about him by the following year. Nelson told us that he "really didn't give a shit."

Wang Y and Teacher Li had put themselves in a classic dilemma. They *could* have communicated, shared information and agreed to support each other so both might have been able to go to the US. But they didn't trust each other so they each undermined the other, trying to prevent what they feared most—that their rival would get the prize and they wouldn't. They were both willing to settle for the next worst alternative—that neither of them would get anything.

A folk-saying characterized what Chinese thought of their own national character: One Chinese was a tiger, two Chinese were dogs and three Chinese were worms. When we first heard this saying, we didn't understand it but our students explained: One Chinese was as strong and clever as a tiger, but put two Chinese together and they became so overwhelmed with petty jealousies they lost their power. And for three it was even worse.

We foreigners were not supposed to see this side of China and we usually didn't. What we saw most of the time was extraordinary affection and cooperation and group spirit, people undergoing great inconvenience to help and intervene for others, taking days out of their lives and using their precious *guanxi* for their friends. But China also had its wormy side—of jealousy, spite, and revenge.

Trust and Skepticism
These stories called for a little philosophizing. College undergraduates are often introduced to philosophy with these challenges: How do you know what you see before you is real? How do you know you're not dreaming? Philosophical skepticism celebrates baroque doubts. Undergraduates either love this crazy game and go around infuriating their friends by challenging the basis of all their beliefs, or else they hate it and drop the course. In the real world

there are ways of updating and verifying information, ways that we use all the time so automatically we can't really specify how we do it. We have sources we trust and those we don't, and we have theories to help us interpret information.

But in China, to us a new country and a new culture, we no longer had our old sources. Even some of our old theories about why and when people told untruths had to be abandoned. All we had left were some general principles about how to verify information. For example, we trusted Xiao Song. We remembered that even Pierre believed she was trustworthy. We remembered hearing that Li Meili thought well of her. So we believed that Xiao Song was trustworthy because we had several converging sources of information. But in China we didn't know enough about what trustworthy people did. It was possible that Xiao Song really did harangue Eleanor Fu about a sexual liaison with Nelson, believing she was protecting Eleanor and the moral standards of the university, and then denied she did so because the foreigners were offended.

We thought we had learned a lot about China from the Saga of Driver Li, Nelson's Tale, and the Wang & Li Dilemma, but what we learned most was how information functioned. Since information was such a valuable currency, we shouldn't have been surprised to find some of it counterfeit.

We heard from Wang Wei that there had been a suicide in the Education Department—a teacher upset by recent promotion decisions had killed herself. We asked other people but no one else confirmed the story, so we were not sure it really happened. It was not that we thought Wang Wei lied to us, but only that he didn't check the truth of the story before he passed it on.

But should we have accepted stories that were confirmed and rejected stories we could not confirm? Maybe there *had* been a suicide in the Education Department and no one except Wang Wei would tell us because no one else wanted the foreigners to know.

Information spread so fast in China that perhaps we should have been more skeptical even of widely repeated stories, especially when they fit the ideology of the moment. Maybe we should have been suspicious of the universal deprecation of the Cultural Revolution. Everyone told us that the Cultural Revolution was terrible—everyone except one worker at the university who said wistfully and privately, "In those days we got to travel all over the country."

As foreigners we didn't have enough information about Chinese culture to be sure of what people would do or how they would act. Implausible stories could have been true. Behavior that shocked us might have been normal. Conflicting reports might have been rendered compatible by a piece of information we did not possess and that no one would tell us. Not only were there missing pieces of information, but we didn't know how to find the missing pieces, we didn't know what to look for. And even if we had found them, we might not have known what they meant.

Often this uncertainty was fun, as if we were walking through a mystery story, if not a who-done-it at least a why-done-it. Ordinary interactions were exciting because the behavior of others was unexpected, and we had to puzzle out the explanation, make up theories about why this was done instead of that. But every so often the uncertainty got out of hand. There were times when we really wanted to know why we were being told a certain story and how much of it was true.

Information as a Commodity
One of the official secrets that everybody knew was the existence of the second floor of the Foreign Language Bookstore. The staircase was guarded by a sign that said "FOREIGNERS PLEASE DO NOT ENTER." The first time we saw the sign, we dutifully turned back. Later Pierre explained the mysterious prohibition. The second floor was filled with photo-offset copies of foreign books sold for a tiny fraction of their home-country prices. We returned to the store wearing our university badges, Robin in his Mao jacket. Janice had practiced *"Je ne parle pas Anglais"* ready to pretend we couldn't read the sign. We walked past the sign and to the second floor, but no one stopped us.

Inside were shelves and tables and cases filled with books in English mostly, but also in Russian, Japanese, and German. These were the pirated editions, printed without permission of the original publisher, without permission of the author, sometimes without even the author's name. Science books, novels, self-help books, technical books: *Earthquake Engineering, Wordstar on the IBM PC, Cytology, Electron Microscopy, Reisz Spaces, Lineman's and Cableman's Handbook, VLSI - Fundamentals and Applications, Gone with the Wind, Airport, Frankenstein, The Moon and Sixpence, Dr. Morrison's Amazing Healthy Foods with Miracle Health Promoter M, Electron Fractography Handbook, The Language of Restaurants and Catering, Working with Acrylic Sheet Plastics*. Next to this last book was one entitled *KGB*.

There were photo-offset volumes of the *Reader's Digest*, whose short stories and single paragraph anecdotes made it one of the most popular English language readings in China. Somerset Maugham spy stories had study questions at the end. A book called *Bridge Squeezes* in the engineering section turned out to be about the card game. A thick Tibetan-English dictionary was available with cloth or paper binding.

China clearly did not adhere to the International Copyright Convention. Books were photocopied without permission or royalties and sold for a fraction of their original cost. Such books were marked "not for export." Other Asian governments didn't even bother with this nicety. The pirating of written material, music cassettes, and computer software in Hong Kong, Thailand, and Taiwan was notorious.

The sign on the bookstore stairwell suggested that China was not proud of its pirating. We bought a few books, more to participate in this National Sin than to save money. Our books were wrapped in newspaper and tied with string; our foreign faces were not questioned. We didn't know why we were granted special privileges and allowed to see the extent of the piracy while other foreigners were not. Certainly the publishing community in the West already knew that China did not honor international copyright agreements. Pierre believed that as long as we bought something the bookstore didn't care.

The motivation for the pirating seemed pretty good to us at first: to provide inexpensive books that Chinese couldn't otherwise afford. If Western books were imported at their original prices, the cost of a single book in terms of Chinese salaries would be the equivalent of hundreds, or even thousands of dollars. When we heard that our linguistics book was slated to go into China's "ancillary publication" we were not bothered. We'd rather have a billion readers than get rich.

Still we weren't too happy that copies of *The Human Factor* didn't have Graham Greene's name on them. Money wasn't important (said we who in China had so much) but credit was, we thought.

And then we began to see a larger picture. Students told us about a radio serial that was a clear rip-off of a famous novel, with only the professions of the protagonists changed to disguise the source. Piracy was not confined to foreign writers. Chinese pirated each other.

Our students, who had been taught that learning meant memorizing, rarely paid attention to the source of their ideas. Four renditions of "The Gift of the Magi," only one with a new ending, were handed in as original compositions. When we told them it was wrong to copy another's work, they said they hadn't copied, they had remembered.

In China, information is treated as a commodity, something to exchange to develop *guanxi*, something to give to friends. Credit for the information is transferred from one person to the next, just like ownership of a physical object. If we give you a bottle of wine, it is yours to keep, share or give to another. If you pass it along, you are not under any obligation to tell the new recipient that you got it from us. Similarly if we tell you a good story, in China it becomes yours. You don't have to credit the source if you want to pass it on to someone else.

The practice of not listing sources was reinforced by that other Chinese social custom—one never revealed a special relationship with another person. Naming anyone we met, ate with, or talked with was a form of boasting about the connection and an invitation to jealousy. Public praise of another person could get them in trouble. It was Just Not Done.

Therefore, if someone told you a story, you could repeat the story, but you did not say who told you, for that would be announcing your special connection with the source. Stories were repeated the way Chinese passed around cigarettes, as freely as Americans exchanged greetings, but the sources were concealed.

In the West listing your sources usually enhances your credibility. It might not always be easy to remember where information came from, but making that extra effort is a sign of competence, a sign of reliability. In China, we learned that revealing your sources was bad manners. And besides, keeping your sources a secret enhanced the value of your information, gift-wrapping it in mystery.

If we recognized that information was a form of merchandise, attitudes and customs in China that bewildered us could be explained. When people told us a story embellished so much it bore little resemblance to the truth, at first we felt misled, upset at being told a lie. Now we understood that receiving a story was like receiving the gift of a cake. Our informants meant no harm, they just wanted to entertain us, to satisfy our appetite for knowledge, to give us a gift of information. Embellishing a story was like decorating a cake to suit the taste of the recipient. Inventing a story was like cooking up a cake from ingredients that in their original state were much less delicious. Our informants thought it no more important to tell us their sources for a story than we would tell where we bought the flour and eggs for a cake.

At last, we thought, we understood. But we had more to learn. Much more.

13

CULTURE SHOCKS

Troubles in the Guest House

The approach of the end of our stay in China amplified our emotions. We concentrated on every event and interaction so we wouldn't miss anything. The good experiences were joyous, the bad ones were devastating. They seemed to alternate, making the good and bad seem more extreme by contrast.

Just before the May Day holiday, Old Dong, the front desk guard, ordered all Chinese visitors to show identification and to sign an official register.

Ten months earlier, when we first arrived on campus, Golden Zhou had asked if we objected to having visitors checked by the front desk guards. It was to prevent theft, he said, to keep strangers from stealing our tape players and the university's new color TV sets. It seemed no different from the security arrangements for buildings in many large American cities, until we learned that only Chinese visitors had to identify themselves. Pierre explained that the security measures were not for our benefit but to keep a record of which Chinese visited the foreigners. When Chinese friends confirmed this, we objected to the sign-in policy and it was stopped right away.

Now the sign-in policy had been reinstated. We asked our student, Jeannie (the Party-Member-to-be), to translate the sign posted in the Guest House lobby (written in Chinese cursive which we couldn't read). It said that the foreigners living in this building wanted their Chinese guests to sign in. As she translated, the surly technician came out from the office and muttered in Hubei dialect. Again Jeannie translated for us. He had called her a traitor for telling the foreigners about the sign.

The surly technician's action pushed us to revolt against the new policy. We realized that any anger directed against Old Dong would be misplaced. He hadn't initiated the policy; older workers, even those who had worked for Public Security, did not make such decisions on their own. We posted our own notice in the lobby—written in English, which the Guest House workers could not read:

> The foreigners in this building have *not* agreed that you should sign in. If you are asked to sign in, please inform the person you are visiting.

Our poster was torn down overnight.

We asked the Waiban who had made the new policy. Xiao Pu said it had been done for our safety. "Then how come only Chinese visitors had to sign in," we retorted. "There are a lot of strange foreigners walking into the Guest House; why don't *they* have to sign in?"

Unappeased by our encounter with Xiao Pu, we made another poster to replace the one torn down and this time we added a large silver star to make it look official. One day. Two days. The poster remained.

Daniel wasn't satisfied with our success in semiotics. To him just repudiating the sign-in policy was inadequate; he wanted to get rid of it. It was unjust, he said, and good people fought against injustice. Daniel's protest took the form of an ultimatum: Either the sign-in policy stopped, or he would leave. He wouldn't stay in a country that did this to its people.

Golden Zhou was assigned to handle Daniel's ultimatum. He tried to explain to Daniel that the sign-in policy was no different from what fancy apartment and office buildings did in New York, but Daniel was unfamiliar with the crime controls of New York City; he was from suburban California where people consider anonymity an inalienable right. He had seen his students and friends upset by Old Dong's badgering and wanted to explain this to Zhou.

"Making people sign in is part of the intimidation process that hurts people in China. It adds to the gossip and rumors that people here use to hurt each other."

Zhou did not appreciate Daniel tutoring him about morality. In fact, few Chinese saw the sign-in policy as an infringement of anyone's rights. Such monitoring was a regular part of Chinese life, sometimes more, sometimes less, but never entirely absent. To them it was just one more thing to circumvent; they would meet us someplace else.

Zhou replied calmly, "I know about this and it is not the same. I do not worry about this signing-in."

Daniel felt frustrated that Zhou did not see his point. He tried again: "The record of who visited us could be used in a new Cultural Revolution to hurt people. Things like this were done in the Cultural Revolution and people were killed because they had a record of associating with foreigners. We can't let it happen again."

"I know about the Cultural Revolution," Zhou responded sharply. "I too suffered during the Cultural Revolution. Every Chinese suffered."

Daniel realized his arguments were not working. He tried to give Zhou specific examples, tried to explain his personal reasons for opposing the signing-in policy. "Old Dong has accused my friends of immoral behavior with me. In China everything is so closely controlled, so completely recorded, these stupid rumors can ruin people's lives. They make people afraid to do anything."

Daniel had never officially reported Old Dong's harassment. He didn't like to say bad things about people. He didn't tell Zhou that some of his friends had wept, that some no longer visited him because they were afraid. Daniel had expected Zhou to share his outrage at the new policy.

But Zhou was angry at being told how Chinese ought to behave, angry at being patronized by this young foreigner. He hit back:

"And these rumors, are they true?"

Daniel was shocked, outraged. Tears came to his eyes. He could think of nothing to say and he lost control. "Get out. How can you say that? Get out of my apartment. Get out! Get out now!"

Zhou left. Much loss of face by both. Daniel was very upset by Zhou's accusation. Zhou was not his friend anymore. Zhou was no better than the rest of the evil old men who were ruining this wonderful country.

Never had Zhou lost control before, never had he said anything hurtful. How could such a masterful diplomat have lost his cool?

To Zhou it was arrogant and inappropriate of Daniel to try to protect Chinese from their own social practices. No one was asking foreigners to sign in, and what the Chinese asked of their own people was none of the foreigners' business.

It was not only Zhou's personal pride that was insulted by Daniel's moral lecture. He probably could have weathered that. But Daniel had insulted China as well, saying that Chinese did not know how to treat each other, and in effect, that outsiders should monitor Chinese behavior to prevent another Cultural Revolution.

It is one thing for Chinese to complain about their own country, as we can complain about members of our own family, but it is quite another thing for outsiders to do it. Americans know how serious it is to insult someone's mother. In China criticizing the motherland might be worse.

Daniel was adamant about going home if the sign-in policy continued. Zhou came back to make friends and work out their differences but Daniel wouldn't talk to him. Such a difficult social problem called for a Double Indirect Approach. Xiao Han became Golden Zhou's emissary; we represented Daniel. Xiao Han said that Zhou was very unhappy about his fight with Daniel but it was not right for Daniel to tell Mr. Zhou how to run China.

Diplomatically, we acknowledged that Daniel should not have tried to interfere with how China treated its citizens. But, we explained, the sign-in policy made our job harder if students and other teachers were afraid to visit us. We felt very bad that the government thought we were dangerous and wanted to keep track of who made contact with us. We didn't say anything about the new policy hurting Chinese—we emphasized that it hurt *us*.

In the end the Waiban, the Security Office and the Guest House agreed on a compromise. They would rescind the sign-in policy until Daniel left Wuhan, but they would do this only as a personal favor to Daniel and not because they accepted his criticism.

Later we found out why the sign-in policy had been reinstated. A student demonstration had been scheduled for May fourth and Public Security suspected someone was keeping the foreigners informed. Official "concern for our safety" took other forms during that time. Our friends and families back home wrote that our recent letters to them had been opened.

Fed Up in Three Gorges
As June neared its end, Wuhan began to show us why it was called one of the "three furnaces of China." The mosquitoes from the campus swamp had learned the way to the Guest House and every morning we found covens of them hanging inside our mosquito netting, fat as beetles. When we fought back, bloody streaks appeared, a scene from a slasher movie.

Golden Zhou's talents were recognized by those higher up and he was appointed Educational Attaché to the Chinese Consulate in San Francisco. He said it was a wonderful opportunity but he worried that his little boy would forget him while he was away. We gave another party to celebrate his good news, but it wasn't good news for us. We thought his little boy could get along without him better than we could.

When classes were over, we had a few weeks to travel and use up our Chinese money. The Waiban arranged a trip to the Little Three Gorges, reputed to be even more beautiful than the Big Three Gorges and only recently opened to foreigners. Since Golden Zhou had already left for the United States and Xiao Han was in charge of a tour group, Little Lin was to be our escort and the university would provide a car.

We felt lucky to get Driver Tang, our favorite driver, the only one who preferred the music of his tape cassettes to the honking of his horn. He drove his new air-conditioned Toyota smoothly and considerately, and in addition, he was very handsome, with a striking face of angles and dimples and a pair of designer sunglasses that made him look like a movie star. He put our bags in the trunk alongside a case of orange soda and two twenty-liter cans of gasoline.

We drove out of town with the air conditioner on low, listening to Driver Tang's tapes of Chinese popular music, some in accented English: "Rah-Rah-Ras-pu-teen, lover of the Russian queen. Rah-Rah-Ras-pu-teen, Russia's greatest love machine."

We drank warm orange soda as we passed through villages where new stucco homes with curly roof eaves announced the prosperity of their peasant owners. Between villages we saw people plowing, planting, harvesting, building roads, working at lime kilns—large stone cairns filled with white powder. Driver Tang cooperatively drove over piles of wheat being dried and threshed on the road. As we got farther from Wuhan the coolie hats and clothing of the field workers made it seem as if we were going back in time.

The orange soda finished its journey long before we finished ours so we used one of the many small brick buildings with slotted concrete floors along the road. Under these buildings our deposits would be aged and then used to fertilize the farmland. We contributed our share to the agricultural prosperity of China, remembering not to breathe through our noses. It was the end of the year and we barely turned our heads at the movement of small creatures sharing the facilities.

An hour later, a white-uniformed traffic officer standing in the road waved at us to stop. He spoke to Driver Tang and we pulled over to the shoulder. Little Lin said the officer claimed we had "overpassed" another car.

"But we haven't overtaken another car since we left Wuhan," we said.

"No matter," she said, "that's the way it is in China, the police can say anything they want and you must never disagree; just say please, please, do not fine me. In China the police can do anything they want," she said emphatically.

Driver Tang opened the trunk and took out his work unit card, his license and the vehicle registration papers. We got out of the car, almost a habit by now, displaying our foreign faces to the authorities in order to make things easier for our driver. Other cars pulled up behind us, each driver showing papers to the cop. Driver Tang returned cheerful and we continue our trip.

After ten hours the car arrived at the city of Yichang and we boarded the ship that would take us up the Yangtze River to the Little Three Gorges. Little Lin joined us at the rail to announce that the ship would probably arrive too late the next day for us to make the Little Three Gorges trip.

"Don't worry," we told her, "let's see what happens. We can always stay another day, can't we?"

"Yes," she said, "but perhaps we cannot."

"*Maybe* we can," we replied, refusing to be daunted by her attempts to change the plans, and mischievously turning some of her "maybes" and "perhapses" back on her. Our latest theory was that when Little Lin said "maybe" she meant "yes," and when she said "perhaps" she meant "no," and when she said "I don't know" she meant "I will not tell you."

That night the ship went through the locks of the Yangtze River Dam, called *Gezhou Ba*, the pride of Chinese engineering. We went out on the deck to marvel at the colossal structure glowing in pale green from mercury plasma lamps. The giant doors of the lock opened in slow motion to receive us, a magical scene from *Star Wars*.

We disembarked at the city of Wu Shan just before noon, in plenty of time for the boat trip up the Little Three Gorges. In great spirits we went first to the Wu Shan Hotel to book a room for the night. We were about to ask the clerk if they offered a discount to foreign experts, but Little Lin stopped us.

"I will talk with him," she said with such determination that we stepped aside to let her. She spoke softly to the clerk, head turned away from us, and we couldn't hear what was said. In fact, we were grateful that Little Lin was willing to deal with business while we looked around.

The hotel clerk, a pleasant young man with dark skin, escorted us back down to the waterfront where Little Lin began to make arrangements for the boat trip through the gorges. We waited with Driver Tang and the hotel clerk as Little Lin talked to the boatmen and then came over to us with a big surprise—the boat ride would cost two-hundred yuan! Director Fang had told us the cost would be ten or twenty yuan a person. Two hundred was ridiculous, we thought—even the best overnight cabin on the Yangtze River steamer was only twenty-four yuan and this little boat was no more than a large whaleboat with a canopy over some benches in the middle. The boatmen wanted more for this three-hour ride than a university teacher earned in three weeks. Little Lin shrugged innocently, as if there were nothing that could be done.

"No," we said. "That is too much. We will not go if it is that much."

She said, "But you have come all this way just to go on this ride," forgetting that last night she expected us to be too late to go on the boat at all.

Janice asked Driver Tang which man was the boat boss. He indicated the one with two stainless steel teeth and a vinyl pouch strapped around his waist. Janice walked over to the boatmen, ignoring Little Lin's objections, unwilling to let these boatmen take advantage of Little Lin's inexperience.

"We will give you one hundred yuan," she said. "If you want two hundred, we say good-bye."

They listened attentively, smiles appearing for the first time on their stern faces. One boatman turned to the others and said, "She knows how to speak Chinese!"

Little Lin interrupted in English, "No, no, you must not ask to pay so little money." Then she stepped in front of Janice and began talking so fast we couldn't understand.

Little Lin turned to us and said they would take us for 150 yuan and the university would pay for her and Driver Tang so our part would be only eighty yuan. Would we accept that? She looked so anxious that we accepted.

The trip was spectacular, much better than we had imagined. The boat had a crew of three—Captain Steel Teeth in the stern controlled the outboard motor and two men up front used long bamboo poles to fend away from rocks. The boat floated high in the water and the skills of the boatmen were evident as the river twisted and foamed over rocks and shoals. The captain lifted the motor out of the water whenever the hull scraped over the rocks and the two men in front struggled to punt the boat up river. At times the boat was motionless against the rapids while the punters strained horizontal against their poles.

The haze over the river created an ethereal mood. Mountains rose fast from the water's edge, their flanks so steep that corn stalks grew nearly parallel with the surface of the earth. Herds of white goats foraged on the mountainsides, their coats bright against the dark rock as if they were illuminated from within. Sacred golden monkeys moved slowly across the face of a cliff whose walls were pierced by thousands of regularly spaced holes that once held beams for an ancient roadway high above the water. Rocks and caves and goats and rows of corn, stalactites, trees, walls, all combined in a wonderful kaleidoscope of beauty. Even Little Lin seemed happy.

Large boulders and mountain peaks had special names, often bearing their Chinese characters painted in white: Monkey King Mountain, Baby Goat Hill. Some resemblances were so faint that we began renaming them, laughing at our own jokes. One mountain became Director Fang Peak—there was a sort of huge round face in it. Across the river was Napoleon Mountain, shaped like his famous hat. One ridge we called Toothpaste Crest because it didn't look like anything and we liked the pun.

On the return trip we went with the current, shooting rapids in a white-water adventure completely different from the up-river trip, the majesty of the gorges undiminished at high speed. The skill of the boatmen and the grand scenery was worth every *fen* of the two hundred yuan we had refused to pay.

When we got back to the hotel, Little Lin told us she and Driver Tang could not eat dinner with us because it was the hotel's policy not to let Chinese eat with foreigners. Intolerant of such racism, we suggested that we all eat at one of the restaurants outside the hotel and that she and Driver Tang would be our guests. Little Lin said, "Never mind, the hotel agrees we can eat together in the dining room." We said, fine, but we did not want a full banquet, only one or two dishes. She agreed to tell them.

Our table was already set with four cold dishes, the way banquets usually start, but we were still too high from the magnificent boat ride to realize what this meant. As we began to eat, a group of foreigners led by a Chinese man entered the dining room. They were Canadian hydroelectric engineers visiting the great *Gezhou Ba* dam and celebrating their arrival with a tour of the Little Three Gorges and a banquet. The engineers sat down to eat and their Chinese host sat with them. Had this group also objected to the mealtime racial segregation policy?

We were served exactly the same food as the other table, only in smaller amounts. We thought the first dishes were appetizers, but our request for a menu was ignored and dishes of French fries, steamed fish pieces, slices of pork, vegetables of several kinds were brought to the table. When a large tureen of soup arrived we asked Little Lin if the soup was the last dish. She said yes but then the waitress brought us three more dishes. It was clear that we had gotten the standard banquet, the wasted food enough to feed a family of six.

The steamer taking us down river was scheduled to leave at six-thirty so we got up very early and waited with Driver Tang for

Little Lin, ready to check out. Little Lin spoke to the clerk and told us how much we had to pay. It was so much more than the sum of the hotel room and the meal that we asked for an explanation. She said there was an eighty-yuan charge for the "tour guide," six yuan for each of the four-page brochures, and a charge of ten yuan for procuring a pair of boat tickets that cost only thirteen yuan.

Little Lin presented these charges as if she were outraged, as if we were all being taken advantage of. The hotel clerk was demanding an exorbitant salary as a "guide" when we thought he had merely been getting a free boat ride. Little Lin tried to prevent us from talking directly to him and told us we had to pay whatever he asked for, that we had no way out.

We were so angry the clerk had not told Little Lin in advance about these charges that we wanted to object to something, however small, to let him know our displeasure. Sternly, we told him we would only pay one-yuan as a service charge for each boat ticket (the going rate). If he insisted we pay a five-yuan service charge for each ticket, we would call the police. It was petty but we were so ill-tempered from the obvious fraud that we couldn't help ourselves.

Little Lin got agitated and started talking to the clerk in rapid Chinese. She said the clerk agreed to lower the fee to three yuan, but as she was talking he handed us the receipt showing a service charge of one yuan per ticket. We paid the rest of the exorbitant bill, feeling hurt by the rip-off and sullied by our own behavior.

On the ship, we leaned over the rail, brooding about how much trouble we were having on this trip compared with the trips we had made on our own. We were beginning to consider the possibility that some of the things Little Lin told us had not been completely true. She always seemed to be the victim, so innocent and cute, but the prices and the stories changed so often. It seemed everyone she dealt with had tried to cheat her. When we traveled on our own, even though we were linguistically handicapped aliens, those problems never happened.

In the city of Yichang, Little Lin told us that she and the driver had been invited to dinner by the head of the Peach Blossom Hotel, but we could eat in one of the hotel dining rooms. Fine, we didn't want to eat with her either. We left the hotel compound, walked down the street and found a small family restaurant that had a menu with prices clearly marked. The family of restaurant workers came over to talk with us, bringing their small child from its grandmother's care. When we gave our order they brought a bowl of hot peppers to our table and asked how many we wanted in our food. We picked up one small chili pepper and they laughed good naturedly at our culinary cowardice. There was no problem about the price, no additional last minute charges. The friendly people, good food and beer made us forget our past irritations.

We returned to the hotel, full from the first good meal we had eaten on this trip, and were in bed when Little Lin knocked on our door. She came in to talk, cheerful and charming. We described our wonderful meal and said that we promised the restaurant people we would return for breakfast. She said she and Driver Tang would eat breakfast with us at our restaurant. We told her about the hot peppers and our comic refusal. Her charm won us over again.

The next morning we checked out of the Peach Blossom Hotel and climbed into the Toyota, ready to go to our restaurant for breakfast. But Little Lin directed Driver Tang to stop at a different restaurant, much seedier. We sat at one of the picnic benches while Little Lin went to get noodles for us all. She brought back two bowls for us and then went back to get bowls for herself and Driver Tang. Our noodles were fiery hot, sprinkled with chopped red peppers. There were no peppers in Little Lin's noodles.

On the drive back, suspicions and resentment came boiling to the surface. Little Lin had been lying to us all along. No restaurant personnel had ever told her that Chinese couldn't eat with foreigners. No one had been cheating her. Little Lin had been telling us anything that came to her mind, inventing prices, slandering other people, acting with the charm and mentality of a seven-year old and the morality of The Bad Seed.

We should have known better—all year long we had plenty of evidence that Little Lin was not a truth teller, that she was spoiled and willful. She entertained us with stories about the lies she told others, the tricks she played on them. Why had we thought she would treat us differently? Her coworkers told us that she shirked her jobs, never volunteered to help others. Why had we thought she would go out of her way to bargain for us, to help us do something she had no interest in doing?

We had been especially gullible because her stories so often presented an unfavorable picture of China, stories of corrupt officials and stupid public policies—that the traffic police would wrongly stop us for "overpassing;" that drivers would lie and hotel workers cheat at every opportunity. We believed these had to be stories of the real China, the China behind the scenes, because we couldn't imagine any motive for her making up stories that put her country in a bad light.

We imagined what her fantasies about this trip must have been, her first trip in charge of foreigners. She would lead the rich Americans, passive, dependent and grateful, showing them off, reveling in her power to control them, to speak their language and make them give out unlimited amounts of money. She could even provoke them a little, the way circus trainers prod their tigers to growl for the crowd before they jump through hoops. We obliged her by getting angry in front of the clerks and workers, performing as barbarian foreigners were supposed to. But we spoiled her act by trying to do things on our own, refusing to follow her commands, having the gall to try to teach *her* how to negotiate.

She must have thought of us as the kind of nerds who deserved to be misled because they were so gullible. To her we were like the giant salamander, the *wawa yu*—strange creatures who did funny things when in distress, funny things she wanted to see. The *wawa yu* was luckier than we, for she had been afraid to provoke it.

All those Saturday shopping hassles, all those arbitrary changes of plans that we attributed to the van drivers. It was Little Miss Mischief all along, not telling the drivers what she told us and not telling us what she told the drivers. When we thought the drivers were changing the agreed-upon plan at the last minute, they must have thought we were doing the same. No wonder the drivers got angry. Did any of them know Little Lin was responsible, or had they blamed us?

We thought of poor Helen, so dependent on Little Lin for shopping on Saturdays, always complaining that the shopkeepers were cheating her. We attributed this to penny-pinching, but now we knew that Helen's paranoia was not without a catalyst. We wondered about all the other things Little Lin told us. What was really true? We searched through our memories, trying to recall all the things we learned from her. What else? What else?

Fraying Ties
When we got back to the university, our problems did not end. Little Lin knew we were unhappy with her but she didn't know we were ashamed of ourselves for being taken in and had no intention of complaining about her behavior. She was sure we were going to "criticize" her and she did not like to be criticized. And she believed that offense was the best defense.

At the Waiban office, Director Fang asked us about our trip to the Three Gorges. We thanked him for arranging the trip, praised the magnificence of the scenery and encouraged him to organize the trip for the foreigners the following year. Little Lin hurried over and interrupted: Whatever we had said was not true. We were astonished, uncomfortable. Even Director Fang was surprised.

The next day Janice went to the Waiban office to pick up our departure allowance. Director Fang, Little Lin, Xiao Han and Xiao Song were in the office. Little Lin did not look up. Director Fang asked Xiao Han to handle the matter and left the office. Xiao Han told Janice that we would get the money soon but we would only get half as much money as the other foreign experts because we were a couple.

"Wait. That's not right," Janice said.

Xiao Han was agitated; he raised his voice. "It is right, it does not sound right, but it is right."

"No, it is not, we each worked for the university, we each should get what the other foreign experts get."

"Yes it is right, it has been decided. The Waiban does not have to give you this money." He was very angry.

"Certainly, and we appreciate this," Janice conceded, even though she knew the allowance was mandated by the State Education Committee. "But if there is a policy to give all foreign experts a certain amount, it is unfair to give us half."

"This money is like a gift," Xiao Han shouted, "it is not right for you to ask for a gift."

Janice responded to his anger by lowering her voice and speaking very slowly and calmly, "I am not asking for a gift, just for the departure allowance that Little Lin and Director Fang said all of us were getting."

This provoked Little Lin. "I did not tell you anything. That was only for Daniel."

And even more slowly Janice answered, "We were in Daniel's room when you said that each of us would get a departure allowance."

"I did not say this thing! You are telling people I said things I did not say!" Little Lin was standing now, scolding Janice loudly.

Janice's voice was shaking but unlike theirs it was slow and quiet. "I know Americans get angry and are rude, but Chinese are supposed to be more polite. You are being rude to me and that is not right. You should be ashamed to be Chinese." She began to leave the office.

Little Lin followed Janice, screaming that we told lies about her to everyone. Janice turned around and said just loud enough for the others to hear, "Lower your voice when you talk to me."

Little Lin stopped, her face reddening as the public criticism from an elder finally evoked its traditional power.

Back at the Guest House we learned from Daniel and Julie that Little Lin had tried to protect herself from the criticism she expected from us by making up stories about our behavior on the trip. We were horrible, she told everyone. We fought with hotel clerks, objected to every bill, every fee. We bargained shamelessly and embarrassed her.

And that's why Xiao Han had been angry with Janice. He had believed everything Little Lin said about us. How could he believe her? Why did he think we would do that? Weren't we his friends? We had always been fond of Xiao Han; we trusted him and enjoyed his company and cared about what he thought of us. We believed he felt the same about us, but now we had to reevaluate our friendship with him.

It wasn't a symmetric relationship; it couldn't have been. His job involved handing us our enormous salaries, watching us spend money each month it took him years to earn. He got the plane tickets for us to zip around China, in and out of the country, but he couldn't travel like that himself—he even had to get permission to leave the city. When he did travel it was always as the caretaker, sometimes the gofer for foreigners. It was his job, his "duty" to be nice to us, to suffer abuse and be called "dog's leg" by other Chinese because he served us.

If the roles had been reversed we're not sure we would have liked us either. But if we were Xiao Han, we wouldn't have been so kind and friendly in the first place.

Still, hadn't we blamed the van drivers, hotel clerks, merchants and even our own Helen because we had believed charming, pretty Little Lin? We had been willing to accept that dining room workers were racists, that merchants were cheats, that the university drivers were willful and irrational. We may have deserved to be treated in kind, but it still hurt.

The next day Little Lin came to the Guest House with a detailed list of her expenses on the Three Gorges trip, showing it to all the other foreigners, trying to prove that she hadn't cheated on her university expense account. Little Lin's own handwritten list was supposed to convince everyone that she actually incurred those expenses.

Her action rekindled our suspicions. Why had Little Lin always tried to negotiate costs and payments out of our hearing? Why had she falsely claimed that Chinese and foreigners were required to eat separately? She and Xiao Han had said the same thing on the Lu Shan trip in the fall. Maybe they got a kickback for bringing in the foreigners; perhaps they were even skimming a few extra yuan from their university expense account.

If so, it was Xiao Han who taught Little Lin on the Lu Shan trip to hide a padded expense account by saying restaurants did not allow Chinese to eat with foreigners; it was Xiao Han who fiddled the ticket prices on the boat; it was Xiao Han who had learned to steal from the peasants during the Cultural Revolution and years later might not be above pocketing a few extra yuan.

This provided us a new explanation of Xiao Han's hostility toward Janice: He was afraid she would turn him in. And it was just because we would never think of turning him in that we hadn't realized his anger might have been self-defense. He probably didn't know that we, who had been so scrupulously honest in China, conscious of our position as guests, were used to people back home skimming and padding and fudging to get a little extra from their employers, customers, or the IRS. Somehow this explanation made us feel a little better. It made it seem possible that we could renew the friendship, but, alas, we never saw Xiao Han again.

Director Fang came to visit. He tried to mollify us, making excuses for Xiao Han and Little Lin, explaining that she was the "baby sister" of the Waiban. We said we understood, but it was really Director Fang whom we saw in a new light. He was the harried father in charge of a difficult family, one that included some willful children. And the very children he was now trying to protect were the ones who made fun of him, criticized his administrative skills and told anecdotes about his English language mistakes.

14

HOMEBOUND REFLECTIONS

What Tourists

It was our last morning in Wuhan. As we carried our bags downstairs, the surly technician hovered around the electric heater Nelson had left with us for safekeeping. The technician wanted it for himself, but his obvious greed foiled his plans. We got some small revenge as Director Fang issued orders for the heater to be moved to the Waiban office and stored for Nelson's replacement.

A crowd came to see us off—students, colleagues and everyone from the Waiban except for Little Lin and Xiao Han. A teacher who had once given us "medicine" to kill roaches brought us a bag of wood-ear mushrooms. We gave him the last of our firecrackers and he set them off as the van pulled away for the airport. Everyone applauded. Li Meili and Julie came to the airport with us and we parted with tears and hugs and promises to write.

From Wuhan we flew to Shanghai for our last bit of travel in China. We met Nelson, who had just returned from Thailand, and he took us to the bar at the Shanghai Hotel. This was his last chance to get us drunk in what he called "the best bar in China." He ordered rounds of brandy alexanders and asked us for news of back home. We knew he meant Wuhan so we told him about the Three Gorges trip and the trouble we had with Little Lin and Xiao Han. Nelson said he could never be sure when Little Lin lied to him. "And Poor Xiao Han, that young Old Man."

The air conditioned bar with its luxurious appointments and another round of brandy alexanders moved us on to exchange more pleasant news. Nelson reported seeing Bud on the beaches of Thailand hanging out with hippie transvestites. Bud had changed his mind about returning to Wuhan to teach next fall, saying he just wanted to live on the beach and play. Helen had left for home by way of Turkey in order to visit friends in the foreign service. There had been anti-American demonstrations in Ankara, but we knew she could take care of herself. Fiona and Nick had decided to live near each other back in the US; she would move from the West Coast to get a teaching job in Boston. Judy Liang, Nelson's lovely tutor, would no longer be an "old girl." She was getting married, he told us, both proud and wistful.

We toured Shanghai with Nelson who knew the city from previous visits. "I love Shanghai. It's a civilized town," he said.

And he was right. The crowded streets reminded us of New York, the Nanjing Road shopping district a cross between Fifth Avenue and Fordham Road. The shops were well stocked and varied, some decorated and appointed with sophisticated taste. We walked for hours on Shanghai streets, exploring everything from the crowded poverty of the Old District to the luxury of the new Jiujiang Hotel complex. We admired Yu-the-Mandarin's Garden and stepped gingerly on real lawns, the first well-kept grass we'd seen in a year.

The next day Nelson left for the US. We hugged him and held on a bit longer and squeezed a bit harder trying convey some of the emotion we felt. We had shared so much with him over the year, cheered and sustained by his insightful wit, our feelings validated by his rages at our shared frustrations.

Nelson's taxi left for the airport and we took a bus to *The Bund*, Shanghai's waterfront boulevard. When we got there we drank three cans of *Ke Kou Ke Le* (Coca Cola), and waited in the heat to board the excursion ship that sailed the Huang Po River to the sea. Many of the waiting passengers were foreigners herded by tour guides. Occasionally a stray wandered from the flock; a woman in a flowered dress pushed into line and shouted in English at the ticket sellers:

"Excuse me. Excuse me. I need to find someone who speaks English."

The ticket sellers stared at her, uncomprehending. She turned up the volume, "I need to find my group. Are they on the boat?" And even louder, "Is there a group of sixty people on the boat?"

The ticket sellers, still unable to understand despite the increase in volume, ignored the woman. She turned away in disgust and strode up the gangplank, pushing through the ticket takers as if they were curtains, still shouting, "Excuse me. I need to find a person who speaks English."

We usually volunteered to help fellow foreigners but this time we did not, lest anyone think we came from the same country, probably even the same city as that loud woman in the loud dress. In compensation we gladly agreed to help a French couple purchase tickets for the excursion. When we got to the window, the ticket sellers said there were no first class tickets.

"Oh please," we said, smiling, "perhaps there are still some left."

"First class is filled."

"But we need first class tickets," we said, still smiling, refusing to give up. We enjoyed playing Golden Zhou in front of these innocent French tourists.

"How many do you want?"

"Four."

We showed our White Cards and paid with *renminbi*. The French couple reimbursed us with FEC, which we pocketed as the ticket sellers watched impassively. Xiao Han could not have done it better.

As soon as the ship got under way, the dining attendants served watermelon, preserved plums, beef chips, chocolate covered ice cream bricks, Coca Cola canned in Macao, Sunkist drinks, and Japanese beer. We stood at the rail watching the sights go by: First the view of the old European section of Shanghai, then the activity of one of the largest ports in the world—container ships from Panama, Egypt, US, Iran, Liberia, Monrovia, Germany; cranes and unloading equipment that resembled Imperial walkers in the *Star Wars* movies; tugs, barges, junks with cooking stoves smoking in the stern, passenger ships, and a military vessel of World War One vintage.

A steward warned tourists not to take pictures of the military craft. "It is against the law." As soon as he left, the photographers shot away. The interesting picture was not the rusty guns on the mothballed destroyer but a band of Chinese sailors playing steel drums and cymbals, reggae with an Asian flavor. The musicians waved happily at the picture takers, indifferent to the breach of military security.

Most of the tourists in first class were from the US, England, Australia, Germany, Spain or Hong Kong. We couldn't help eavesdropping, especially when most of the conversations were so loud.

> . . . completely transparent but they wear shorts, sometimes miniskirts underneath. And the blouses, they might as well not be wearing anything. They wear bras but they're not anything much. They look like they come from J C Penney or something, so what's the point? . . .

> Boy, it's really amazing. China is doing all right, the way they're going. I was talking to this woman and she was so open, I was so surprised. I told her—you know the way I am—that I didn't care about socialism or anything but you look at our system and look at your system and how can anyone say your system is better? It's not, just look. And she said, "Nobody believes that stuff anymore." I was so surprised she could say that. It's really great. And she's a professor and she can say something like that. China is really changing.

> I don't understand why they take the risk, the young people. As Sam said, "When you sleep with someone you don't know, you're sleeping with everyone they've slept with for the past five years." It's really scary . . .

> You speak English better than ninety-nine percent of the Chinese people but you want to be better than that. Just

> think, there's only one percent to go and it's all up to you. You can do it but only you, all by yourself. Nothing's standing in your way. Now you have to get rid of your Chinese accent so people won't know you're Chinese when you speak. Our guide in Beijing had a British accent. I have a New England accent...
>
> You know, you go on these tours and stay at the Shanghai Hotel, but this isn't the real China, man. You gotta go out and get in with the people. These people, they all think they're seeing China, but this isn't really China. All this isn't real.

We turned away so they couldn't see us laugh, smug that we knew enough about China not to worry about which part of it was "real."

Chinese Changes
The next day we went to the airport to begin our twenty-one hour plane ride. Nearly a year ago the passenger terminal seemed austere, alien, unfriendly. The People's Liberation Army officer who said we couldn't walk into the departure lounge was a character out of a cold-war espionage novel.

Now the feeling of the passenger terminal was different. Chinese army uniforms looked friendly and bicycles on runways were normal. We were not the same people who walked through those doors a year earlier.

However, inside the airport we were tourists once again, not always an easy role in this country. There were a few more hassles to work out—our Green Cards had already been taken by the university but the border police insisted we surrender the cards to them before they let us leave the country. This time we knew how to negotiate, how to keep our cool, how to concede and insist at the same time. The border police turned friendly and supportive, making telephone calls to check that we had indeed turned in the precious documents. We doubted the problem would be solved in time to board the plane but as Old China Hands we were not upset—

HOMEBOUND REFLECTIONS

"The cart will get to the other side of the mountain when it gets there."

While waiting we thought of how much we had learned about getting around in China. For example, we finally understood why the Chinese travel system had no round-trip tickets. All tickets were one-way and had to be booked and purchased from the city of departure. There were no technological barriers to round-trip ticketing—China had an extensive telex network and the airline offices had modern computer booking systems.

The barrier was a social one. The people who worked in each ticket office controlled access to transportation from their city, and in a land where some resources were still scarce, control of those resources was power. Power was the chief currency in the great system of *guanxi*. To allow someone from a distant city to sell or reserve *your* tickets was to give up power, and as you lost power, you lost your ability to keep and develop your network of relationships, your *guanxi*.

Fortunately, the very system that resisted the introduction of round-trip booking was beginning to find a way around the problem. When we wanted to travel to Xian and back to Wuhan, our Waiban telephoned a university in Xian. This other university, a member of our informal network of connections, bought return tickets for us in Xian and we picked up the tickets when we got there. We appreciated this *guanxi* when we overheard a conversation between tourists at the airline ticket office in Xian:

"I'm so relieved. I got a ticket to Nanjing for tomorrow."

"I thought you wanted to go to Guilin."

"Yeah, but I've been trying for three days. There are no tickets. I'll go anyplace just to get out of here."

The problem of our missing Green Cards was solved sooner than we expected. The border police wished us a good journey and warmly welcomed us to return to China. The Boeing 747 was filled so we couldn't spread across the seats to sleep, giving us plenty of time to think about the country we were leaving.

These days many Chinese were better off than we had been when we were graduate students in Chicago. Chinese might complain about the *guanxi* system because it was needed for everything. But in China everyone gets to use the system, at least to some extent, allowing power to be distributed more fairly, more democratically than it was in Chicago in the 1960's. And there aren't as many roaches.

We had lived on the border between the turfs of two rival Chicago street gangs. Gunfire sounded nearly every night; used cartridge cases lay on the streets and bullet scars marred buildings and mailboxes. We lived in fear of violence every day, fear of arson for more than a year, and in the reality of a war zone when armed National Guard troops patrolled the streets.

In contrast, one of the great pleasures we had in China was the feeling of personal safety. We hiked and cycled through the countryside, strolled in lonely parks, walked down unlit streets, even explored the poor back alleys of Shanghai, once notorious for murder and kidnapping. Never did we feel afraid.

The conviction that no Chinese would hurt us was challenged only once and this incident stood out because it was the exception. At all other times we felt safe and comfortable, even while being stared at or shoved onto buses. On our return from the Three Gorges, we were driving through a remote area when the traffic ahead of us stopped. Driver Tang got out and walked up the road along the stopped trucks and buses to find the reason for the delay. We also got out and as we followed him, everyone on the road stared, school children hung out their bus windows, adults gaped open-mouthed. Many had never before seen a foreigner.

At the end of the stalled traffic, the road was blocked by a truck and a small tractor smashed together. We walked back to the car, opened the windows and waited, knowing we might be stuck there for quite a while.

People began to gather around our car to stare at us. We said hello. One girl replied but the others just stared. As the crowd grew, we became uncomfortable. Robin said, "To look at the foreigners, please pay thirty *fen*." Most of the adults laughed, waved and went away but younger people stayed, staring without smiles. When they pressed closer to the car, we rolled up the dark tinted windows. A few people left because they could no longer see us, but the rest of the crowd moved closer. Someone knocked on the glass the way children tap on the glass to get a reaction from snakes in the zoo. We ignored it. More knocking. Then it got louder. Driver Tang opened his door and sternly told the crowd to go away, that they were giving the foreigners a bad impression of China. A few young men started knocking on the glass again. "*Liu mang* (hoodlums)," we said to Little Lin and Driver Tang and they laughed nervously. The car began to rock and someone kicked the fender. Driver Tang said nothing. Janice made a move to get out. Robin grabbed her arm. We were frightened.

And then suddenly it ended. A police officer in a white summer uniform appeared, walking up the line of stalled traffic. No pistol, not even a billy club. He waved over the most hostile looking of the young men and turned away. The young man meekly followed the officer and the crowd backed off.

Unlike US peace officers, the Chinese police did not carry firearms on ordinary duty. Certainly a greater proportion of people wore military uniforms, but in China the military included an enormous number of people in non-combative jobs—factory workers, school teachers, transportation services and airport personnel. The ceremonial guards on the Yangtze River Bridge did carry AK-47s, noteworthy because they were unusual. With rare exceptions, such as the Tiananmen tragedy, it was social pressure rather than firepower that kept the peace in China.

Although we feared no physical violence, there were thefts. On one of our Saturday shopping jaunts, a young boy tried to steal Nelson's leather shoulder bag from the van but Driver Tang chased and caught him. When we returned to the van, a policeman invited us to the Block Committee Room, the place where people from the neighborhood went when they had trouble. The policeman gave us cold bottles of soda from the community refrigerator as Driver Tang filled out a report. Nothing was missing from Nelson's bag but the police still wanted to know the price of the whiskey, how much the bag cost and how to spell "Seagram's." We asked Little Lin if the thief would get a red check, that is, be executed. She said not if the amount was less than a hundred yuan. The report listed the value of Nelson's bag and its contents as 120 yuan.

Years ago in China there had been little point in stealing; everybody knew what you had and what you could afford to buy. If you started carrying a new bag or had a bottle of imported whiskey, it would have been so unusual that everyone in the neighborhood would know about it.

Now Chinese stores offered things people couldn't have imagined back then. Television ads and billboards made consumer goods even more attractive. Teachers thought it unfair that others (like rich peasants) could afford to buy more than they. Newspapers and magazines increased the jealousy by reporting that people were getting rich from the free market, lionizing the new "millionaire" class and headlining the success stories. What was not reported, of course, were all the people who weren't getting rich, people whose salaries were fixed while the new products they wanted were getting more expensive.

Inflation was soaring as we left China. Meat had doubled in price over the year. Fruit prices doubled in the last month. Bicycles increased thirty percent and were rumored to be going up again. Airfares climbed by a third on April first. It used to be that everyone knew the prices of the items they bought but when inflation hit, merchants started to use price tags for the first time and to call out the cost of their wares. Full employment also dwindled, creating a growing number of "waiting-for-work people," the Chinese euphemism for the unemployed.

We had been fascinated by the changes in China's economy, the excitement of new products, the improvements in living conditions. But we were disturbed by the effects of the new motivation to turn a quick yuan: a tidal wave of advertising that created a flood of false needs, product adulteration, brand-name counterfeits, and an increase in theft.

We had mixed feelings about changing social customs. When we first arrived in China, male and female rarely touched in public, unless it was a parent carrying a small child. By spring the greater freedom allowing young people to choose their own romantic partners had also resulted in couples holding hands and brushing shoulders on evening walks. All this we approved, but by July the practice of buttock-fondling appeared on the city streets. We walked behind couples kneading each other in X-rated delight, wondering about our own ambivalence toward these changes.

In Wuhan, crowds gathered around displays of purported "art"—harshly lit, badly composed photographs of blond *Playboy* rejects, clad only in make-up and earrings. Because these were passed off as art, the authorities didn't rip them down. The city of Guangzhou passed a law against performers wearing bikinis, making an exception for bodybuilders. The job titles of nightclub go-go dancers were quickly adjusted and postcards of thin-armed bikini-clad women in bodybuilding poses sold better than pictures of the formerly revered Mickey Mouse.

We sympathized with official worries about Western "spiritual pollution," perhaps more than did many of our Chinese friends. Sure, China was a puritanical country and official repression stifled creative expression. But unlike other puritan cultures, Muslim fundamentalism, for example, Chinese Puritanism allowed, even celebrated, sensuality and personal beauty. These qualities were displayed, appreciated and admired without the leers and crude sexual aggression so common in the West. How much of this would change?

Family Values

As we flew toward the United States we thought back to China—about teachers who were also advisers, comforters and surrogate parents, about the child-parent relationship of worker to supervisor, about the frequent last minute changes in plans and ad hoc rules—

and we had an insight that explained many things both frustrating and delightful. The entire country of China, with more than a billion people, is run not like a country, but like a family (shades of Confucius).

What does that mean? In a family, nothing has to be done formally; nothing has to be written down, few things have to be preplanned. Family plans and promises don't require contracts or other paperwork, no matter how many people are involved. Decisions are made as problems arise, and these decisions needn't always follow a system of rules applied impartially to all. In a family, one doesn't need laws. The needs and peculiarities of each case can be taken into account.

Whenever Vice Chairman Wang Y or Director Fang informed us that there was a "new rule," we never knew whether there really was such a rule or whether we were victims of an ad hoc decision. With the aid of the China-as-Family Theory, we realized that there was little difference between official policy and administrative whim. If a supervisor or leader decided that something should be done a certain way, then that *was* a new rule. And because rules, including national policies, were so often general and vague, interpretation was more important than code.

For example, the supervisor who was supposed to enforce the one-child policy was the same person who advised that you *ought* to have that one child soon. Having no more than one child was national policy, while having that one child soon might be only friendly advice. But when the same person delivered both messages, there was little difference.

Just as parents might be inconsistent and break their own rules or decide not to enforce them, so in China any policy or law could be ignored or reinterpreted for a particular case. Some supervisors risked everything to protect their charges while others repudiated and punished the slightest offender. The system of *guanxi* was essential in all this, because it was personal connections and personal trust (or lack thereof) that determined how policies were enforced.

Using social pressure to enforce compliance added to the Family character of China. Social pressure could be more ruthless and more effective than official command, but it also could be more delicate. We admired how well it worked in China. During the Sports Day races, fans and spectators ran along the edge of the track to be near the runners, cheering them on. Some of the runners who were well behind the leaders cut across a corner of the track, lessening their own times but not changing the outcome of the race. No one raised an official objection to this cheating, no one talked of disqualification. Yet when one runner tried a shortcut to pass a competitor, the jogging spectators quickly blocked the corner-cutter, preventing the cheater from getting through. No official intervention took place, no reprimand or shaming procedure was needed. The Family had made sure no competitor took unfair advantage. What we had witnessed was a paradigm of Chinese society.

And because Chinese society was run like one big family, no aspect of personal life was irrelevant to public concern. Job assignments for graduating students were made by people who acted as parents, taking into account the personal lives of the students. Official duties included discouraging premarital sex and protecting reputations by sending troublemakers out to the countryside far from temptation. And if Public Security read our mail, they had only been acting like overprotective parents.

Private Property and Revolutionary Ideals
As the flight continued, we began thinking fondly of home, our American home, our cozy, newly renovated house. We talked about what projects we should tackle next, about the flowers that must be blooming, worried a little about things we had stored in the cellar. We'd have to weed what the tenants had been too timid to pull up. We'd have to check for leaks in the roof. Was the old dishwasher still working? The clothes dryer? They were such comfortable worries about a piece of the world that was all ours and that we could make into anything we wanted.

Comparing the home we just left to the one we were returning to reminded us how Chinese who loved their country in the abstract took so little care of it. We remembered the contrast between the immaculate clothing of our students and their dirty classrooms and dormitories; the polished refrigerators and audio systems of our friends contrasting with the stained and marred walls of their apartments; the image of Xiao Li, almost sparkling in her delicate white dress, her hair shiny clean and perfectly arranged, throwing food and candy wrappers out her apartment window.

We thought of the Chinese intellectuals we'd met who had contempt for labor; the academics who knew nothing about the simplest mechanical problems; the people who couldn't believe that we professor-types did our own plumbing and bicycle repairs; the welder who looked surprised when we showed him how to attach his ground wire by wedging it under the I-beam. Even Xiao Han, who knew us well, didn't trust us when we telephoned to report a broken steam line gasket, just because we weren't supposed to know about such things. The Great Proletarian Cultural Revolution, "re-education through labor," was supposed to rid intellectuals of their elitist attitudes. It seems to have had the opposite effect.

American academics are not less arrogant or elitist, but few are contemptuous of manual labor. Some even brag about their do-it-yourself abilities. Maybe that's because of private property: If you own something, you are more likely to take care of it. Either you learn to do the work, as we had, becoming workers ourselves—painters, carpenters and mechanics on weekends—or you hire someone else to do it. And Americans who need the services of a plumber or an electrician—no matter how great they think they are in their own professions—dare not show contempt for such workers if they want the project completed.

If we were right, private ownership could accomplish what the Cultural Revolution had failed to do. Give the intellectuals and professionals in China responsibility for the upkeep of their own housing, let them see routine maintenance as a financial investment, and they might learn to respect labor and craft. If we were right, those condos in Beijing and the private homes built by peasants in the countryside were going to serve the Communist ideal of breaking down class distinctions better than all the political slogans and campaigns against elitism. Respect for Labor! Honor to the Workers!

Lettuce and Longing
How were we going to feel when we landed in the US? One returning foreigner wrote that she'd burst into tears when she saw the lights of the George Washington Bridge. She said returning was just as exciting as traveling to a foreign country for the first time. What would be different about the US? What would we be surprised at?

The luxury of the San Francisco airport was startling—clean carpeting and sparkling fountains, large plants and shiny surfaces all around. The air was so clear that the distant hills stood out as if they were only across the street. The first thing we did after landing was to run to a public water fountain and drink the cold, clean, unboiled water—exuberant and grateful for such a miracle. When we got to a friend's home we gorged ourselves on a head of fresh lettuce, stuffing wads of it into our mouths. We hadn't eaten raw vegetables in a year. Then we stood in front of a washing machine, watching in appreciation as it filled up and began agitating *all by itself.*

Our own country was strange to us. Current news about American politics seemed like excerpts from a "Saturday Night Live" mock newscast. At a shopping mall in the cosmetics department of Macy's, we saw a young woman lying on a chaise, apparently nude, her entire body covered in mud. But strange also were the ordinary people—their noses too large, eyes sunken into their faces, hair an unruly jumble of colors, and so many fat people.

The first day we returned to campus, Smith College shut down the electricity and sent everyone home. Then the computer center closed for a week of renovation. Just like China, we thought. But because we had *guanxi* we were able to use the laser printer in another office.

The mailbox was full of bills, things we hadn't seen for a year: telephone, electric, fuel oil, city taxes, television cable. And we got another letter from the IRS claiming they never received our tax return from two years ago. We sent them a certified letter with a copy of the refund check for that year but our letter was ignored. We sent them another certified letter but it too had no effect. They continued sending letters and we continued answering by certified mail, telephoning, driving to their "Problem Resolution Office" in Springfield for help. Nothing did any good.

The IRS began "penalty withholding" on our bank accounts. A friend who had a similar experience suggested we write to our congressional representative to ask for help. Of course! We needed *guanxi*. We should have known that. Our Rep came through and the IRS wrote that since we had paid our taxes for that year we did not need to have penalty withholding anymore. No admission of error, no apology. All of our experiences with Chinese bureaucracy—currency exchanges, reentry visas, hospital food bills, border police—suddenly got a new perspective.

We heard from Fiona, who now lived in Boston near Nick, that Bud was back at Central China University, but he thought none of the new foreigners were interesting and he was bored. Helen was writing a book on China and had called Nick because she wanted to use excerpts from his journal. She was planning to return to China, but wanted to go to Kunming where there were more national minorities.

Adjective Boy wrote to us that Nelson's graduate student, Eleanor Fu, won a province-wide contest in translation. Adjective Boy, although only an undergraduate himself, was a finalist. We wondered if the translation Eleanor submitted was the one she had done jointly with Nelson and whether she had given him credit.

Daniel returned to California to decide what to do with his life. He planned to work hard and save enough money so a certain young Chinese woman could come to this country. Nelson and his wife bought a boat with his sabbatical salary. It was in dry dock but he practically lived on it, polishing the brasswork along with his year's poetry and making plans to live in Hong Kong.

Bud left Wuhan at mid-term, telling people his brother was in jail and his mother needed him. But he couldn't stay away from the Orient and returned to teach in Hong Kong.

Li Meili and her husband Ming Yong wrote to us. They were taking Chinese medicine so they could have a baby. Ming Yong made a business trip to steel mills in Pittsburgh and marveled at American supermarkets. Li Meili wanted to study abroad but was afraid of making plans that might conflict with the birth of a baby.

We now bought rice in ten-pound bags instead of one-pound boxes. We looked forward to the Smith College President's Annual Reception, the only place we knew with traditional ballroom dancing, so we could show off our new skills, but when we got there we found the old dance band had been replaced by a punk rock disk jockey.

We missed our friends, especially Julie and Li Meili and Golden Zhou. We wrote to Julie and Li Meili and asked for news. They did not mix with this year's foreigners, they said, and the foreigners had little to do with the Waiban. Old Dong had been relieved of his comfortable job in the Guest House and reassigned to another place on campus because he was caught blackmarketeering in bicycles. Julie had married her boyfriend, but they could not live together until the university assigned them an apartment. Inflation was still terrible, the price of meat had doubled again. The black market and the *guanxi* system were stronger than ever and frustration was increasing.

We received letters from our students written in cursive Chinese script that we laboriously deciphered but they were like official reports. We couldn't recapture the warmth and laughter of filling jiaozi dumplings and sharing meals and taking walks over the causeways of South Lake. We missed the closeness of Chinese faces, and even the smell of garlic.

It was hard to describe our US lives in letters to our friends in China. We didn't bother to explain the IRS foul-up; the system was so alien and complex. We tried to describe the simple joy of using our new leaf blower but Li Meili wrote back that it must be wonderful in the West with electric-powered everything, and we felt we had been bragging.

We got an emergency phone call when eighty-year old Aunt Maggie fell out of bed and could not get up from the floor. We drove to Vermont to convince her to go to a hospital and then into a convalescent home while she healed. We felt that our concern for her was admirable, but we could not explain to our Chinese friends why we didn't bring her to live with us, why we didn't alter our lives to take care of her.

We watched the tragedy of an alcoholic relative deteriorating but never confronted him, never tried to convince him to stop drinking. He would sneak out of the room to put vodka in his coffee, confident we did not know his secret. We came close to tears in his presence, but never did we come close to acting as any Chinese would, carrying out our responsibility to interfere in his life.

Over and over people asked us, "What was it like? Have you changed?"

Yes, we had changed, but not completely. We were caught between two worlds. We had learned a different way of behaving but it didn't fit the culture we had returned to. We escaped into our memories, trying to recapture the world we had left.

And then we got a phone call from Golden Zhou. The Chinese Consulate in San Francisco had a WATS line and he said he could call us often. Was that all right with us?

Oh yes, certainly, we said in unison, eager to talk to someone who understood what we missed about China.

Zhou said he had just gotten a driver's license and was eager to visit Las Vegas.